The Effects of Gamification on Motivation and Performance

Anna Faust

The Effects of Gamification on Motivation and Performance

Springer Gabler

Anna Faust
Wirtschaft und Management
Technical University of Berlin
Berlin, Germany

Zugl.: Berlin, Technische Universität, Diss., 2021

ISBN 978-3-658-35194-6 ISBN 978-3-658-35195-3 (eBook)
https://doi.org/10.1007/978-3-658-35195-3

Responsible Editor: Marija Kojic
This Springer Gabler imprint is published by the registered company Springer Fachmedien Wiesbaden GmbH part of Springer Nature.
The registered company address is: Abraham-Lincoln-Str. 46, 65189 Wiesbaden, Germany

Foreword

In recent years, gamification has become a common buzzword in business and research. The concept that implements game elements in non-game contexts is associated with mixed effects on motivation and performance. In this context, Anna Faust embeds gamification in the field of management control and investigates how the design of gamification affects motivation and performance. Further, her research focuses on the interaction of different compensation schemes and gamification. This research consists of three studies: a systematic literature review and two laboratory experiments. Based on these studies, she identifies causes for the mixed results concerning the effects of gamification reported in previous studies. In her experiments, she investigates whether the number of implemented game elements results in different effects of gamification on motivation and performance. Moreover, she explores the effects of gamification in combination with different forms of compensation.

Results provide insights on why gamification results in inconsistent and partly contradictory effects on motivation and performance. Thus, researchers and practitioners should be aware of the interaction effects between compensation and gamification. Further, depending on their objectives, practitioners should examine whether gamification is a suitable instrument to incite desired behavioral effects. Further, the three studies contribute to closing the research gap in management control concerning gamification as a non-monetary incentive scheme. Results show that monetary incentives can affect learning more effectively than previously expected.

Against the background of the ongoing discussion on how to motivate employees to perform in the pandemic-related home office, this research considerably contributes to a deeper understanding of the effects of gamification on motivation and performance and thereby addresses a timely and innovative topic. I am therefore convinced that this book will find an interested and broad readership.

Prof. Dr. Maik Lachmann

Acknowledgment

This dissertation was submitted for obtaining the degree Doctor of Philosophy (in German Dr. rer. oec.) at the Technical University of Berlin. The research described herein was conducted under the supervision of Prof. Maik Lachmann at the department of financial accounting and management control, Technical University of Berlin, between January 2015 and January 2021.

First, I would like to thank Prof. Maik Lachmann. I am grateful for his supervision, the financial support of my projects, and the creation of a very family-friendly work environment that greatly contributed to the dissertation's success. Further, I would like to thank Prof. Arnt Wöhrmann for being the second assessor of my dissertation.

Special thanks go to Dr. Theresa Herrmann, Dr. Hanna Schachel, and Franziska Spallek for truckloads of good times and for always encouraging me in bad ones. Moreover, I would like to thank my former and current colleagues Prof. Karola Bastini, David and Sofia Dang, Dr. Fares Getzin, Christopher Growth-Tonberge, Ranna Iraki, Lisa-Marie Wibbeke, Susan Mehr and Dr. Claudia Lemke.

Also, I want to thank everyone involved in the project. Dr. Michael Sailer who generously made available the software programmed by Peter Arndt, Vanessa Herbst, Katrin Kehrbusch, and Sebastian Klingenbeck; Vincent Wyszynski who patiently re-programmed the software; Prof. Sofia Lourenço for her highly constructive feedback and suggestions during my stay as a visiting researcher at Lisbon School of Economics in Portugal; as well as Florian Wiek and Nina Bonge for their organizational help with my experiment.

Finally, I would like to express my gratitude to my family for their support and love. Specifically, I am very grateful for the support of Tilmann Rocha. Looking back, you helped me like Ariana Luterman helped Chandler Self in Dallas in

2017. As my partner in crime you endured a fair amount of my frustration and supported me unconditionally through this challenging time.

I dedicate this work to my amazing daughters Mathilde and Ronja. You are my reason. You are my light. I love you with all my heart.

Dr. Anna Faust

Abstract

In this thesis, I examine the effects of gamification as a non-monetary incentive scheme on motivation and performance. In practice, gamification gained increasing importance, comprising an estimated market size of USD 6.33 billion in 2019 (Fortune Business Insight 2020). At the same time, predictions expect that up to 80% of the implemented gamification applications fall short of their objective to increase motivation and performance (Kumar 2013). In academia, the concept has received increasing attention, resulting in a rapidly growing body of literature (Patricio 2017). Findings present a mixed picture of the effectiveness of gamification (Seaborn/Fels 2015). A primary concern of managerial accounting are systems and practices that increase motivation, effort, and performance (Bonner et al. 2000, Zimmerman 2011). However, in the field of management accounting and management control, previous research has focused on the effects of monetary incentives at the expense of non-monetary incentives (Bonner/Sprinkle 2002). Gamification, as a non-monetary incentive scheme, has received little to no attention so far in the field of management accounting and management control. To address this gap, I conduct three studies to investigate the influence of gamification on motivation and performance. In doing so, I identify factors that caused mixed results in previous literature and shed light on the interactive effects of gamification, monetary incentive schemes, and task complexity.

In the first study, I conduct a systematic literature review to analyze the literature on gamification. Findings show that studies still need to overcome shortcomings concerning their theoretical background and research design. Further, results suggest that the form of compensation as well as the measures used in the experiments are, to date, underappreciated factors influencing the effectiveness of gamification.

In my second study, I conduct a laboratory experiment to contribute to the scientific discourse on the number of game elements necessary to create effective gamification. Subjects receive fixed wage compensation for performing a real effort task. In this arrangement, I manipulate the level of gamification through the number of implemented game elements between groups, resulting in four conditions. Results from contrast analysis show that gamification based on one element leads to significantly lower levels of perceived competence compared to gamification based on a multitude of game elements. However, results from the ANOVA show no significant main effect of gamification on motivation and effort.

In my third study, I examine how gamification and task complexity can influence the effectiveness of monetary incentives schemes. Therefore, I utilize a laboratory experiment in which task complexity (less complex vs. more complex), gamification (absent vs. present), and compensation scheme (fixed pay vs. piece-rate) are manipulated. Results show that the effect of monetary incentives on effort duration is moderated by gamification. Effort duration under performance-contingent compensation is lower in the gamified task compared to the non-gamified task. Effort duration under fixed pay is higher in the gamified condition compared to the non-gamified condition. Moreover, results suggest an interaction between gamification and compensation: While a piece-rate compensation in combination with gamification is effective in increasing the pace of learning (measured as performance improvement rate), a piece-rate compensation in a non-gamified task has no effect on the pace of learning.

Overall, this thesis offers new insights into the complexity of gamification as an incentive scheme. It provides explanations for the mixed findings of previous studies and contributes to a better understanding of the interaction of monetary incentives and gamification.

Zusammenfassung

Diese Arbeit befasst sich mit den Effekten von Gamification als nicht-monetäres Anreizsystem auf die Motivation und Leistung. In der Praxis gewinnt Gamification zunehmend an Bedeutung und erzielte im Jahr 2019 ein geschätztes Marktvolumen von 6.33 Milliarden US-Dollar (Fortune Business Insight 2020). Gleichzeitig gehen Prognosen davon aus, dass bis zu 80 % der implementierten Gamification-Anwendungen ihr Ziel, die Motivation und Leistung zu steigern, verfehlen (Kumar 2013). Auch in der Forschung erhält das Konzept zunehmend Aufmerksamkeit, wie die stetig steigende Anzahl an Veröffentlichungen zeigt (Patricio 2017). Hierbei kommen Studien, welche die Effekte vom Gamification auf die Motivation und Performance untersuchen, zu teils widersprüchlichen Ergebnissen (Seaborn/Fels 2015).

Ein Hauptanliegen des Controllings ist es, Methoden und Systeme mitzugestalten, die auf eine Verbesserung der Motivation, erhöhte Leistungsbereitschaft und Performance abzielen (Bonner et al. 2000, Zimmerman 2011). In Fachzeitschriften mit einem Fokus auf Management Accounting und Management Control erhielt Gamification bislang trotz seiner praktischen Relevanz kaum Beachtung. Im Rahmen der vorliegenden Dissertation werden drei Studien vorgestellt, die zur Schließung dieser Forschungslücke beitragen. Im Rahmen der drei Studien wird der Einfluss von Gamification auf Motivation und Performance untersucht. In diesem Zusammenhang werden Faktoren identifiziert, welche die widersprüchlichen Ergebnisse vorheriger Studien erklären können. Darüber hinaus werden die Interaktionseffekte zwischen Gamification, Task Complexity und monetären Anreizsystemen ergründet.

In der ersten Studie wird eine systematische Literaturanalyse durchgeführt. Die Ergebnisse zeigen, dass Studien zum Thema Gamification Mängel hinsichtlich ihrer theoretischen Fundierung und des Forschungsdesigns vorweisen.

Darüber hinaus deuten die Ergebnisse darauf hin, dass die Form der Vergütung sowie verwendete Indikatoren die Ergebnisse von Studien zu den Effekten von Gamifizierung beeinflussen.

In der zweiten Studie wird ein Laborexperiment durchgeführt. Dieses trägt zum wissenschaftlichen Diskurs hinsichtlich der notwendigen Anzahl von Spielelementen, die für eine effektive Gamification erforderlich sind, bei. Die Probanden werden für die Bearbeitung einer *real-effort task* mit einem fixen Betrag entschädigt. Dabei wird der Grad der Gamification mithilfe der Anzahl implementierter Spielelemente manipuliert, was zu vier experimentellen Gruppen führt (no game, low game, med game and high game). Die Ergebnisse der Kontrast-Analyse zeigen, dass eine Gamification auf der Basis eines Elements zu einem signifikant niedrigeren Kompetenzempfinden führt im Vergleich zu Gamification auf einer Vielzahl von Spielelementen. Insgesamt zeigen die Ergebnisse der Studie aufbauend auf einer ANOVA allerdings keine signifikanten Haupteffekte von Gamification auf Motivation oder Anstrengung.

Im Rahmen der dritten Studie wird untersucht, wie Gamification und Aufgabenkomplexität die Wirksamkeit monetärer Anreizsysteme beeinflussen können. Hierfür wird ein Laborexperiment durchgeführt, in welchem die Komplexität der Aufgaben (weniger komplex vs. komplexer), die Gamifizierung (nicht vorhanden vs. vorhanden) und das Vergütungsschema (fix vs. variable) manipuliert werden. Die Ergebnisse zeigen, dass die Wirkung monetärer Anreize auf die investierte Arbeitszeit durch Gamification moderiert werden. Unter leistungsabhängiger Vergütung ist hierbei ein geringerer zeitlicher Aufwand zu beobachten, wenn die Aufgabe gamifiziert ist im Vergleich zur nicht gamifizierten Aufgabe. Unter leistungsunabhängiger Vergütung ist die investierte Arbeitszeit bei der gamifizierten Aufgabe höher im Vergleich zur nicht gamifizierten Aufgabe.

Darüber hinaus deuten die Ergebnisse hinsichtlich der Leistungssteigerung auf Interaktionseffekte zwischen Gamification und Vergütung hin. So hat eine leistungsabhängige Vergütung keinen Einfluss auf Lerneffekte, wenn die Aufgabe nicht gamifiziert ist, beeinflusste die Leistungssteigerung jedoch positiv, wenn die Aufgabe Spielelemente enthält.

Basierend auf diesen Erkenntnissen bietet die vorliegende Arbeit neue Einblicke in die Komplexität von Gamification als Anreizsystem. Sie identifiziert mögliche Ursachen für die teils widersprüchlichen Ergebnisse früherer Studien und trägt zu einem besseren Verständnis hinsichtlich des Zusammenspiels von monetären Anreizen und Gamification bei.

Contents

Abbreviations

COVID-19	Coronavirus disease
IMI	Intrinsic motivation inventory
MDA	Mechanics, dynamics, aesthetics
RAI	Relative autonomy index
RPI	Relative performance information
RQ	Research question
SLR	Systematic literature review

List of Figures

List of Tables

1 Introduction

1.1 Motivation and Scope

Over the last few years, an increasing number of firms have implemented gamified systems and services to increase customer engagement (e.g., Coca-Cola and Starbucks) or employee's motivation and performance (e.g., Applebee's and SAP) (Esteves 2017, Mandl et al. 2015, SAP 2011). Deterding et al. (2011, p. 9) define gamification generally as "(…) the use of game design elements in non-game contexts." Service providers claim that a gamification of everyday work, which often leads to demotivated and over-stressed employees, results in increased enjoyment as well as higher performance quality and quantity (Robson et al. 2016).

Practitioners utilize gamification as a non-monetary incentive scheme in a broad range of contexts, including education and learning, marketing and customer relationships, health and exercise, innovation, and creativity. Companies such as Bayer or Applebee's use the non-monetary incentive scheme to recruit, motivate and train employees (Kappen/Nacke 2013). Practitioners' interest in the concept of gamification is reflected in a growing market size, which grew to an estimated worth of USD 6.33 billion in 2019 (Fortune Business Insight 2020).

Despite the practical relevance of gamification, minimal attention has been paid to the concept as an incentive scheme within the field of managerial accounting and organizational control so far. A rapidly growing body of research on gamification from fields other than management accounting and control has found that gamification does not always improve motivation and performance (Seaborn/Fels 2015). These findings underscore the importance of understanding the conditions under which gamification will produce positive, negative, or no effects on motivation and performance.

A. Faust, *The Effects of Gamification on Motivation and Performance*,
https://doi.org/10.1007/978-3-658-35195-3_1

Managerial accounting focuses on the systems and practices that motivate individuals within an organization and ensure that employees act in the best interest of the firm (Sprinkle 2000, Zimmerman 2011). Scholars emphasize the importance of empirical studies showing how managerial accounting systems and information affect the individuals' behavior (Sprinkle et al. 2008, Kunz/Linder 2012). In this context, understanding the mechanisms of monetary and non-monetary incentives is critical for determining how to maximize their effectiveness (Bonner/Lewis 1990, Bonner/Sprinkle 2002). Previous research suggests that task characteristics, such as task complexity, can influence the effectiveness of performance-contingent monetary incentives on performance (Bonner/Sprinkle 2002, Jung et al. 2010).

However, up until now, researchers have lacked studies that embed the concept of gamification in the context of managerial accounting and control. Further, there is little information on what factors are responsible for the previously mixed findings concerning the effectiveness of gamification and how gamification must be designed to affect motivation and performance effectively.

In this thesis, I will address these research gaps and analyze the effects of gamification, as a non-monetary incentive scheme, on motivation, effort, and performance. To this end, I conduct a systematic literature review on empirical studies of gamification. Furthermore, I conduct two laboratory experiments. The first experiment focuses on the optimal design of gamification, and the second experiment examines the effects of two task characteristics, namely gamification and task complexity, on the incentive-effort-performance relation induced by different forms of compensation. This thesis is the first work to combine gamification, compensation, and task complexity in a laboratory experiment and hypothesize interactions that contribute to the effectiveness of monetary and non-monetary incentives on motivation and performance. Moreover, findings shed further light on the factors that have led to mixed findings in prior research. Thus, the three studies that comprise my thesis contribute to the streams of literature on monetary incentives and gamification.

For the development of my hypotheses, I rely on two widely used frameworks. First, Deci and Ryan's (2012) self-determination theory that originates in the field of psychology seems particularly suited to explain the interplay of rewards, motivation, and effort. Second, I utilize the framework on the effects of monetary incentives provided by Bonner and Sprinkle (2002). This framework originates in the field of accounting and draws on a compilation and integration of prior evidence and theories (e.g., agency theory, goal-setting theory, expectancy theory). Therefore, it is suitable to examine the incentive-effort-performance relations and respective moderators.

Building on these theoretical foundations, I predict that gamification will increase motivation, effort, and performance, whereby I expect a multitude of game elements to be more successful as compared to gamification based on one game element. Moreover, I predict that the monetary incentives affect total performance while leaving performance improvement unaffected. I expect that this relation is moderated by task complexity. Further, I expect that the relationship between monetary incentives and the rate of performance improvement (e.g., learning rate) is moderated by gamification. In other words, I expect gamification to support a positive effect of monetary incentives on the performance improvement rate.

To test my hypotheses, I conduct two laboratory experiments. In my first experiment, I use a 1×4 between-subject design that manipulates the level of gamification in the form of the number of implemented game elements (control, low gamification, medium gamification, high gamification). Participants receive a fixed compensation for performing a real effort task. Relying on evidence generated from a post-experimental questionnaire on motivation and effort, I show that gamification based on a multitude of game elements leads to higher motivation and effort compared to gamification based on one game element.

In my second experiment, I use a $2 \times 2 \times 2$ mixed factorial design, where I manipulate gamification between subjects (absent vs. present), compensation scheme between subject (fix vs. piece-rate), and task complexity within-subject (less complex vs. complex). As in the first experiment, participants perform a real effort task. The effects of the manipulations on motivation, effort, and performance are analyzed based on behavioral and motivational data. Motivational measures are collected via a post-experimental questionnaire. In contrast to the limited number of studies that investigate the effects of gamification on performance based on a single performance measure, I provide a differentiated view on performance effects, including different parameters such as total performance, performance errors, pace of performance improvement, and efficiency. Results suggest that gamification moderates the relation between monetary incentives and performance improvement. Whereas in the absence of game elements, monetary incentives do not affect performance improvement, they significantly increase the pace of improvement in the gamified environment. At the same time, gamification does not result in significant main effects—neither on motivation, nor on performance, nor on performance improvement rate. Further, in accordance with previous literature, I find that the effectiveness of performance-contingent monetary incentives is moderated by task complexity. Thus, increased task complexity attenuates the relationship between monetary incentives and performance.

1.2 Contribution

This study contributes to the existing literature in at least five ways. First, it introduces gamification as a non-monetary incentive scheme into the body of accounting and management control literature. Whereas the concept of gamification has already received attention in other fields of study, it remains a blind spot in accounting and management control. Thus, this study provides a theoretical foundation for further research on gamification and makes clear that there are several unanswered research questions on gamification that need to be addressed in the field of accounting and management.

Second, the study responds to a still valid call for more research on non-monetary incentives (Bonner/Sprinkle 2002, Bonner et al. 2000). The existing body of research concentrates mainly on the effects of monetary incentives, neglecting non-monetary incentives. In this way, this thesis also meets the call for a more sophisticated perspective on human motivation in management research (Adler/Chen 2011). This is achieved by including the psychology-based self-determination theory in the theoretical frame and by analyzing corresponding measures of extrinsic and intrinsic motivation. Thus, from a scientific perspective, the study provides new insights and contributes to a more comprehensive understanding of the functioning of gamification as a non-monetary incentive scheme.

Third, as the study includes both, gamification as a non-monetary incentive scheme and monetary incentives, it contributes by adding to a limited number of publications that explore combined incentives (monetary and non-monetary incentives) and their interaction effects (Hammermann/Mohnen 2014). Such findings are useful for practitioners who are considering implementing gamification in the future or search for factors resulting in a malfunctioning gamified application. From the research perspective, this study demonstrates the importance of understanding the interaction effects of monetary and non-monetary incentives.

Fourth, the study adds to a limited research body on gamification that analyzes not only the effects on motivation (Cheong et al. 2014, Hamari et al. 2015, Monterrat et al. 2017, Leclercq et al. 2017) but also the effects on performance (Smith 2017, Liu et al. 2018, Frost et al. 2015). It breaks with previous studies by considering several performance measures of qualitative and quantitative nature. From the perspective of research, the inclusion of diverse motivational and performance measures contributes to a comprehensive understanding of the effects of gamification and compensation. Further, examining the effects of gamification on diverse performance measures is particularly valuable from a practitioners' perspective as it allows a detailed assessment of potential utility.

Finally, this study offers several explanations for the mixed findings on the effects of gamification in previous studies that report increased motivation (Goehle 2013) and demotivation (Cramer et al. 2011), increased engagement (Snyder/Hartig 2013), and no effect on engagement (Guin et al. 2012) as well as increased performance (Foster et al. 2012) and decreased performance (Domínguez et al. 2013). The study therefore makes an essential contribution to further research on gamification.

1.3 General Structure

This thesis is structured as follows: The next chapter (chapter 2) provides a comprehensive overview of the concept of gamification. First, it provides an overview of existing definitions and explain related terms. Further, it presents gamification-related theoretical frames developed in prior literature and delimits gamification with respect to other similar concepts. Moreover, I will highlight the concept's practical relevance by showing cases and areas of application. Following this fundamental background on gamification, I present my first study: a systematic literature review of empirical studies on gamification. In doing so, I contribute to the existing body of literature on gamification by identifying possible reasons for the mixed findings concerning the effectiveness of gamification. One reason identified that accounts for the contradictory results relates to the use of different compensation schemes. Based on this finding, the necessity of further research to explore the interaction of gamification and compensation becomes clear.

Thus, in chapter 3 I provide an overview of the theoretical foundations of the effects of monetary incentives on motivation and task performance. To this end, I rely on self-determination theory and the framework developed by Bonner and Sprinkle (2002). Since Bonner and Sprinkle (2002) identify task complexity as an important moderator of the relationship between monetary incentive, effort, and performance, I pay particular attention to task complexity in this chapter.

In chapter 4, I present my second study: a laboratory experiment on the levels of gamification. To do so, I rely on the above-mentioned theories to develop hypotheses, describe the utilized method in detail, and present respective findings. Chapter 5 contains my third study—a laboratory experiment on the moderating effects of gamification and task complexity on compensation.

In chapter 6, I summarize and integrate the results of the three studies. Based on these findings, I highlight several important implications for practitioners and scholars. Finally, I will discuss the limitations of my studies and provide suggestions for future research.

Literature and Theoretical Background of Gamification

2

This chapter deals with the theoretical background on gamification and provides an overview of the current state of research. I begin by explaining the concept of gamification and related terms. I then move on to provide insights into the variety of theoretical frames used in the context of gamification and delimit the concepts with respect to others. The practical relevance of gamification will be demonstrated by pointing out areas of application. Moreover, I derive research questions, and based on them, conduct a systematic literature review. Finally, I present the utilized methodology and findings in this chapter.

2.1 Theoretical Background

In academia, the term gamification was introduced in 2010 (Liu et al. 2017, Garcia et al. 2017, Gatautis et al. 2016, Robson et al. 2015). Since its introduction, an increasing interest and correspondingly growing body of research has been observable across fields such as education, healthcare, computer science, and innovation (Seaborn/Fels 2015).[1] Studies evaluate the effects of gamification on training experience and learning performance (Baxter et al. 2017, Su 2017), knowledge sharing and idea generation (Agogué et al. 2015, Suh/Wagner 2017), system use (Hamari/Koivisto 2015, Jung et al. 2010), patients' health compliance (Lin et al. 2013) as well as the effects of gamification on motivation and engagement (Bittner/Schipper 2014, Siemens et al. 2015).

[1] According to Hamari et al. (2014), in 2014 there were 399 publications found on the EBSCOhost database when searching for gamification or related verbs. Nonetheless, in the subsequent four years until April 2018, an additional 2,196 publications were accessible on EBSCOhost based on the same keyword search.

A. Faust, *The Effects of Gamification on Motivation and Performance*,
https://doi.org/10.1007/978-3-658-35195-3_2

Findings in these fields show a mixed picture of the effects of gamification. Positive findings report significantly more data provided by survey participants, increased engagement, and increased time taken to complete a survey without affecting data validity (Bailey et al. 2015). In the fields of education and computer science, gamification has been linked to enhanced motivation as well as increased engagement, perceived effort, and performance (Reiners/Wood 2015). Other studies report negative and neutral findings such as poor writing performance and participation in class (Domínguez et al. 2013), the demotivating effects of game elements (Cramer et al. 2011), inconsistent effectiveness of gamification (Witt et al. 2011) or statistically non-significant results (Liu et al. 2011, Massung et al. 2013).

These mixed findings can partly be explained by different experimental designs varying in time frame and duration, the demographics of participants as well as the number and type of implemented game elements. However, questions concerning these mixed findings remain unanswered, and more work is necessary to fully understand the effects of gamification and influencing factors. In particular, it remains unclear whether gamification is effective as an incentive and reward system for employees. Also, aiming at reliable motivational and behavioral effects, it remains an open question as to how gamification should be designed and implemented in an organizational context.

Simultaneously, practitioners are increasingly interested in gamification. The worldwide gamification market was valued at USD 6.33 billion in 2019 and is expected to be worth USD 37.00 billion in 2027 (Fortune Business Insight 2020). Practitioners' interest in gamification is based on the expectation that it positively affects motivation and allows for the mediation of behavior (Buckley et al. 2019). Despite the great practical and theoretical relevance of gamification, minimal attention has been paid to the concept as an incentive system within the field of management control. Before investigating the effects of gamification on motivation and behavior, a clear definition of the concept is needed. Thus, the next section focuses on the definition of gamification.

2.1.1 Definition(s) of Gamification

As might be expected from the early conceptual stage of gamification, various definitions have been proposed. These definitions can be clustered into two main perspectives: the structural viewpoint and the interactive viewpoint. In the structural viewpoint, gamification is defined based on the structure of the task or system. The interactive viewpoint emphasizes that gamification results from a human-task interaction, and therefore also depends on individual perception.

As a representative of the structural viewpoint, Deterding et al. (2011, p. 9) define gamification generally as "(...) the use of game design elements in non-game contexts." Also, the definition of Werbach and Hunter (2012) can be classified as a structural viewpoint, as they define gamification as "embedding game features into activities that are not games" (2012, p. 27). Later, Nelson (2012) proposes an extension of the definition of gamification to include the intended purpose of motivating employees and increasing productivity. This is contrary to Deterding et al. (2011), who consciously refer to non-game contexts regardless of their specific usage intentions. Another definition proposed by Robson et al. (2014) emphasizes behavioral effects and centers on the impact of gamification on productivity, defining it as "the application of lessons from the gaming domain in order to change stakeholder behaviors and outcomes in non-game situations." (Robson et al. 2014, p. 352). Cardador et al. (2017) characterize gamification as a performance management approach that improves motivation and performance through two levers. The first lever is the provision of information; the second one is described as increased task attractiveness, referring to an affective lever that gamification activates (Cardador 2017). According to these definitions from within the structural viewpoint, gamification acts as an incentive instrument based on ludic techniques.

As representatives of the interactive viewpoint, Huotari and Hamari's definition focuses on the user experience rather than the task or system design as they define gamification as "a process of enhancing a service with affordances for gameful experiences in order to support user's overall value creation" (Huotari/Hamari 2012, p. 19). This definition is commonly used in studies with a focus on intra-organizational design or marketing (Kamel et al. 2017, Hamari et al. 2018, Liu et al. 2018, Seiffert-Brockmann et al. 2018). Followers of the interactive viewpoint stress that a gamified system or task is designed for and should create a gameful experience, but also that the gamified system cannot guarantee this experience.

As I proceed, I will refer to gamification in accordance with the definition provided by Deterding et al. (2011) for two reasons. First, in their conceptualization of gamification, Deterding et al. (2011) emphasize the implementation of gamification through game elements, a game-like design, and gameful interactions rather than designing a complete game. Second, it presents the most frequently cited definition in the research literature (Armstrong/Landers 2017, Monterrat et al. 2017, Wang et al. 2017, Nobre and Ferreira 2017, Leclercq et al. 2017).

As the definition of Deterding et al. (2011) refers to the term game element, the next section will shed more light on game elements and their classifications as described in the existing literature.

2.1.2 Game Elements

Gamification is based on the implementation of game elements in a real-world context. In the following, the term "elements" is crucial to distinguish the concept of gamification from serious games. In contrast to serious games, gamification is not a fully developed game but instead refers to the implementation of design elements that are characteristic of games (Deterding et al. 2011). Here, characteristic means that those elements are pervasive across games and contribute significantly to the meaning of the game (Sailer et al. 2017).

Researchers use different approaches to subclassify the term "element." Whereas Cheong et al. (2014) differentiate between concrete elements, such as points and leaderboards, and abstract elements, such as game mechanics and dynamics, Werbach and Hunter (2012) distinguish between components, mechanics, and dynamics. A classification into mechanics, dynamics, and aesthetics is also commonly used. Some authors avoid sub-classifications and refer to each element directly (Eickhoff et al. 2012, p.872, Guin et al. 2012, p.615).

Several studies focus on compilations of game elements as basic building blocks of gamification (Kapp 2012, Robinson/Bellotti 2013, Werbach/Hunter 2012, Werbach/Hunter 2015, Zichermann/Cunningham 2011, Zichermann/Linder 2012, Reeves/Read 2009). These lists of elements are partly identical but, at the same time, reveal different views on the importance of game elements as they vary widely. Werbach and Hunter (2012) focus on 15 components, while Reeves and Read (2009) identify ten. Amongst those components are avatars, badges, leaderboards, points, narrative context, feedback, competition, and teams, to name a few.

In this study, I do not aim to provide another compilation of game elements. Instead, for purposes of my study, I focus on a selection of several elements whose effects will be investigated. The game elements discussed in more detail below are (1) leaderboard, (2) avatar, (3) points, (4) time restrictions, (5) progression bar, (6) level, (7) search and discovery. I focus on these specific elements for four reasons. First, according to Ferro et al. (2013) and Bartle (1996), different player types exist. Depending on the player type, an individual prefers certain game elements (Kocadere/Özhan 2018). The chosen combination of game elements aims to satisfy the preferences of a broad range of player types. Second, the focus on these specific elements is explained by their direct visibility to the user. They can be displayed on a surface and thus foster the perception of game elements by the users. Third, to avoid the influence of interpersonal effects, no team-specific elements or elements related to direct communication were chosen. Fourth, the selected elements are the ones most frequently employed in existing literature (Seaborn/Fels 2015, p.23). In sum, relying on this set of elements ensures that similar effects on motivation and behavior can be observed, and that the results are comparable to other studies.

(1) Leaderboards rank players according to their performance in a certain activity. They are also referred to as high-score lists, rankings, or scoreboards. They are often implemented to display results based on accumulated points (Buckley et al. 2019). Displaying relative success in the form of a leaderboard allows comparison to others, which leads to a competitive mechanism such as a desire to outperform others (Buckley et al. 2019). The element allows for a quick identification of high performers (Crumlish/Malone 2009). Despite their motivational potential, there are also studies that suggest that leaderboards have a negative effect on motivation and performance. While being on top of the list may encourage further performance, being on the bottom can promote frustration and giving-up (Cherry/Ellis 2005). Nevertheless, the implementation of leaderboards (as well as points and levels) aims to provide a clear connection between individuals' actions and performance. Previous research suggests that this feedback is effective in increasing motivation and promoting certain behaviors (Von Ahn/Dabbish 2008, Denny 2013, Hamari 2013, Wang/Eccles 2013).
(2) An avatar refers to a character, icon, or figure that represents a user. Avatars enable users to adopt or create a fictive identity and allow them to participate in a virtual community (Annetta 2010). In gamified environments, they are usually chosen or created by individuals (Kapp 2012). The visualization can vary from simple pictograms to complex multidimensional animation or uploaded pictures of the individual (Sailer et al. 2017). Avatars are required to allow a clear identification of the user. Frequently, making progress is linked to further options to customize an avatar (Buckley et al. 2019). The visual representation of a player's character fulfills several functions, such as personalization of an individual's experience of a gamified activity and increasing emotional attachment to the activity (Buckley et al. 2019, p. 26).
(3) Points serve as a numerical record to indicate progress in gamified activities or processes and are frequently used in applications (Zichermann/Cunningham 2011). They represent a reward for specific activities, processing, completing

a task, or reaching certain goals within the setting (Sailer et al. 2017, Werbach/Hunter 2012). Points are numerical feedback for player performance. In contrast to the relative ranking through leaderboards, points present an absolute metric (Buckley et al. 2019). Depending on the gamified environment and related objectives, various kinds of points exist, such as experience points, redeemable points, or reputation points (Werbach/Hunter 2012). As a performance measure, points provide continuous and immediate feedback and reward (Sailer et al. 2013). Depending on the form of implementation, points can have several functions, such as to indicate prowess, status, or to serve as a social function (Buckley et al. 2019).

(4) A time restriction or time limit is an imposed restriction on activities within a gamified environment. It requires finishing a task or performing required actions within a specified passage of time and can be visualized in the form of a countdown. As an integral part of goal achievement, time constraints can be used to adapt task difficulty and create pressure (Buckley et al. 2019).

(5) A progression bar refers to a graphical element used to visualize and/or control an operation in digital computing. It is frequently used to indicate the progression of digital operations such as program installation and file transfer. A distinction can be drawn between determinate progress bars, showing a percentage of completion, and indeterminate progress bars, indicating that an operation is ongoing. Depending on the context, progress-bars might be accompanied by user options such as a "cancel" or "stop" button, information on the indicated operation, and metrics (percentage or number of items).

(6) Within the context of games and gamification, a level is often linked or defined by missions or storylines. As an inter-related set of achievements, it indicates increasingly difficult environments and is also referred to as a "stage," "area" or "world." Levels allow for the system to group individuals in accordance with their skills and, thus, to provide challenging tasks appropriate to their experience and expertise (Buckley et al. 2019). By completing a task, they may gain access to another, more difficult level. This process of "leveling-up" can be indicated through feedback in the form of a pop-up window, changes in page theme, colors, amongst others. The implementation of a level serves diverse purposes, such as bundling activities to promote skill development and learning; or to indicate progression (Buckley et al. 2019).

(7) Search and discovery refer to the possibility of reaching a goal via several distinct paths. The purpose of this element is to engage and motivate individuals through enabling exploration and discovery. Process optimization and skill

development often require a high number of repetitions. As such, implementing search and discovery decreases the level of boredom and fatigue emerging from repetitive activities (Buckley et al. 2019).

Additionally, elements such as badges, boss fights, combat, gifting, multi-player function, virtual goods, time constraints, content unlocking, quests, social graphs, and performance graphs are frequently used. These will not be discussed in greater detail here. For further reading on these elements, the studies of Werbach/Hunter (2015), Buckley et al. (2019), and Robinson/Bellotti (2013) provide helpful insights. Buckley et al. (2019) investigated 97 empirical studies to identify relative frequencies of implemented game elements. Results show that points, achievements, progression bars, and quests were the most commonly used elements, as they were represented in over 70% of the studies, whereas levels and leaderboards were used in 59.8%, time constraints in 56.7%, and avatars in 29.9% of the studies. Gifting, as the least frequently implemented element, was found in 13.8% of the studies. Moreover, the authors found significant differences in the usage of elements depending on whether applications aim at individual or group effects (Buckley et al. 2019).

After having provided information on the definition of gamification and the related term of game elements in this section, the next section presents a broad overview of underlying theoretical frameworks.

2.1.3 Theoretical Frames of Gamification

Conceptual and theoretical papers on gamification have been published in different fields of study, such as business, information systems, marketing, software development, and education. Among these various studies, we can distinguish between those that focus on designing gamified environments or systems and those that focus on examining the effects of an existing gamification. Frameworks are mostly compilations of existing theories, whereby underlying theoretical models are applied in a context-sensitive manner depending on the field of studies (e.g., learning, customer loyalty, creative processes, health sector). In the following, I will first provide an overview of theories on the design of gamification. Afterward, I will summarize the theories utilized to examine the effects of gamification. Figure 2.1 provides an overview of the theoretical frames of gamification.

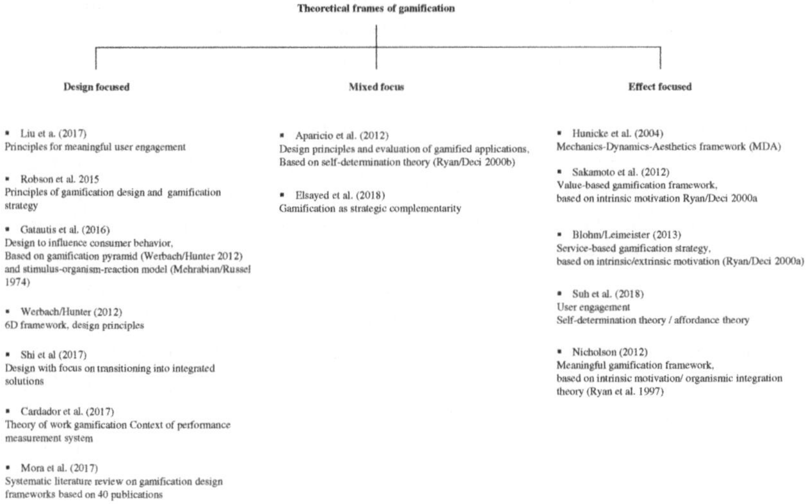

Figure 2.1 Overview of theoretical frames of gamification

Mora et al. (2017) provide a systematic literature review of gamification *design frameworks*. They analyzed 40 publications, of which 18 focus on business environments. The remaining studies were classified based on their context as either environmentally unspecific, learning, or health related. Among the publications focusing on the business environment, the authors found that non-theoretical frameworks emphasized iterative processes as a focal point. Moreover, the majority of frameworks included either user-centered design principles (Burke 2014, Gears/Brown 2013, Kumar 2013, Li 2014, Popa 2013, Raftopoulos 2014) or technological design principles (Brito et al. 2015, Harms et al. 2014, Herzig 2014, Kumar 2013, Li 2014, Raftopoulos 2014, Ruhi 2015). The first considers users and their goals as a crucial basis of design and development; the latter focus on technological artifacts such as architecture, modeling, and systems as a foundation for any deployment of gamification. Other publications used the 6D framework as the underlying concept (Brito et al. 2015, Julius/Salo 2013). The 6D framework presents a design process that consists of six phases: define business objectives, delineate target behavior, describe players, devise activity loops, don't forget the fun, deploy appropriate tools. Further, frameworks and theories from the field of psychology provided a basis for frameworks that focus on designing gamification (Gears/Brown 2013).

In the field of information systems, Liu et al. (2017) propose a taxonomy and framework for the research of gamified systems. The framework includes a design approach and principles that aim to stimulate meaningful user engagement. In the area of marketing, Gatautis et al. (2016) combine the gamification pyramid proposed by Werbach and Hunter (2012) and the stimulus-organism-reaction model by Mehrabian and Russel (1974). The resulting framework explains how gamification can influence online consumer behavior, whereby game components basically act as stimuli on the individual and lead to a consumption decision (Gatautis et al. 2016). Within the business domain, Robson et al. (2015) discussed the principles of gamified company practices, specifically focusing on customer engagement effects. The proposed framework covers the optimal design and implementation of gamified applications as well as the gamification strategy of companies. Cardador et al. (2017) provide a similar framework in the context of performance measurement. Thus, gamification is theorized to be an extension of traditional performance management systems that facilitates access to performance information for employees. Moreover, Carador et al. (2017) investigate several characteristics of individuals that mitigate or even hinder the effects of gamification. Furthermore, Shi et al. (2017) provide a gamification framework targeting the context of transitioning to integrated solutions.

Besides the frameworks with a design focus, scholars proposed frameworks that explain the *effects of gamified environments* and outline how gamification systems can be analyzed. In these studies, frameworks predominantly refer to theoretical foundations grounded in the field of psychology. Thus, a part of the literature relies on the Mechanics-Dynamics-Aesthetics (MDA) framework by Hunicke et al. (2004). This framework provides a formal structural approach to understand gamification. It allows for games to be dissected into rules, systems, and fun, which are mirrored within the framework by the three components: mechanics, dynamics, and aesthetics. Mechanics refer to particular parts at the level of data representation and algorithms. Dynamics describe the interaction of player input, mechanics, and outputs during run-time. Aesthetics refer to the emotional effects of the elements on players who interact with the game or gamified system.

Moreover, Sakamoto et al. (2012) introduced a value-based gamification framework. Building on the theoretical background of intrinsic motivation, it consists of five values: (1) informative value—providing necessary informational content at the right time, (2) empathetic value –creating sympathy and positive relationship, e.g., through implementing virtual characters, (3) persuasive value—providing feedback to the user, (4) economic value—providing ownership of digital objects and (5) ideological value—including metaphors to promote ideological concepts and values such as friendship. Blohm and Leimeister (2013) developed a service-based gamification strategy. To explain the effects of gamification on motivation and behavior, they draw on Ryan and Deci's theory on intrinsic and extrinsic motivation (Ryan/Deci 2000a). Moreover, they integrate theories on social recognition, cognitive stimulation, and intellectual curiosity (Blohm/Leimeister, 2013). The framework describes service bundles, which consist of game elements and mechanics. These bundles are related to certain motivational and behavioral outcomes.

Nicholson (2012) introduces a user-centered framework for "meaningful gamification."[2] Within this framework, he builds on organismic integration theory, a sub-theory of self-determination theory, to emphasize the importance of intrinsic motivation (Ryan et al. 1997). According to this, meaningful game elements are associated with intrinsic motivation regardless of external rewards (Nicholson 2012). He follows a user-centered approach, as meaningful gamification requires situational relevance and situated motivational affordance. Situational relevance demands an assessment of meaning by the user. Situated motivational affordance stresses that users' backgrounds and the gamified setup should be evaluated in a specific context. To ensure that various types of users are affected by gamification, it should be implemented based on a universal design, which includes various forms of content presentation, a diverse set of activities to explore, and various options to demonstrate skills. Suh et al. (2017) first draw on affordance theory to explain the effects of gamification. In a subsequent publication, Suh et al. (2018) provide a framework that draws on cognitive evaluation theory as a sub-theory of self-determination theory. Thus, gamification is effective due to the satisfaction of psychological needs (autonomy, competence, relatedness).

Next to the frameworks that focus either on the design of gamified environments or on explaining the effects of gamification, there exist *frameworks that cover both, design and effect aspects* of gamification. The framework developed by Aparicio et al. (2012) is based on self-determination theory. It builds on the concept of autonomy, competence, and social relatedness (Ryan/Deci 2000b). The framework consists of four parts that describe the whole cycle from design to later evaluations of applied gamification systems. First, an identification of the main objectives and reasons for implementing gamification is carried out. Secondly, the

---

[2] Nicholson (2012) defines meaningful gamification as "the use of gameful and playful layers to help a user find personal connections that motivate engagement with a specific context for long-term change." He further makes a distinction between reward-based gamification which focuses on the short-term and involves no personal connection or intrinsic motivation of the user.

"identification of the transversal objective" provides insights on targeted motivating factors (Aparicio et al. 2012, p. 2). The third step determines which game elements should be implemented. Therefore, elements' contribution to the fulfillment of psychological needs according to self-determination theory is assessed. The final step deals with the evaluation of the applied gamification system (Aparicio et al. 2012). Further, Elsayed et al. (2018) provide a comprehensive conceptual model that refers to gamification as strategic complementarity that contributes to building capabilities within organizations (e.g., learning, talent management). The concept covers design aspects of gamification, as well as psychological and behavioral outcomes, and explains how gamification can be used to build organizational capabilities and performance metrics.

In summary, a variety of frameworks on the design of gamification and evaluation of the effects of gamification can be found in the existing literature. However, none of the frameworks has proven dominant. This seems consistent with the early stage of gamification as a concept. Nonetheless, a common denominator among these frameworks can be found in underlying theories. In particular, affordance theory and sub-theories of the self-determination theory are used to derive and justify the design of gamified applications or explain the effects of gamification on psychological and behavioral measures.

In the remainder of this chapter, I will delimit the concept of gamification with respect to other related concepts.

2.1.4 Delimitation of Gamification with Respect to Other Concepts

The concept of gamification is often difficult to distinguish from other concepts. This can create confusion. Gamification is often referred to as a serious game, or gamifying an activity is called "framing an activity as a game" (Lieberoth 2015). Hence, in this section, I will delimit the concept of gamification to distinguish it from the concepts of serious games, pervasive games, game-based learning, advergames, as well as from the concept of framing and task attractiveness.

2.1.4.1 Serious Games, Pervasive Games, Game-based Learning, and Advergames

The terms serious games and gamification are occasionally used synonymously (Landers 2015). While both concepts aim to increase user engagement and interest in a given system, serious games are full games, predominantly used in educational contexts (Terlutter/Capella 2013, Landers 2015). Serious games refer to fully developed games and have a particular non-entertaining purpose (Deterding et al. 2011, Xu et al. 2013). Also, the concepts of pervasive games, digital game-based learning, and advergames are based on an implementation of a fully fledged game. Like serious games, these concepts should be considered standalone concepts. In comparison, gamification describes the implementation of some game elements without claiming to create a full game and, consequently, is distinct from the above-mentioned concepts (Deterding et al. 2011).

2.1.4.2 Framing Effect

Framing and gamification can be differentiated by their effect on the perception of a task or information. The framing effect was first introduced in decision-making literature; it described the fact that despite facing identical decision problems, individuals often behave differently depending on how the problem is presented (Kahneman/Tversky 1979, Chang et al. 2002). Levin et al. (1998) differentiate three types of framing effects: standard risky choice, attribute framing, and goal framing. Most studies in the field of managerial accounting focus on the risky-choice framing effect (Chang et al. 2002). Risky choice framing refers to the different descriptions of a choice problem with equivalent outcomes and affects preference orders (Tversky/Kahneman 1981). Attribute framing refers to highlighting a characteristic of an object as either positive or negative (e.g., labeling beef as 75% lean versus 25% fat) (Levin/Gaeth 1988). Goal framing describes the different descriptions of a logically equivalent outcome as either desirable (e.g., 50% success rate) or undesirable (e.g., 50% failure rate).

Framing functions as a socio-cognitive filter to direct attention and change the understanding of a task or information (Davidson 2002). In contrast, gamification does not change a user's understanding of the task or information. This difference can be illustrated by SAP's gamified application, "Lead-in-One." (SAP 2011). Initially, managers perceived the task of assigning new sales requests to a responsible account executive as cumbersome and exhibited evasive behavior towards the task. SAP introduced a gamified version of the process that provided a golf-themed user interface (golf balls representing the request, while holes representing the sales representatives). Through the gamified version, the managers' understanding of the task as a professional duty remains unchanged. Managers are fully aware that completing a hole is equivalent to assigning a sales lead. In contrast, framing this task as a game would change the understanding of the task as a professional duty. If it was a true game, this would also mean managers could choose to participate in a "game" and correspondingly exclude any consequences should they decide not to participate or perform a task.

Lieberoth (2015) experimentally tested framing and gamification concepts for their psychological impact. Both concepts yielded similar cognitive and behavioral effects. Results suggest that both, framing and gamification, encourage task engagement, while gamification results in a slightly higher engagement increase compared to framing. At the same time, a change in self-reported intrinsic motivation was neither observable in the framed nor in the gamified task. Nevertheless, the characterization of gamification highlights that the concept differs from that of framing. To sum up, gamification differs from framing in that it implements game elements and mechanics, yet gamification leaves the understanding of the task itself unchanged.

2.1.4.3 Task Attractiveness

Task attractiveness describes the perception of a task as being interesting and creating task enjoyment. In this sense, task enjoyment captures the individual's experience of a task being pleasurable, and thus, creating a feeling of joviality and happiness (Cardador 2017, p. 357). An attractive task is more likely to be performed based on intrinsic motivation. Within an interactive, web-based experiment with participants from U.S. universities, Bailey and Fessler (2011) demonstrated that the absolute benefits of monetary incentives decrease when the task is attractive. Gamification can increase the perceived attractiveness of a task (Rybak et al. 2015). However, gamification and task attractiveness should not be equated. Whereas task attractiveness describes a subjective perception (Bailey/Fessler 2011), gamification refers to an objective change of the environment or task (Deterding et al. 2011).

Next, I will shed light on the various application areas of gamification to demonstrate its practical relevance.

2.1.4.4 Relative Performance Indicators

The concept of gamification and relative performance indicators (RPI) are not identical, yet they do overlap. RPI are frequently used by firms in order to provide performance feedback and allow comparison between employees. The theory behind RPI suggests that competitive feedback can positively affect motivation and performance even without monetary incentives linked to performance (Festinger 1954, Hannan et al. 2013).[3]

Depending on the chosen game elements, gamification can include RPI (e.g., leaderboards, public display of badges). However, gamification can be

[3] Depending on endogenous and individual factors, relative performance information can also cause demotivation (Collins 2000, Mussweiler 2003).

implemented based on elements that do not inherently provide information on performance (avatar, narrative elements) and/or elements that provide feedback but are presented in absolute form on an individual level (progress bar, level upgrades, and points). Based on the broad spectrum of elements involved, gamification is able to trigger more/other dynamics than RPI (exploring, fun, creativity, cooperation) (Hunicke et al. 2004). Thus, the concept of gamification is more comprehensive compared to RPI.

2.1.5 Areas of Application

Gamification is implemented in a broad range of areas and contexts, including education and learning, military training, marketing and customer relationships, health and exercise, innovation, and creativity. Although the majority of gamified applications are implemented in a digital context, the concept itself does not necessarily require such technology or systems (Buckley et al. 2019).

In accordance with the setting and goals, gamified implementations focus on individuals or groups. Examples of individual-oriented gamification applications include "Goalbook," a gamified education tool kid, "FitRPG," an application with a focus on health, fitness and wellness, and "Habit List," a personal productivity and goal tracker (Buckley et al. 2019). As examples for group-oriented applications, "Battle of Concepts," "Greenbean Recycle," and "Magnum Pleasure Hunt" can be listed.[4] From an organizational perspective, gamification can be oriented towards consumers and/or employees. Depending on the implementation context, there are diverse objectives, ranging from increasing customer loyalty, creating brand awareness, enhancing employees' engagement and motivation as well as improving their performance. For the latter purpose, employees are confronted with a gamified work-related environment, including game elements such as badges, points, leaderboards, missions, and levels, to name a few.

In recent years, many organizations have implemented gamified information systems or applications to support business activities (Suh et al. 2017). Companies from various sectors such as IBM, Microsoft, Siemens, Bayer, or Applebee's have implemented gamified applications to recruit, motivate and train employees (Kappen/Nacke 2013). Nike, Starbucks, McDonald's, Coca-Cola, Magnum, Seat, and Heineken adopted gamified platforms to increase customer engagement (Nobre/Ferreira 2017, Chou 2016). SAP even includes employees' performance

[4] For an extensive list of individual and group oriented gamified activities see Buckley et al. 2019 p. 30.

within a gamified community network into promotion considerations. AirBaltic, a state-owned Latvian airline company, introduced gamification via a business game aiming to increase employee engagement. The management of this company claims that the application results in better communication, increased employee commitment, and improved quality of management decisions that have the potential to save expenses amounting to up to one million Euros annually. Employees perceived themselves as better informed of the company's plans, actual projects, upcoming decisions, and key targets (Ērgle 2016, 2015). The industry behind gamification grows due to the increasing interest in its practical implementations (Cardador 2017). Before the COVID-19 pandemic, the gamification market size was predicted to grow from USD 9.1 billion in 2020 to USD 30.7 billion by 2025 (Markets and Markets 2020). During the pandemic, digitalization as a trend has continually gained strength (Soto-Acosta 2020). As the majority of gamified applications is based on digital design, one might speculate that the pandemic will have a positive influence on the market growth of gamification.

2.2 Systematic Literature Review

Neither management literature nor research on organizational control has paid much attention to gamification. However, the concept has already been examined in the fields of education, computer science, and psychology (Reiners/Wood 2015). Previous quantitative studies focus on the implementation of specific elements and observe positive, neutral, or negative effects on motivation and performance. Two literature reviews assessed the previous literature on gamification. Whereas Hamari et al. (2014) concentrated on motivational affordances in empirical studies, Seaborn and Fels (2015) opted for a more holistic approach, including theoretical and empirical papers. Since the publication of these two literature reviews, research on gamification has generated a considerable body of literature. Before presenting the respective research questions and analyzing subsequent studies, I will provide a brief summary of the findings from Hamari et al. (2014) and Seaborn and Fels (2015).

In 2015, Seaborn and Fels published a meta-synthesis-based literature review in which they clustered and analyzed the first wave of scientific literature on gamification with a holistic approach.[5] Their results demonstrated that scholars across diverse domains and fields of study have engaged with the concept. However, a

[5] The first wave of literature refers to publications on gamification up to July 30, 2013, which served as the closing date of literature search by Seaborn and Fels (2015).

lack of consistency concerning the use and interpretation of the concept's theoretical foundations became obvious. Rather, Seaborn and Fels (2015) observed that conceptual research and empirical research on gamification were carried out in parallel without connecting. Empirical studies that examine the effects of gamification on participants provided a rather mixed picture. The authors suggest that the divergence of results might be traced back to different application domains and emphasized the context-sensitive character of gamification.

Another literature review on gamification was carried out by Hamari et al. (2014). Empirical studies on gamification were analyzed using the information on the context of implementation, study methodology, results, investigated motivational affordances (independent variables), and examined psychological and behavioral outcomes. Results show mixed effects of gamification, with the positive effects being more frequent. Hamari et al. (2014) identified different contexts of application and differences among users as the sources of the varying effects of gamification.

Both literature reviews find that the effects of gamification varied widely. One reason for these mixed findings could be the novelty factor. Scholars claim that in the beginning, a perceived innovative character of a gamified system drives positive effects, but as users get used to the system, this effect declines over time (Seaborn/Fels 2015). Also, some studies observe a varying effectiveness of gamification amongst individuals (Gasland 2011, Passos et al. 2011, Witt et al. 2011). Bagley (2012) found that age and familiarity with gaming are related to the interest in and the use of gamified systems. McDaniel et al. (2012) identified gender as an influence on the effects of gamification in a study of an online course: After receiving information about a classmate earning a badge, female participants showed marginally significant more engagement in earning a badge compared to males.

However, neither the literature reviews nor any other studies focused on reasons for the diverging effectiveness of gamification. The following literature review addresses this research gap and investigates the factors that may have led to varying results concerning the effects of gamification on motivation and performance. An additional impetus for this research stems from the fact that since the publication of the two literature reviews by Seaborn and Fels (2015) and Hamari et al. (2014), the discourse on gamification has taken on new dimensions, yielding a correspondingly high number of studies. Therefore, the following study aims to review this second wave of literature on gamification with the objective of classifying, evaluating, and assessing publications from diverse fields of studies and thus providing an extensive picture of the state of research on gamification.[6] The analysis of previous literature includes factors that are deep-seated in the field of management accounting and control (e.g., compensation and performance measures). These criteria are chosen based on the need to introduce and establish a basis for further research on gamification in the field of management accounting and control. Based on this motivation, I conduct a systematic literature review (SLR) examining empirical papers.[7]

2.2.1 Research Questions

The first review question is derived from the insights of previous studies, which called attention to flawed study design, missing theoretical frameworks, and a lack of statistical analysis (Hamari et al. 2014, Seaborn/Fels 2015). Further, most of the previous studies implemented a cross-sectional design (Seaborn/Fels 2015). However, the results from a limited number of longitudinal studies suggest that the positive effects of gamification on motivation may decrease over time, or that gamification may even carry negative effects occur over a longer observation period (Hanus/Fox 2015, Putz et al. 2020). Thus, the effectiveness of gamification might be linked to a novelty effect (Sanchez et al. 2020). Only a more balanced ratio of cross-sectional and longitudinal studies would provide insights on whether gamification affects motivation and performance in the long and/or short-term. To evaluate whether the second wave of studies on gamification overcomes these shortcomings, my SLR aims to answer the following question:

> *RQ1: To what extent do recently published papers feature a longitudinal or cross-sectional design and sufficiently explain theoretical underpinnings?*

Further questions focus on the mixed findings concerning the effectiveness of gamification implementations. Examining the effects of gamification in a learning system, Domínguez et al. (2013) observe positive effects on motivation, but at the same time, negative effects on performance. Similarly, the study of Guin et al. (2012), which examines the effects of gamification within marketing questionnaires, found that gamification resulted in an increased sense of satisfaction among users while at the same time no effects on engagement occurred.

---

[6] The second wave of literature refers to literature on gamification published between 1st August 2013 and 30th April 2018.

[7] I deliberately decided against performing a traditional literature review, as this method is criticized for its subjective approach and lack of methodical rigor (Tranfield et al. 2003).

Results from examining two cases of gamified healthcare services show that patients experience challenge, entertainment, social dynamics, and escapism and show positive engagement effects. However, when tasks level of difficulty exceeded patients' abilities and skills, positive engagement effects were deferred or moderated negatively (Hammedi et al. 2017). Moreover, it has been demonstrated that applying game elements in online surveys can significantly increase the richness of spontaneous data, participant engagement, as well as the time that participants take to complete a survey without significant differences concerning data validity (Bailey et al. 2015). However, these results were only partly reproducible in a longitudinal study. In the first session, respondents found it more enjoyable and easier to complete the gamified survey. In doing so, no differences in participation rates were observable compared to the control condition. In the second session, a higher breakoff was found among participants in the gamified condition. The positive gamification effect found in the first session faded in the second one (Mavletova 2015). The results of other studies support the assumption that the effects of gamification on motivation and work performance are in part temporarily limited. Whereas cross-sectional study designs led to positive effects on motivation and performance, such effects vanished in longitudinal studies (Suh et al. 2017). Up until now, there is no sufficient explanation for the broad spectrum of results.

From the perspective of accounting and management control, it is particularly interesting to explore whether gamification can be utilized to increase performance under recurrent forms of compensation. Against the background of mixed findings on the effectiveness of gamification, it is moreover important to examine whether contradicting results can be explained by participants' compensation within empirical studies. In general, studies differ widely concerning the compensation of participants, ranging from no compensation over non-monetary compensation (e.g., credit points, material goods) to monetary compensation (e.g., tournaments, fixed pay, performance-contingent pay schemes) (Bonner/Sprinkle 2002). Theory and evidence from diverse disciplines show that these forms of compensation affect motivation, effort and performance differently (Awasthi/Pratt 1990, Lee et al. 1997, Deci/Ryan 1985, Jenkins et al. 1998, Kunz/Linder 2012). Monetary incentives are frequently used to increase motivation, effort and performance (Bonner/Sprinkle 2002). Theories, such as agency theory (Baiman 1982) and expectancy theory (Vroom 1964), predict that performance-contingent monetary rewards leads to increased effort and performance as compared to fixed compensation.[8] As previous literature reviews on gamification failed to investigate the effects of participants' compensation as an influencing factor, my SLR addresses this research gap by answering the following questions:

RQ2: Which compensation schemes were used in recent studies, and is there a relationship between the compensation scheme and the effects of gamification?

RQ3: Which other factors (e.g., implemented elements, applied measures) might explain the mixed results of gamification on effort, motivation and performance?

2.2.2 Methodology

As a secondary study, this SLR follows a structured, clear cut methodology to ensure an unbiased and objective approach. The method aims at providing a summary of existing literature, identifying research gaps and establishing a framework for future research (Kitchenham/Charters 2007). In light of the broad range of empirical methods and domains concerning research on gamification, SLR represents an appropriate method (Kitchenham/Charters 2007).

The literature search follows a six-step approach and is based on a specific review question (Jesson et al. 2011, p. 108). In the first step, the scope of the search is sharped, review questions are phrased, keywords for the literature search are determined, criteria for the inclusion of papers are defined, and data extraction sheets are designed (Booth et al. 2012, p. 58 ff, Davis/Crombie 1998, Tranfield et al. 2003).

To answer the questions derived in the previous section, I will rely on empirical studies on gamification available in EBSCOhost and Google Scholar. The timeframe for my SLR is oriented around the previous literature study of Seaborn and Fels. As they ended their search on July 30, 2013, my SLR started directly after August 1, 2013 and ended on April 30, 2018.

For the purpose of maintaining comparability with the study of Seaborn and Fels (2015), databases were searched for the terms: *gamification* and *gamif**. The use of the latter term allows the query to identify studies that use an adjective or verb form of gamification. Further, the following inclusion criteria were defined, whereby papers were only included if they met all of the stated criteria:

[8] However, previous research shows a mixed picture on the effectiveness of monetary rewards on effort and performance (Bonner et al. 2000, Jenkins 186, Jenkins et al. 1998, Gupta/Shawn 1998). A detailed overview of underlying theories and evidence will be provided in chapter three.

- Original, full paper, peer-reviewed, published in an international journal (in English)
- Research on gamification, rather than on fully-fledged games
- Published between August 1, 2013 and April 30, 2018
- Inclusion of empirical study involving human participants
- Research methods specified and substantial (data collection with validated instruments)

In the second step, a comprehensive literature search through databases was performed. Results were assessed regarding relevance to previously defined research questions. Jesson et al. (2011, p. 108) note that if necessary, keywords for search should be modified in this step. Due to the use of the broader search term *gamif**, an adaption of the search terms was not necessary.

In step three of my SLR, a quality assessment of the papers is performed. At this point, Jesson et al. (2011) recommends reading the full paper, while Booth et al. (2012, p. 99) suggest a successive three-stage approach: title screening, sifting based on abstracts and full-text evaluation. In this thesis, I rely on Booth's approach. The quality assessment can be based on the nature of the review process, type of publication, date of publication, and journal impact factor (Jesson et al. 2011, p. 120 f.).[9]

Step four of SLR covers the extraction of the relevant data based on a previously developed extraction sheet. In doing so, studies were scanned for numerical data as well as statistical analysis and interpretation.

In step five, the extracted data were synthesized to identify patterns in the literature and integrate knowledge across different fields of studies. This step is particularly useful for identifying possible explanations for mixed findings (Booth et al. 2012, p. 125). For a synthesis of the literature, there are three methods that are often employed: meta-analysis, meta-synthesis, and narrative review. A condition for conducting a meta-analysis is homogenous numerical variables and comparable research questions and methods of measurement. Consequently, a meta-analysis is predominantly used for further developed, homogenous bodies of research (Kitchenham/Charters 2007, Booth et al. 2012, p.153). Unlike the

[9] The journal impact factor was no criterion for inclusion of a paper nor its quality assessment. This decision against the recommended procedure by Jesson et al. (2011, p. 120 f.) was made for two reasons. First, no ranking did cover all journals of the identified papers (e.g. VHB Jourqual 3, Scimago Journal and Country Rank (SJR and InCites Journal Citation Reports (JCR)). Second, as the field of gamification is relatively young and previous studies were criticized for methodological flaws, including the ranking would preclude an objective overview of the current research state.

meta-analysis, the meta-synthesis is suitable for heterogeneous bodies of literature, as it is not limited to comparable study design but synthesizes data in an interpretative way by displaying similarities and differences. Particular attention is given to theories and findings in a narrative form (Sandelowski et al. 1997). A meta-synthesis differs inherently from a meta-analysis since the former summarizes previous literature on a qualitative basis, and the latter relies on statistical data yielding in a quantitative overview of effects (Heyvaert et al. 2013, Tranfield et al. 2003). A third technique to synthesize the literature can be found in the narrative review. The narrative review builds on a descriptive approach and is mostly used for primary, qualitative studies. The method is the least systematic of the three mentioned above and is often criticized for its inability to detect consensus across findings (Booth et al. 2012, p. 147).[10]

As mentioned before, research on gamification is highly diversified concerning domains and design. As the body of literature does not meet the homogeneity requirements of a meta-analysis, this SLR adopts a meta-synthesis approach. The final step of the SLR includes a write up of synthesis findings.

Throughout the six steps of the literature review process, transparency, reproducibility, and auditability were ensured by protocols (Jesson et al. 2011, p. 103, Kitchenham/Charters 2007). Moreover, with the implementation of cross-checking and a test–retest procedure performed independently by two researchers, I followed the approach of Kitchenham and Charters to ensure consistency of data extraction and replicability (2007). Table 2.1 (p. 31) provides an overview of the included papers. Hereby, the included papers are categorized by the application domain.

2.2.3 Findings of Systematic Literature Review

In the following, I present the results of my literature review. I start by providing some general findings before presenting the findings that respond directly to the research questions.

[10] Further techniques to synthesize include: mixed methods research synthesis, Bayesian meta-analysis, critical interpretive synthesis, and realist synthesis (Heyvaert et al. 2013, Booth et al. 2012, p. 147 ff.).

Table 2.1 Basic study information

Nr.	Domain	Author and year	Type of Study	Purpose
1	Digital Design	Sutcliffe/ Hart (2016)	Mixed method	Exploring effect on website's perceived usefulness
2		von Rechenberg et al. (2016)	Quantitative	Evaluating the effect of rewards in online Q&A community
3		Kwon et al. (2015)	Quantitative	Understanding the motivation behind users' sharing of badges in media
4		da Silva Brito et al. (2018)	Quantitative	Developing gamification measurement scale for app users
5	Human Computation	Wang et al. (2017)	Mixed method	Exploring influence of game elements in Human Computation System
6	Information Systems	Suh et al. (2017)	Quantitative	Exploring aesthetic and flow experience in gamified IS
7		Hamari et al. (2018)	Quantitative	Comparing the influence of users' goals & motivations with regard to gamification
8		Hamari/ Koivisto (2015)	Quantitative	Exploring the effects on attitude towards and continued use of gamified systems
9	Education / Learning	Monterrat et al. (2017)	Quantitative	Predicting gamer types and adapting game mechanics

(continued)

Table 2.1 (continued)

Nr.	Domain	Author and year	Type of Study	Purpose
10		Landers/ Landers (2014)	Quantitative	Increasing student motivation through game elements
11		Armstrong/ Landers (2017)	Quantitative	Increasing students' declarative and procedural knowledge
12		Baxter et al. (2016)	Quantitative	Enhancing knowledge gain through gamified training
13		Frost et al. (2015)	Quantitative	Exploring the effects of gamified Learning Management System
14		Smith (2017)	Quantitative	Analyzing effect of gamified statistics course on the students' attitudes
15		Baxter et al. (2015)	Quantitative	Enhancing knowledge gain through a gamified training
16		Lambert (2017)	Mixed method	Exploring effects of attitudes and knowledge on the use of gamified learning tools
17		Fisher et al. (2014)	Quantitative	Investigating knowledge, experience and attitude from teachers towards gamification

(continued)

Table 2.1 (continued)

Nr.	Domain	Author and year	Type of Study	Purpose
18		Cheong et al. (2014)	Mixed method	Exploring students' perception of various game elements
19		Liu et al. (2018)	Quantitative	Exploring gamifications' effects on job performance, motivation and satisfaction
20	Business	Suh/ Wagner (2017)	Quantitative	Exploring effects of gamification on knowledge-sharing and underlying affordances
21		Leclercq et al. (2017)	Mixed method	Exploring effects of gamification on co-creation, identifying different user types
22		Seiffert-Brockmann et al. (2018)	Quantitative	Exploring the effect of gamification on stakeholders' behavior
23		Nobre/ Ferreira (2017)	Qualitative	Exploring the relation between gamified and brand co-creation experiences
24		Kamel et al. (2017)	Mixed method	Investigating the user attitude towards a gamified system in an enterprise context

(continued)

Table 2.1 (continued)

Nr.	Domain	Author and year	Type of Study	Purpose
25		Bittner/ Shipper (2014)	Quantitative	Exploring the effect of gamification slogans in advertising of sports products
26	Surveys / Market Research	Mavletova (2015)	Quantitative	Exploring the effect of game elements in longitudinal surveys
27		Scheiner (2015)	Mixed method	Exploring the longitudinal effect of gamification in idea competitions
28		Rapp et al. (2015)	Mixed method	Exploring the effect of gamification on field evaluation
29	Other (Health)	Kim et al. (2017)	Quantitative	Motivating users via gamified app to stretch more

2.2.3.1 General Findings

The allocation of the 29 studies shows that research on gamification is predominantly performed within the fields of Education and Learning (34.5%); and Business (24.1%). Studies in other domains occurred less often: 13.8% Digital Design; 3.4% Human Computation; 10.3% Information Systems; 10.3% Market Research; and 3.4% in the Healthcare domain.

Consistent with previous literature reviews, mixed findings are observable concerning the effects of gamification across all domains. Some studies reported positive effects of gamification (Landers/Landers 2014, Baxter et al. 2017, Nobre/Ferreira 2017, Rapp et al. 2015); others reported negative (Kamel et al. 2017, Kim et al. 2017) or mixed effects (Sutcliffe/Hart 2016, Bittner/Shipper 2014).

Table 2.1 (p. 31) shows that with regard to the type of studies, a notable dominance of quantitative and mixed studies is observable. Only Nobre and Ferreira

(2017) uses a purely qualitative study design while exploring the relation between gamified experiences and brand co-creation experiences.

The purposes of the studies can be clustered into three types: effect-focused, design-focused, and instrument-focused. The former either investigates the effect of gamification on psychological or/and behavioral measures or examines how attitude and prior knowledge affect the use of gamified systems (e.g., Scheiner 2015). The second focuses on how gamification should be designed, including individuals' needs according to gamer typology (e.g., Armstrong/Landers 2017). The latter test a scale developed to measure effects (e.g., da Silva Brito et al. 2018). 93% of the studies can be categorized as effect-focused (83% investigating the effect of gamification on psychological and behavioral measures, 10% focus on the effects of attitude and prior knowledge on the use of gamification). 3.4% of the studies can be categorized as instrument-focused; 3.4% are design-focused.

2.2.3.2 Findings on RQ1

(1) *To what extent do recently published papers feature a longitudinal or cross-sectional design and sufficiently explain theoretical underpinnings?*

A previous literature review voiced the criticism that most of the research on gamification is not grounded in theory and does not refer to appropriate frameworks (Seaborn/Fels 2015, p. 28). Moreover, a lack of longitudinal studies was observable (Seaborn/Fels 2015). These two criticisms remain unchanged when looking at the second wave of published papers. Table 2.2 provides information on the theories and timeframes used in the studies. Thus, 58%of the reviewed papers did not provide a reasonable theoretical frame. The remaining studies use either gamification specific frames; such as BrainHex gamer typology (Monterrat et al. 2017), the framework of successful gamification (Suh/Wagner 2017), the theory of gamified learning (Smith 2017); or more generally, renowned theories, such as self-determination theory (Frost et al. 2015) or the job characteristics model (Liu et al. 2018). Deterding et al.'s (2011) definition of gamification is the most frequently referred to in research. However, some studies forego defining the concept itself (Baxter et al. 2015, Mavletova 2015).

Regarding the timeframe of the studies, the cross-sectional design remains dominant in gamification research. Of the 29 studies analyzed, only three use a longitudinal study design (Leclercq et al. 2017, Mavletova 2015, Scheiner 2015). It is worth mentioning that studies utilizing a longitudinal design suggest that gamification has positive or neutral effects on motivation and behavior. These findings seem surprising as previous publications suggest that longitudinal studies

Table 2.2 Theory used and timeframe of studies

Nr.	Theoretical Frame and definition	Timeframe; Duration
1	n/a	Cross-sectional
2	Prospect Theory Value function (Heath et al. 1999)	Cross-sectional
3	n/a	Cross-sectional
4	Octalysis (Chou 2014)	Cross-sectional,
5	n/a, definition from Deterding et al. (2011)	Cross-sectional, 15 min
6	Affective Affordances model (Van Vugt et al. 2006)	Cross-sectional
7	Goal-setting theory Social comparison theory	Cross-sectional
8	Self-Determination Theory (Deci/Ryan 1985), Theory of planned behavior (Ajzen 1991)	Cross-sectional, 3 months
9	BrainHex gamer typology (Nacke et al. 2011) Typology of game design elements (Deterding et al. 2011)	Cross-sectional Three sessions of 45 min
10	Theory of gamified learning (Landers 2014)	Cross-sectional, 10 weeks
11	Technology-Enhanced Training Effectiveness Model (Landers/Armstrong 2017); definition from Deterding et al. (2011)	Cross-sectional
12	n/a	Cross-sectional, 30 min
13	Self-Determination Theory (Ryan et al. 1997)	Cross-sectional, 1 semester
14	Theory of gamified learning (Landers 2014), Taxonomy for gamification in learning Bedwell et al. (2012)	Cross-sectional, 1 or 2 semesters
15	n/a, definition from Deterding et al. (2011)	Cross-sectional
16	n/a, definition from Deterding et al. (2011)	Cross-sectional

(continued)

Table 2.2 (continued)

Nr.	Theoretical Frame and definition	Timeframe; Duration
17	n/a	Cross-sectional
18	n/a, definition from Deterding (2012)	Cross-sectional
19	Game element hierarchy (Werbach/Hunter 2012), Job Characteristics Model (Hackman/Oldman 1974)	Cross-sectional, 2 days
20	Framework of successful gamification (Hamari et al. 2014)	Cross-sectional
21	n/a, definition from Deterding et al. (2011)	Longitudinal, 6 months
22	Concept of gamer motivation (Yee et al. 2012)	Cross-sectional, 4 weeks
23	n/a, definition from Deterding et al. (2011)	Cross-sectional
24	n/a, definition from Deterding et al. (2011)	Cross-sectional
25	Theory of planned behavior (Ajzen 1991) Modified technology acceptance model (Herzig et al. 2012),	Cross-sectional, 20 min
26	n/a	Longitudinal,10 days + 1 month
27	n/a, Definition from Deterding et al. (2011)	Longitudinal
28	n/a, definition from Deterding et al. (2011)	Cross-sectional, 4-day event
29	n/a	Cross-sectional, 5 days

on gamification result in negative results concerning motivation and performance (Hanus/Fox 2015).

2.2.3.3 Findings on RQ2

(2) *Which compensation schemes were used in recent studies, and is there a relationship between the compensation scheme and the effects of gamification?*

While analyzing the papers with regard to compensation aspects, a methodical information gap became obvious. Out of 29 studies, only 14 provided information on whether compensation was provided to the subjects of the study and if so, which type of compensation was provided. The studies reviewed used non-monetary compensation, monetary schemes (including fixed and variable compensation and lotteries), or no compensation. In the following, I will analyze these studies categorized by the type of implemented compensation scheme. Table 2.3 (p.39) provides more details on implemented compensation schemes and findings from studies that reported on the use of compensation.

Three of the studies provided no compensation to participants: Firstly, Smith (2017), who investigated the effects of gamifying a statistics course on students' attitudes towards it, used questionnaires and a skill assessment. Results suggest that gamification has a positive influence as it yielded significantly higher assessment scores after two semesters compared to the non-gamified condition. Secondly, Cheong et al. (2014) conducted a study in which they explored students' perception of various game elements through questionnaires. Findings suggest that despite a lack of knowledge concerning the concept of gamification, the majority of students had a positive attitude towards the concept and expected increased learning due to gamification. Also, Monterrat et al. (2017) forego compensation but provide free access to a fee-based learning environment instead. Based on the corresponding data logging and questionnaires, they explore how the adaptation of game mechanics affects different gamer types. Findings show that learners have different player profiles and preferences for proposed gaming features. Moreover, the learning environment becomes more complicated with added game elements. Surprisingly, gamification features that did not match the player profile were perceived as more fun and useful than compatible features (Monterrat et al. 2017). Further, a fourth study written by Baxter et al. (2015) used different forms of compensation: whereas bank employees received no compensation, students gained course credits for participating in the experiment. Baxter et al. (2015) examined the effects of gamified training on knowledge gain. They find that the gamified condition was perceived as more enjoyable and less boring but also less informative. The performance in the gamified condition was worse than in the non-gamified one. In this case, performance was measured as knowledge gained using multiple-choice questions and essay questions (Baxter et al. 2015).

The remaining 11 studies that provided compensation used different schemes, including monetary, non-monetary, fix, and variable compensation schemes or lotteries. In the following, first, the eight studies with non-monetary compensation are introduced, whereby three of them use a lottery. Afterward, those three with monetary compensation are presented.

Kwon et al. 2015 performed a field study to understand the motivation behind users' sharing of badges on social media platforms. 142 participants answered a questionnaire that gathered data on self-efficacy, social intentions, inattentive sharing, support, and passing time based on Likert scales. In return, participants entered a lottery and had the chance to win one of several $50 gift cards. They identified self-efficacy and social incentives as main drivers for users to share badges. Moreover, results suggest that different badge types are associated with different motivations (Kwon et al. 2015). Two more studies refer to lotteries to compensate participants; Hamari and Koivisto (2015) provide the opportunity to win one $50 Amazon gift certificate, and Seiffert-Brockmann et al. (2018) provide a material prize through a lottery. Hamari and Koistivo (2015) used questionnaires to analyze the effect of utilitarian, hedonic, and social motivations on attitude and continued use of gamified systems. They find that hedonic and utilitarian factors prompt the use of a gamified system, whereas social factors had no influence. Seiffert-Brockmann et al. (2018) explored the effect of gamification on stakeholders' behavior based on a questionnaire on engagement, perception of game mechanics, and sponsor recognition. Results suggest that gamification enhanced behavioral and psychological engagement. Recapitulating, all three studies utilizing a lottery for compensation yielded positive or neutral results.

Besides lotteries, course credits were used as a non-monetary compensation in three of the studies (Landers/Landers 2014, Frost et al. 2015, Baxter et al. 2016). Hereby, Landers and Landers investigate the effect of game elements on students' motivation. Based on analyzing data logging and a student assessment, they find that students provided with leaderboards interacted more frequently with their project than those in the control condition. Moreover, the time spent on the task predicted the outcomes of the assessment (Landers/Landers 2014). Baxter et al. (2015) conducted a laboratory experiment with students and a field study with bank employees to investigate the effects of gamification on knowledge acquisition through training. In this study, students were compensated with course credits; bank employees did not receive any compensation. They find that although participants in the gamified condition perceived the training as significantly more enjoyable and less boring, the gamified training did not improve knowledge acquisition. Actually, the gamified version of the training was perceived as significantly less informative and yielded significantly fewer correctly answered questions than an un-gamified version of the training (Baxter et al. 2015). Also, Frost et al. (2015) provided course credits to the participating 80 college students as they examine the effects of a gamified learning management system. Analyzing questionnaires and course grades, they find no effect of gamification on competence, motivation, perceived autonomy, and satisfaction. However, results suggest that relatedness (as a sub-construct of motivation) and students' interest were significantly higher with gamification (Frost et al. 2015). Overall, compensation with course credits yields positive, neutral, and negative effects of gamification on psychological and behavioral measures.

Two studies provided material compensation (Liu et al. 2018, Rapp et al. 2015). Liu et al. (2018) investigated the effect of job gamification on job performance, motivation, and satisfaction. The field experiment collected data in the form of questionnaires and data loggings. In return, a gift worth $10 was provided to 60 participating machine operators. Results suggest that gamification improved not only job motivation and satisfaction but also operational performance. Hereby, no correlation between consent to the concept of gamification and operational performance was observable (Liu et al. 2018). Whereas Liu et al. (2018) provided material compensation regardless of performance, Rapp et al. (2015) decided to link compensation to performance as they provided a T-shirt to those who gained a minimum amount of points. The latter study investigates the effects of gamification using data from loggings and semi-structured interviews collected in a field experiment. Results show a higher contribution in the form of social interactions in the gamified application compared to the non-gamified version (Rapp et al. 2016). Both studies using material compensation yielded positive or neutral results.

Three studies provided monetary compensation (Armstrong/Landers 2017, Leclercq et al. 2017, Kim et al. 2017). Armstrong and Landers (2017) investigated the effect of gamified training on declarative and procedural knowledge. The 273 participants of the field experiment received a variable compensation of $4 per hour. Based on a multiple-choice test, essay assessment, and a questionnaire on satisfaction, attitude and knowledge, they found gamification to increase the level of satisfaction. Furthermore, no effect on declarative knowledge acquisition was observable, but results showed a lower level of procedural knowledge compared to the control condition (Armstrong/Landers 2017). Kim et al. (2017), who tested the effects of a healthcare application for a smartwatch on stretching behavior, provided a fixed monetary compensation of $20. Analyzing data from data logging and questionnaires, they found that subjects in the gamified version performed less stretching than subjects in a comparable non-gamified app (Kim et al. 2017). Leclercq et al. (2017) explored the effects of gamifying a co-creation site on motivation and behavior. They found that two of four player-types identified value gamification features, whereas the other two were indifferent to them. In this case, participants received a percentage of the profits generated through the sale of the products and services created (Leclercq 2017). The three studies providing monetary compensation also show a rather mixed picture as their results include positive, neutral, and negative effects of gamification on different measures of motivation and performance.

To sum up, only 14 of the 29 studies provided information on compensation: three provided no compensation at all (Monterrat et al. 2017, Smith 2017, Cheong et al. 2014); three offered course credits (Landers/Landers 2014, Baxter et al. 2015, Frost et al. 2015); two provided material compensation either linked to performance (Rapp et al. 2015) or not linked to performance (Liu et al. 2018); three offered the opportunity to enter a lottery and win a gift card (Kwon et al. 2015, Hamari/Koivisto 2015) or a material prize (Seiffert-Brockmann 2018); and three offered monetary compensation which was either fixed (Kim et al. 2017) or variable (Armstrong/Landers 2017, Leclercq 2017). These forms of compensation yield a rather mixed picture concerning the effects of gamification.

2.2.3.4 Findings on RQ3

(3) *Which other factors (e.g., implemented elements, applied measures) might explain the mixed results of gamification on effort, motivation and performance?*

Several other possible causes might explain the mixed results. In the following, I will examine the effects of the choice of implemented game elements, measures used, and data capture in more detail.

Investigated studies implemented a wide variety of game elements, whereby they also differ in the number of elements implemented. Some studies incorporate solely one element, such as badges (von Rechenberg et al. 2016, Kwon et al. 2015), leaderboards (Landers/Landers 2014), or a game narrative (Armstrong/Landers 2017). Other studies implement a broad range of elements at once, such as goals, action language, challenges, points, levels, badges, virtual identity (Smith 2017, Bittner/Shipper 2014, Scheiner 2015). However, the number of implemented elements seems to have no effect on the results as studies find positive, negative, and mixed results. The question of whether certain game elements or combinations of certain elements are more or less effective in encouraging the desired psychological and behavioral outcomes remains open. Data collected within the literature review is not sufficient to answer this question due to the variety of combinations implemented.

All studies investigated captured data to measure the psychological or/and behavioral effects of gamification. Hereby, psychological constructs were measured considerably more often than behavioral measures—23 studies collect data

Table 2.3 Compensation schemes and results of studies

Nr.	Results	Findings	Compensation
3	Neutral	Users shared badges mainly for reasons of self-efficacy and social incentives. Results suggested that different badge types are associated with different motivations	Lottery, $50 gift cards
8	Mixed	Hedonic and utilitarian factors prompt the use of a gamified system. No observed influence of social factors	Non-monetary, prize draw for one $50 Amazon gift certificate
9	Mixed	Learners have different player profiles and different preferences for the proposed gaming features. Game elements increased perceived complexity	No compensation, free access to fee-based learning environment
10	Positive	Leaderboards increases interaction frequency and time on task. Time-on-task as a consistent mediator of the relationship between gamification condition and outcome	Course credits
11	Mixed	No effect on declarative knowledge, less procedural knowledge, higher level of satisfaction in gamified condition	Monetary, $4.00/ h
12	Mixed	Gamified condition perceived as less informative, more enjoyable, more fun, less boring. Performance worse in gamified condition	Non-monetary, course credits for students, No compensation for bank employees
13	Positive/ neutral	No effects on competence, autonomy, motivation, satisfaction, pedagogy and learning constructs; Higher relatedness and student interest under gamification	Non-monetary, course credits

(continued)

Table 2.3 (continued)

Nr.	Results	Findings	Compensation
14	Positive/ negative	Short-term performance slightly worse, long-term performance significantly better in gamified condition	No compensation
18	Positive	Lack of knowledge about gamification, positive attitudes and expectations. Students favored social interaction, engagement, feedback	No compensation
19	Positive/ neutral	Increased job motivation, satisfaction, performance	Non-monetary, gift worth US$10
21	Positive/ neutral	Of four specific player types identified, two value gamification features, the other two are indifferent to them	Monetary, a percentage of the profits generated
22	Positive/ neutral	Gamification enhanced behavioral and psychological engagement	Lottery, material prize
28	Positive	Higher contribution and interaction level in gamified condition	Non-monetary, material
29	Negative	Subjects in gamified version performed worse than subjects in comparable non-gamified app	Monetary compensation: $20

on psychological effects, and 12 studies measure behavioral outcomes. Questionnaires were used most frequently to measure psychological effects. 82.8% of the studies reported psychological effects; for instance, in the form of perceived motivation (Armstrong/Landers 2017), attitude (Smith 2017) or intention to use a system (Hamari/Koivisto 2015) or perceived output quality (Wang et al. 2017). In 24.1% of the studies, questionnaires were used in combination with interviews, which were either semi or fully structured. 3.4% of the studies used interviews and discussion groups only.

Especially data logging information and assessment results were used to analyze behavioral effects; for instance, qualitative or/and quantitative performance (von Rechenberg et al. 2016, Landers/Landers 2014, Liu et al. 2018) and interaction of individuals (Monterrat et al. 2017). In fact, 24.1% of the studies capture data loggings; 13.8% use course grades or multiple-choice tests. Overall, neither of the methods to capture data seems to be connected to whether studies on the effects of gamification yield positive, neutral, or negative results.

However, the construct measured seems to influence results when compensation aspects are included. This relation becomes apparent in Figure 2.2, which presents a matrix of implemented compensation schemes and effects.

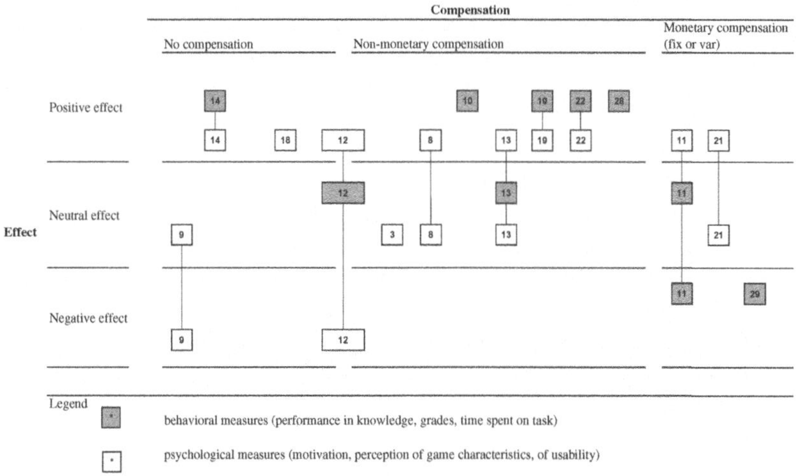

Figure 2.2 Matrix of compensation and effects[11]

Figure 2.2 displays a matrix in which studies were clustered by the type of compensation (no compensation, non-monetary compensation, and monetary compensation) and type of results (positive, neutral, negative).[12] Results were differentiated by their impact on psychological measures and behavioral measures. In accordance with Hamari et al. (2014), psychological measures refer to measures of motivation and other subjective feelings, while behavioral measures refer to objectively measurable variables linked to performance. Figure 2.2 shows that regardless of the form of compensation, psychological measures (such as motivation, perception of game characteristics, perceived usability) are predominantly connected with positive and neutral effects of gamification. Results suggest that

[11] Author's own illustration.

[12] Studies that did not report on compensation used are not included in the figure.

the form of compensation does not influence the effects of gamification when it comes to psychological measures.

Figure 2.2 provides a different picture when it comes to behavioral measures. On the one hand, if no compensation or non-monetary compensation is provided, behavioral measures show either positive or neutral effects of gamification. On the other hand, if monetary compensation is provided, behavioral measures indicate negative or neutral results. In summary, the form of compensation seems to have no effect on the mode of action of gamification when it comes to psychological measures, but seems to have an effect on the mode of action of gamification when it comes to behavioral measures. More specifically, gamification seems to have a positive or neutral effect on motivation, regardless of the form of compensation. In contrast, the effect of gamification on performance seems to be moderated by the form of compensation, whereby only gamification in combination with monetary compensation yields a negative effect on performance measures. These results should be interpreted with caution, as the number of studies on gamification that specify the form of compensation used is limited. However, these observed effects should provide an additional motivation for further research on the interactions between gamification and compensation. In the further course of this thesis, the influence of different compensation schemes on the effects of gamification on motivation and performance will be analyzed in-depth within my second experimental study (chapter 5).

2.2.4 Summary of Systematic Literature Review Results

Previous literature reviews that examined the first wave of studies on gamification showed a rather mixed picture regarding the effects of gamification (Seaborn/Fels 2015, Hamari et al. 2014). Moreover, they criticized a lack of theoretical underpinnings and a lack of longitudinal studies. Against the background of a constantly growing body of scientific contributions, the need for a systematic review of the second wave of studies on gamification was evident. To close this research gap, I performed a systematic literature review. The three underlying research questions focus on: 1) progress of studies with regard to their theoretical foundations and frequency of longitudinal studies; 2) implemented compensation schemes as a possible reason for the mixed findings, and 3) identification of possible other reasons that may explain the occurrence of mixed results.

The examination of the second wave of literature on gamification suggests that the concept is researched in diverse fields of studies, and that scholars predominantly apply a quantitative research design. Hereby, most papers are published in the field of education and learning. In the field of management control, gamification has received little attention so far. Results show that the second wave of literature on gamification did not overcome the shortcomings identified in previous literature reviews. More than half of the reviewed papers failed to provide reasonable theoretical underpinnings. The remaining studies that provided theoretical background used a broad range of theories, depending on the fields of study. Further, most of the studies implemented a cross-sectional design; only three of the 29 studies used a longitudinal design. Moreover, analysis relating to the second research question addressing the applied compensation schemes revealed that more than half of the studies lack to provide information on the compensation of participants. Thus, the shortcomings identified by previous studies (Seaborn/Fels 2015, Hamari et al. 2014) are still prevalent.

Studies that provided information on compensation reveal a broad spectrum of used compensation schemes ranging from no compensation and non-monetary compensation to monetary compensation, whereby monetary compensation might take the form of fixed and variables schemes as well as lotteries. These forms of compensation yielded in a rather mixed picture concerning the effects of gamification. Results suggest that the combination of the type of measure (behavioral or psychological) and type of compensation (no, non-monetary and monetary) affect the effectiveness of gamification. Thus, it becomes clear that psychological measures (such as motivation, perception of game characteristics, perceived usability) are predominantly connected with positive and neutral effects of gamification. In other words, the form of compensation does not influence the effects of gamification when it comes to psychological measures. The picture is different when it comes to behavioral measures. On the one hand, if no compensation or non-monetary compensation is provided, behavioral measures show either positive or neutral effects of gamification. On the other hand, if monetary compensation is provided, behavioral measures indicate negative or neutral results.

These results reveal parallels with findings in the context of the crowding-out effect. Crowding-out refers to the undermining effect of rewards (Frey/Jegen 2001). Self-determination theory provides an explanation for the crowding-out effect as it argues that extrinsic rewards can shift the locus of causality from intrinsic to extrinsic motivation (Deci/Ryan 2012). According to that, monetary incentives can cause a decrease in intrinsic motivation and performance based on a changed locus of causality. However, the literature review suggests that in gamified empirical studies, the negative effect of monetary incentives is limited to behavioral outcomes, whereas the level of motivation remains unaffected. Thus, one could speculate about whether gamification can mitigate the detrimental effects of monetary compensation on motivation. Another possible reason for this relation origins in arousal theory (Broadbent 1971). Thus, game elements might increase the motivation to exert effort towards the task, but at the same time cause stress to perform (e.g., social comparison, countdown). Arousal theory states that if individuals' stress level exceeds a moderate level, then performance decreases. Thus, arousal theory might explain why previous studies on gamification yield in positive/neutral effects on motivation but negative effects on performance.

Due to the limited number of empirical studies that report the compensation scheme used, there arises the need for further research to confirm and explore this interaction. Practitioners and scholars should be aware of the interaction effects between compensation and gamification when designing gamified systems or services for practical or research purposes.

In summary, gamification seems to have a positive/neutral effect on motivation, regardless of the form of compensation. The effect of gamification on performance seems to be moderated by the form of compensation, whereby only monetary compensation yields in negative effects of gamification on performance measures. Additionally, neither the form of data capture (data loggings, grades, multiple-choice tests) nor the number of implemented game elements can explain the mixed results of previous studies. It remains unanswered whether certain combinations of elements are more effective in achieving motivational and behavioral objectives.

3 Effects of Monetary Incentives on Motivation and Task Performance

Results from the literature review (chapter 2) suggest that the effects of gamification on performance differ depending on the compensation scheme used. These findings invite further research on the relation of monetary incentives and gamification. Before examining this relation in-depth through two laboratory experiments (chapter 4 and chapter 5), this chapter will provide a theoretical background on monetary incentives that stem from two fields of research: management accounting and psychology. In many companies management accountants are responsible for the design of monetary incentive schemes (Kunz/Linder 2012). From a practitioners' perspective, the design of incentive systems is a crucial factor that influences individuals and the overall performance of the organization. There exists a large body of literature that examines the effects of monetary incentives (Bonner/Sprinkle 2002).

The following sections provide a theoretical background on the effects of monetary incentives on motivation and performance. Following the chain of effects, I start by examining self-determination theory (Deci/Ryan 2012), which originates from the field of psychology, to shed light on the effects on motivation. Further, I rely on the framework developed by Bonner and Sprinkle (2002) to explain the effects of monetary incentives on effort and performance. Since Bonner and Sprinkle (2002) identify task complexity as an influential factor moderating the effectiveness of monetary incentives, I provide detailed information on task complexity as a moderator of the incentive-effort-performance relation. The final section reinforces the theoretical foundations by presenting findings from related meta-analytical studies.

A. Faust, *The Effects of Gamification on Motivation and Performance*,
https://doi.org/10.1007/978-3-658-35195-3_3

3.1 Monetary Incentives Within Self-determination Theory

Self-determination theory (Deci/Ryan 2012) is a theory of human motivation and personality. The theory was empirically derived and differentiates between controlled and autonomous motivation. As a widely used frame in the field of psychology, it is accompanied by a large body of empirical literature that investigates the relations among incentives, motivation, and performance (Kunz/Linder 2012, Gagné et al. 2010). Based on its six sub-theories, self-determination theory provides a useful overview of different facets of motivation.

The theory successfully explains influencing factors on motivation in the laboratory and in the field (Deci/Ryan 2012). Like much of the literature since the mid-1980s, self-determination theory emphasizes the importance of intrinsic and extrinsic motivation for employee performance (Benabou/Tirole 2003, Ryan/Deci 2000a). Intrinsic motivation has been used to refer to doing something because it is inherently interesting or creates a pleasure. Extrinsic motivation refers to doing something because it leads to an outcome that is separable from the activity itself (Ryan/Deci 2000a, p. 54). Thus, self-determination theory focuses on individual satisfaction of needs. Following from it, humans strive for the satisfaction of three innate human needs: the need for competence, the need for autonomy, and the need for relatedness. The satisfaction of these needs is a basic prerequisite for emerging motivation. The need for competence describes the need to influence one's environment (Ryan/Deci 2017). Individuals derive the feeling of efficacy from having an effect on their environment. Research that examines competence also refers to efficacy, optimism, achievement motivation, or success expectancies. Ryan and Deci (2017) claim that an individual must perceive actions as initiated and self-organized to feel competent (Deci/Ryan 1985, Nix et al. 1999). There exists a strong intrinsic need to experience the feeling of competence that starts to show in early childhood. In this context, learning and play are typically motivated by an inherent pleasure of the activities themselves. The need for competence provides energy for exercising and extending individual capacities and functioning (Ryan/Deci 2017). Here, the need for competence theorized by Ryan and Deci (2017) is free from expected outcomes. In contrary to this explanation, the conceptualization of competence by Badura (1977) is linked to extrinsic satisfaction associated with goals or outcomes.

The need for relatedness covers the circumstance that behavior is determined within social contexts. It represents individuals' desire to feel a sense of belonging and being perceived as significant or mattering by others. Thus, individuals strive to feel respected by, responded to, and important to others while avoiding rejection, insignificance, and disconnectedness (Ryan/Deci 2017). Behavior and motives are linked to the need for relatedness. This becomes obvious, for example, in social rituals, hygiene, and the dress style. Actions that stem from the satisfaction of this need aim at acceptance, approval, and group membership or another form of feeling connected (Baumeister/Leary 1995).

The need for autonomy refers to the self-regulation of behavior. Ryan and Deci (2017) theorize autonomy as a phenomenological and functional subject. From a phenomenological perspective, autonomy deals with the extent to which individuals perceive their behavior as volitional or self-endorsed. Thus, autonomous actions are experienced as self-expression and do not involve domination or seduction by external forces. From a functional perspective, the need for autonomy involves the resources and capacities of individuals.

Anticipating or perceiving that activities embody satisfaction of these three needs foster motivation. The motivational pull leads to behavioral outcomes such as increased task engagement, effort, and performance (Kunz/Linder 2012). Moreover, self-determination theory provides a theoretical background for different types of motivation, perceived locus of causality, associated degree of internalization, and allocation on the relative autonomy continuum. Figure 3.1 shows the continuum of motivation developed within self-determination theory.

Behavior	Non self-determined					Self-determined
Type of Motivation	Amotivation	Extrinsic Motivation				Intrinsic Motivation
Type of Regulation	Non-regulation	External Regulation	Introjected Regulation	Identified Regulation	Integrated Regulation	Intrinsic Regulation
Locus of Causality	Impersonal	External	Somewhat External	Somewhat Internal	Internal	Internal

Figure 3.1 The self-determination continuum[1]

Concerning the locus of causality, self-determination theory differentiates six regulatory styles on a continuum that ranges from pure intrinsic (autonomous regulation) to pure extrinsic (external controlled regulation) and non-regulation (Deci/Ryan 2000, Kunz/Linder 2012). Behavior that draws on intrinsic motivation, and thus on enjoyment, pleasure, or fun in the absence of discernible reinforcement or rewards, is classified as an intrinsic locus of causality and, therefore, intrinsic regulation of behavior (Lindenberg 2001, Kunz/Linder 2012,

[1] Based on Deci/Ryan (2000, p. 237).

p. 596). There exists an extensive body of research focusing on intrinsic motivation and related motivation-crowding (Frey/Oberholzer-Gee 1997, Frey/Jegen 2001, Kunz/Linder 2012, Amabile 1998). Integrated regulation, also referred to as norm-based motivation, describes behavior that is fully incorporated into the repertoire of need satisfying behaviors. Thus, the behavior is perceived as being in accordance with personal work ethics and as fully congruent with personal beliefs and values (e.g., a person going to church) (Ryan/Deci 2000b, p. 73, Lindenberg 2001). Behaviors based on intrinsic motivation and integrated regulation differ, as the former is based on an inherent enjoyment of the activity and the latter as triggered by a feeling to act in accordance with internalized norms (Kunz/Linder 212). Following self-determination theory, intrinsic motivation and norm-based motivation are nurtured by the fulfillment of three inherent needs: the need for autonomy, the need for competence, and the need for relatedness (Gagné/Deci 2005).

Further, self-determination theory classifies both, identified and introjected regulation as forms of extrinsic motivation, whereby both share a high degree of internalization (Deci/Ryan 2012). According to Ryan and Deci (2012), behaviors within these types of regulation require actions or goals to be accepted as such, but with a mixed locus of causality (partly internal and external). Thus, the type of regulation is based on internally referenced contingency (e.g., a personally held value to learn new skills); and introjected regulation is based on externally referenced approval or/and avoidance of external disapproval (Deci/Ryan 2000).

Moreover, self-determination theory describes extrinsic regulation as underlying behavior with a purely external locus of causality (Deci/Ryan 1985; Ryan/Deci 2000a, 2000b). Thus, actions are "performed to satisfy an external demand or obtain an externally imposed reward contingency" (Ryan/Deci 2000a, p. 61). Extrinsic regulation refers to behavior that is performed "to attain some separable outcome", such as to gain money or avoid penalties (Ryan/Deci 2000a, p. 60). It has been criticized that most literature in performance management and economics focuses on external regulation with the meaning of financial incentives while ignoring non-monetary incentives and the other types of regulatory styles (Kunz/Linder 2012, p. 597, Bonner/Sprinkle 2002).[2]

Following self-determination theory, external incentives such as monetary incentives may irretrievably shift the perceived locus of causality from internal to external (Kunz/Linder 2012). Scholars claim that external factors reduce the level of perceived autonomy as a basic psychological need. External factors

[2] In the field of management performance scholars often build on principal agent theory, which neglects the existence of intrinsic motivation (Frey/Jegen 2001).

refer to monetary rewards (e.g., bonus) and non-monetary ones (e.g., deadlines, pressured evaluations) (Ryan/Deci 2000b). Thus, the implementation of monetary incentives may change a former enjoyment or norm-based behavior into an extrinsically motivated behavior (Kunz/Linder 2012). This effect is also referred to as motivational crowding-out. Finally, self-determination theory describes the case of non-regulation, which refers to a lack of motivation, intentionality, and personal causation; in other words, amotivation.

3.2 Conceptual Framework by Bonner and Sprinkle

Monetary incentives are widely used in research and practice to increase effort and performance (Bonner/Sprinkle 2002, Lourenco 2016). From a theoretical point of view, (performance-contingent) monetary incentives work in two steps. First, they increase effort, which, in a second step, leads to increases in performance (Bonner/Sprinkle 2002).[3] The construct of effort comprises various components. Bonner and Sprinkle (2002) distinguish between effort direction, effort duration, effort intensity, and strategic development. Thus, effort can either be directed to the current performance of the task itself or towards learning. The latter is associated with a delayed increase in performance (Kanfer 1990, Locke/Latham 1990). *Effort direction* captures what an individual does; in other words, the task or activity in which a person chooses to participate. Measures of effort direction in the field include absenteeism and task choice (Kanfer 1990). In laboratory experiments that implement multi-task settings, time spent on task and the total number of tasks solved are measured and compared (Hannan et al. 2013), whereas in single task settings, effort direction is evaluated along dimensions such as quality or quantity since subjects can choose to daydream and refuse to participate in the task (Bonner/Sprinkle 2002). *Effort intensity* refers to how hard an individual works; in other words, how much cognitive or physical resources the participant invests in solving a task (Kanfer 1990, Bonner/Sprinkle 2002). Measures in the field and in the laboratory record performance on timely restricted tasks or tasks that are timed (Bonner/Sprinkle 2002). *Effort duration* refers to the amount of

[3] There are also theories that predict that monetary incentives negatively affect effort and performance. Cognitive evaluation theory argues that monetary incentives redirect individuals' drive away from intrinsic motivation towards extrinsic motivation (Deci et al. 1981, Deci/Ryan 1985). The crowding out of intrinsic motivation leads to decreased effort and performance. Also, arousal theory predicts that monetary incentives can decrease effort and performance if arousal exceeds a moderate level, thus inducing anxiety (Broadbent 1971, Eysenck 1982, 1984).

time an individual is engaged in a task or activity, whereby engagement means cognitive and physical contribution to the task/activity. Measures gathered in the field capture effort duration over more extended periods (e.g., breaks or overtime work). In laboratory experiments, a measurement requires subjects to control the time spent on the task and/or offer the possibility of exiting the experiment at different times (Bonner/Sprinkle 2002). Overall, measures of effort and performance in laboratory studies are hard to differentiate. Depending on the course of argumentation, a measure (e.g., output quantity) can be used as a measure for effort or performance.

Monetary incentives can also encourage *strategy development* (learning). Strategy development includes conscious problem solving, planning, or innovation. Thus, individuals may acquire new skills or optimize processes to increase future performance and rewards (Bonner/Sprinkle 2002, p. 30). Strategy development behavior can be performed on the task as well as off task. Accordingly, one might observe that efforts to improve strategy may first negatively affect performance before yielding performance improvement (Bonner/Sprinkle 2002).

Several theories offer explanations for the effects of monetary incentives on effort, e.g., expectancy theory (Vroom 1964), agency theory (Baiman 1982, 1990, Eisenhardt 1989), goal setting theory (Locke/Latham 1990), and self-efficacy theory. Following expectancy theory (Vroom 1964), individuals act to maximize their expected satisfaction related to outcomes. The theory proposes that there are two factors that determine individuals' motivation, namely (1) the expected relationship between effort and outcome, and (2) the attractiveness of the outcome itself. Created motivation determines the level of effort that individuals expend, as they associate their activity with a desired outcome. Therefore, expectancy theory proposes two cognitive mechanisms by which monetary incentives influence effort (Bonner/Sprinkle 2002).

First, the financial reward as an outcome has a particular valence as it presents an instrument to acquire desired goods and services. Additionally, money itself is related to prestige and status (Furnham/Argyle 1998). In other words, monetary incentives are more attractive than no financial compensation. Depending on the design of the compensation scheme, performance-contingent monetary incentives may have higher valence than non-contingent incentives.

Second, due to the strong link between effort, performance, and pay, monetary incentives are associated with higher expectancies compared to non-contingent incentives or no financial compensation (Bonner/Sprinkle 2002, Locke/Latham 1990). Thus, expectancy theory posits that performance-based compensation leads to significantly higher levels of motivation and effort due to the high valence of the outcome and the strong link between effort and outcome.

Agency theory (Baiman 1982, Eisenhardt 1989) adds a further understanding of the cognitive mechanisms by which monetary incentives affect effort. Agency theory relies on the assumptions of fully rational individuals that possess well-defined preferences and aim to maximize expected utility. In this context, individuals' motivation only stems from self-interest, whereby the underlying utility function comprises two arguments: wealth and leisure (Bonner/Sprinkle 2002). Agency theory postulates that individuals will not exert any effort unless it is expected to increase one of these dimensions. Monetary incentives that are performance-contingent meet this criterion. Agency theory suggests that performance-contingent monetary incentives will affect individuals' motivation, effort, and performance as they derive benefit in the form of increased wealth (Baiman 1982). Thus, output-oriented variable compensation increases individuals' desire to exert effort, which is expected to lead to higher performance and increase wealth (Bonner/Sprinkle 2002).

Further, goal-setting theory and self-efficacy theory explain the cognitive factors that affect effort. Goal-setting theory posits that personal goals determine effort in three ways (Locke/ Latham 1990, Locke et al. 1981). First, monetary incentives incite individuals to set goals. Second, monetary incentives motivate individuals to define more challenging goals. Third, performance-contingent incentives are supposed to lead to a stronger goal commitment than non-contingent incentives, or under the complete absence of incentives. The combination of specific and challenging goals leads to greater effort compared to undefined, easy, or nonexistent goals (Bonner/Sprinkle 2002).

Moreover, social-cognitive theory, also referred to as self-efficacy theory (Bandura 1991, 1997), describes incentive induced cognitive mechanisms that generate effects in effort. Self-efficacy refers to an individual's belief that he/she is able to perform a certain task or cope with challenging situations (Bandura 1997). The theory proposes that the perceived ability to perform a task is a crucial determinant of effort direction, effort duration, effort intensity, and strategy development (Bonner/Sprinkle 2002). Underlying cognitive and motivational mechanisms take account of goal setting, the use of strategies, and expectations.

To sum up, the above-mentioned theories suggest a positive effect of monetary incentives on effort; and increased effort leads to increased performance (Bonner/Sprinkle 2002). However, empirical findings suggest great differences in the effectiveness of monetary incentives reporting positive, neutral, and negative effects (Bonner et al. 2000, Jenkins et al. 1998). Literature reviews revealed that incentives significantly increased performance in about half of the studies (Bonner et al. 2000, Camerer/Hogarth 1999, Jenkins et al. 1998). In the following, scholars focused on examining moderators of the effects of incentives on effort and performance. Bonner and Sprinkle (2002) reviewed existing literature and introduced a conceptual framework for the effects of performance-contingent monetary incentives on individual effort and task performance. Hereby, they provide an overview of the mediators of the incentive-effort-performance relation. Figure 3.2 shows the conceptual framework by Bonner and Sprinkle (2002). According to their findings, person variables (skills, need for achievement, cultural background), task variables (task type, task complexity, task attractiveness, presentation format, framing of a task), environmental variables (time pressure, assigned goals, feedback, features of the regulatory environment), and incentive scheme variables (incentive rewards, timing of incentives, dimensions of performance) can moderate the incentive-effort-performance relation (Bonner/Sprinkle 2002). Figure 3.2 presents an overview of the conceptual framework developed by Bonner and Sprinkle (2002).

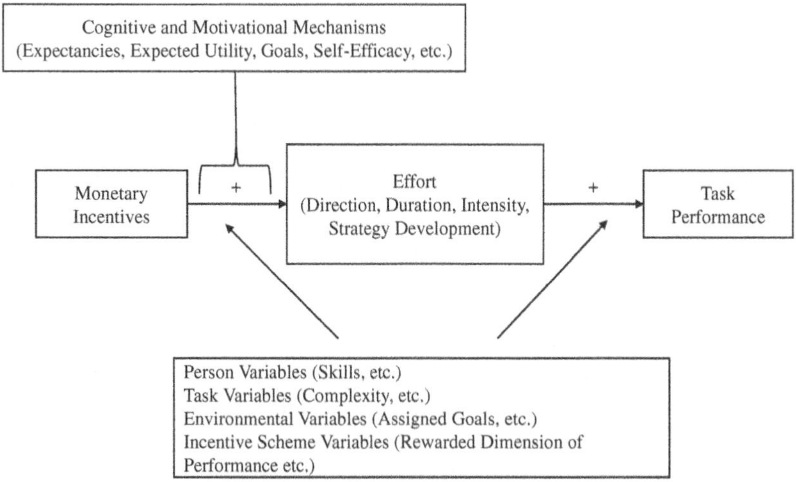

Figure 3.2 Conceptual framework for the effects of performance-contingent monetary incentives on effort and task performance[4]

Person variables encompass individual factors, also referred to as persons' characteristics. They reflect attributes brought to the task by the individual, such as personality, abilities, and basic motivation. Task variables encompass factors

[4] Taken from Bonner/Sprinkle (2002, p. 304).

that relate to the task itself. These factors can vary between tasks. For example, mundane, repetitive tasks are less complex than problem-solving tasks. Task variables can also vary within tasks. For example, calculating the probability of the continued existence of a company may be framed as the probability of a chance of survival or alternatively as a chance of failure (Bonner/Sprinkle 2002). Moreover, environmental variables encompass all factors that constitute the surrounding of a task. Environmental variables include circumstances, conditions, and other influencing factors that characterize the surrounding of a task. These factors are not specific to tasks or individuals; rather they affect all individuals and tasks in a certain setting, such as temperature, time pressure, accountability requirements, and assigned goals. Monetary incentives can also be classified as an environmental variable. However, since the framework by Bonner and Sprinkle (2002) concentrates on the effects of performance-contingent monetary incentives, they focus on variables that interact with incentives. Finally, variables concerning the incentive scheme are included in the framework. They refer to variables that affect the two-step process associated with financial rewards. In other words, they affect either the relation between incentives and effort or the relation between effort and performance.

Comparing the conceptualization of monetary incentives within the framework by Bonner and Sprinkle (2002) with self-determination theory by Deci and Ryan (2000), two things become obvious. First, the model of Bonner and Sprinkle (2002) and, generally, reasoning in the field of managerial accounting is based on the effects of incentives on effort and performance. In other words, incentives directly lead to a behavioral outcome. However, motivation is a central component of models that explain human performance (Campbell/Pritchard 1976, Pinder 2014). In contrast to Bonner and Sprinkle (2002), self-determination theory (Deci/Ryan 2000) and literature in the field of psychology conceptualize the emergence of motivation as an upstream process. Thus, incentives first result in a psychological outcome (increased motivation), which, in a second step, results in a behavioral outcome (increased effort and performance) (Condly et al. 2003).

Second, whereas in the framework by Bonner and Sprinkle (2002), performance-contingent monetary incentives tend to positively affect effort and performance, self-determination theory provides an explanation for the occurrence of the crowding-out effect. Thus, financial rewards can also be the reason for decreased effort and performance due to a shifted locus of causality from an intrinsic towards an extrinsic locus (Deci/Ryan 1985). In sum, the two concepts complement each other and provide a sound theoretical basis to explain the effects of performance-contingent monetary incentives.

The following section will provide more detail concerning the variable of task complexity. The focus on task complexity is chosen for two reasons. First, task complexity is a crucial influential factor influencing the effectiveness of monetary incentives (Bonner/Sprinkle 2002). Second, previous studies on gamification investigate the effect on motivation and performance based on mundane, repetitive tasks. In other words, studies predominantly use tasks with a low complexity to examine the effects of gamification. Addressing this gap, the third study of this thesis (see chapter 5) will explore the effects of gamification in different levels of task complexity. Therefore, the following section provides necessary theoretical foundations.

3.3 Moderating Effects of Task Complexity

Performance in tasks depends on the interaction of several factors. Task characteristics (e.g., complexity and urgency), individuals' characteristics (e.g., knowledge and skill), and characteristics of the environment (e.g., noise and temperature) are expected to significantly influence the behavior and performance of individuals and groups (Liu/Li 2012). Task complexity has been identified to be of special interest as a crucial factor determining performance (Bonner/Sprinkle 2002). Complexity affects the cognitive load and information processing, individuals' intrinsic motivation and perceived satisfaction, decision strategy, as well as the goal-setting effect (Campbell 1991, Gill/Hicks 2006). Moreover, previous research emphasizes the importance of studying task complexity combined with monetary incentives (Bonner/Sprinkle 2002, Young 2001). In light of the increasing task complexity encountered in real life, research on task complexity and its effects on performance and motivation is indispensable (Liu/Li 2012, p. 553).

3.3.1 Definition of Task Complexity

Several definitions capture the construct of task complexity focusing on one of the following viewpoints[5]: (i) the structure of the task (Wood 1986, Campbell 1988, Bonner 1994, Harvey/Koubek 1998; Ham et al. 2012), (ii) resource requirements imposed by the task (Braarud 2001, Park 2009, Robinson 2001) or (iii) the interaction of individual and task (Gonzales et al. 2005, Byström/Järvelin 1995).

[5] Reviews on definitions of task complexity can be found in Campbell (1988), Gill/Hicks (2006), Jacko et al. (1995), Park (2009) and Liu/Li (2012).

The structural viewpoint describes task complexity as a result of the structure of a task, such as the number of elements that compose a task and their relationship (Liu/Li 2012). Thus, a more complex task may consist of more elements and/or more interconnections between those elements than a less complex one (Funke 2010). Several models on task complexity build on this structural viewpoint.[6]

The viewpoint focusing on resource requirements states that more complex tasks require individuals to invest more resources in performing the task. These resources might be of cognitive nature (Wickens/McCarley 2007; Park 2009; Bettman et al. 1990), visual, auditory, and/or psychomotor nature (McCracken/Aldrich 1984). Task complexity arises from requirements on short-term memory (Jacko et al. 1995), knowledge (Gill 1996), skills (Byström/Järvelin 1995), physical and mental requirements (Li/Wieringa 2000), or time (Nembhard/Osothsilp 2002), among others. Representing the resources requirement viewpoint, Braarud (2001, p. 263) refers to increasing task complexity as "a demand for reasoning and problem-solving resources." Liu and Li (2012, p. 555) argue that resources requirement is often used as a measure of task complexity.

The third viewpoint of definitions focuses on the interaction between task and task performer characteristics. Supporters of this standpoint concentrate on the subjective task complexity as perceived by the individual performing the task and describe task complexity as a relative construct (Gonzales et al. 2005). Therefore, an identical task can be perceived as either more or less complex depending on who is processing it (Campbell 1988, p. 41).

For the remainder of this section, I will rely on the definition of Campbell (1988, p. 43), who follows the structural viewpoint and defines task complexity as "any objective task characteristic that implies an increase in information load, information diversity, or rate of information change." Therefore, increasing complexity is accompanied by an increasing cognitive demand on the task-doer (Campbell 1988).

---

[6] Models that build on the structural viewpoint can be found in Wood (1986), Campbell (1988), Bonner (1994), Harvey/Koubek (1998) and Ham et al. (2012).

3.3.2 Ongoing Debates Concerning Task Complexity

Currently, there exist two unsolved issues regarding task complexity. First, opinions are divided on whether task complexity is an objective or subjective construct. Second, there exist divergent views on the conceptual distinction between task complexity and task difficulty.

3.3.2.1 Objective Task Complexity Versus Subjective Task Complexity

Previous research treated task complexity as an objective and subjective quality (Rouse 1979). From the objective standpoint, task complexity exists regardless of individual characteristics. It is instead linked to intrinsic task characteristics (such as the number of elements, information cues, goals or path-goal multiplicity, clarity, and structure) (Liu/Li 2012, Campbell 1988). The objective standpoint finds support in the results of several studies (Wood 1986, Bailey/Fessler 2011).

As opposed to the objective construct, subjective task complexity arises as a result of an interaction of the task performer with the task itself. Here, characteristics of the individual performing the task (such as experiences, knowledge) are considered as contributing factors. Subjective task complexity is also referred to as experienced, perceived, or psychological complexity (Liu/Li 2012, p. 557). Following this standpoint, a task will be perceived as complex when it exceeds an individual's capacity. The construct of subjective task complexity finds predominant use in the field of information seeking (Byström/Järvelin 1995, Vakkari 1999, Walhout et al. 2017).

Comparing the different definitions of task complexity, the structural viewpoint and the resources requirement viewpoint define task complexity as an objective characteristic, in contrast to the interactive viewpoint, which emphasizes its subjective character (Liu/Li 2012, p. 557).

The concept of objective task complexity is difficult to apply to field studies due to the dynamic environment. However, it is appropriate for laboratory studies (Lui/Li 2012, Byström 1999). Further, Lui and Li (2012, p. 558) state that subjective task complexity depends on objective task complexity. In order to analyze complexity, they suggest beginning by manipulating an objective source of complexity, and thereafter focusing on the effects on cognitive effort invested by the task performer.

3.3.2.2 Task Complexity Versus Task Difficulty

Concerning terminology, there exist several different approaches to differentiate between task complexity and task difficulty. Whereas some concepts classify the terms as interchangeable (Bell/Ruthven 2004, Evangelisti et al. 1986), others describe task complexity as a sub-concept to task difficulty (Byström 1999, Braarud/Kirwan 2010). Thus, a task can be difficult without being complex. Other researchers consider task complexity and difficulty to be completely different from each other, as they refer to task complexity as a cognitive demand and to task difficulty as individuals' resources brought to process the task (Lui/Li 2012, Robinson 2001). A fourth approach classifies task difficulty as a sub-construct of task complexity (Bonner 1994). Bonner (1994) states that task complexity, on the one hand, consists of task difficulty and, on the other hand, of task structure. The first refers to the amount of information and the latter to the clarity of information. A sixth viewpoint states that task complexity refers to the objective measure of task characteristics, while task difficulty refers to the subjective perception of the task (Gwizdka/Spence 2006, Walhout et al. 2017). In the further proceeding of this thesis, task complexity will be understood as an objective construct.

3.3.3 Task Complexity Models

There exist several models that capture task complexity from the structural viewpoint; in particular, the models of Wood (1986), Campbell (1988), Bonner (1994), Harvey/Koubek (1998), Ham et al. (2012), Mosenthal (1998), and Lui and Li (2012) are considered.

As the most frequently used model in auditing literature, Bonner (1994) draws upon a general information processing model and classifies three components (Tan et al. 2002, Bonner 1994). The three components input, processing, and output define task complexity, whereby each component differentiates between two dimensions: the amount of information and the clarity of information. Figure 3.3 shows the elements of task complexity according to Bonner (1994). For example, input complexity can arise from an increased number of action alternatives, the number of alternatives' attributes, and the number of cues given. An increasing input complexity carries a larger information load and requires more capacity concerning human memory and attention (Liu/Li 2012). Besides the number of alternatives, attributes, and cues given, redundancy is a crucial factor, as it can reduce or even reverse the effect on information load and brain capacity (Campbell 1988). This becomes obvious when all action alternatives lead to an identical outcome.

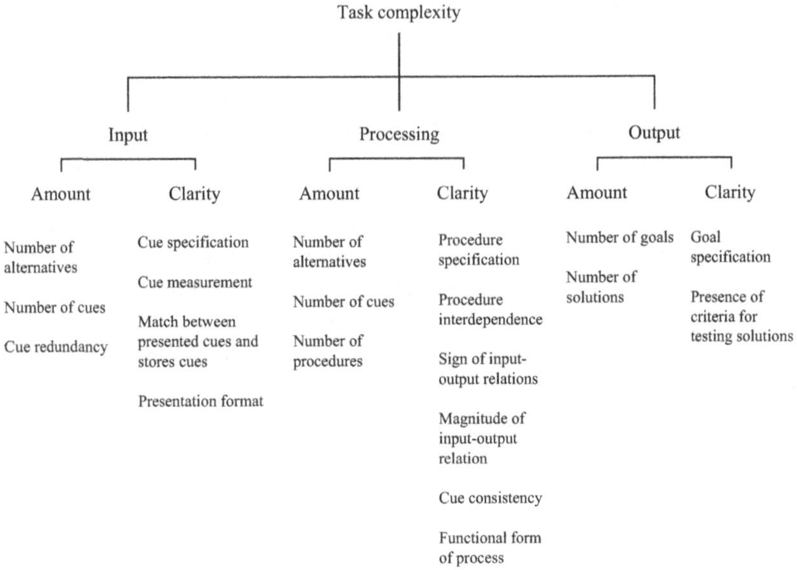

Figure 3.3 Elements of task complexity[7]

Input complexity can also arise due to decreased clarity. Hereby, clarity can refer to the level of specification, cue measurement, a match between presented cues and stored cues, and presentation format (Liu/Li 2012, Bonner 1994). A lack of clarity, for instance, caused by non-measured cues, leads to an unclear input and brings higher requirements concerning human brain capacity. Also, if the presentation format of cues diverges from the information storage in the human memory, a need for representation and recoding of the information emerges, which is tantamount to increased task complexity (Bonner 1994).

Additionally, processing complexity can arise as a result of the amount of processing and the clarity of processing to be carried out. According to Bonner (1994), processing complexity is strongly linked to input complexity as the amount of processing and the number of necessary procedures depend on the amount of input. Overall, an increase in the required steps to process the task and/or an increase in information involved causes a higher degree of processing complexity. Moreover, the clarity of processing plays a crucial role; if the

[7] Taken from Bonner (1994), p. 215.

procedures are either not specified, are dependent on each other, or are based on thinking patterns that are divergent from habitual patterns, then processing complexity increases (Bonner 1994).

Sources of outcome complexity include an increasing number of solutions or goals per alternative. Also, goals that are unspecific or indefinite contribute to an increasing complexity. For instance, giving an architect the goal of designing a more contemporary building as compared to her last design constitutes a lack of output clarity, and thus increases task complexity (Bonner 1994).

In contrast to Bonner (1994), who focused on providing an overview of factors that trigger task complexity, Campbell (1988) clustered task types accordingly. His typology of complex tasks classifies 4 task categories: decision tasks, judgment task, problem tasks, and fuzzy tasks. The complexity can be caused by multiple paths to a desired end-state, multiple desired end-states, conflicting interdependence and/or uncertainty, or probabilistic linkages (Campbell 1988). Following Campbell, complexity in decision tasks (such as employee selection) arises due to the number of desired outcomes, conflicting interdependence among these outcomes, and uncertainty. At the same time, path multiplicity is no relevant factor of complexity in decision tasks. In judgment tasks (such as stock market analysis), complexity is driven by the conflicting and probabilistic nature of task information and uncertainty, whereas at the same time, a multiplicity of desired outcomes and paths are considered irrelevant sources. Problem tasks (such as chess problems) entail complexity due to path multiplicity to a single desired outcome, as well as conflicting interdependence among paths and uncertainty. Simultaneously, outcome multiplicity is classified as an irrelevant factor of complexity for problem tasks. Finally, fuzzy tasks (such as business venture) gain in complexity because of outcome and path multiplicity, conflicting interdependence, and uncertainty.

3.3.4 Previous Findings on Task Complexity

Previous research on task complexity focuses on two directions. Firstly, studies try to prove and expand task complexity models, whereby the primary focus lies on the factors that trigger task complexity. Secondly, researchers investigate how task complexity affects behavior and performance. Previous results show that task complexity is a crucial factor influencing performance (Vakkari 1999). In the following sections, I will summarize both research agendas successively, starting with the *sources of complexity*.

Previous research shows that input clarity and processing clarity are important elements of task complexity (Bonner 1994). Following from this, it is clear that unstructured input requires more cognitive effort than structured input (McDaniel 1990). Task complexity also increases due to a mismatch or inconsistency between the presentation of information and the way it is stored in the individual's memory system (Bonner 1994). Also, the multiplicity of paths to solve a task can be considered a factor that contributes to complexity (Campbell 1988).

Other factors that contribute to task complexity in research settings are based on task presentation. For example, format, heterogeneity, and compatibility are components that are used frequently in computer-based tasks and influence the interaction between individuals and systems (Liu/Li 2012). Different presentation formats of information, such as displaying cues graphically or tabularly, can affect the clarity of input (Bonner 1994). Heterogeneity and compatibility of tasks refer to a match of task characteristics (such as linear or branching procedure) and task presentation (such as language or flowchart description), whereby certain combinations allow a more effective processing of the task (Liu/Li 2012).

Also, time is suggested as a contributing factor to complexity as it creates concurrency, or the need to coordinate task performance in multiple settings (Xiao et al. 1996), and time pressure (Liu/Li 2012, p. 562, Cummings et al. 2010). Time pressure can be caused by time restrictions, a sense of urgency, and risk, among other factors (Liu/Li 2012). Time pressure has been implemented as a complexity contributing factor in several experiments (Braarud 1998, Greitzer 2005, Bedny et al. 2012). Results show weaker performance under high time pressure as compared to low time pressure in strategy development, information selection, and decision efficacy.

As mentioned above, the second line of research focuses on the *effects of task complexity on performance*. Objective task complexity is considered to be easily manipulated within experiments (Liu/Li 2012, p. 558). In many fields of research, task complexity has been identified as a means of influencing and predicting individuals' behavior and performance. In the decision-making field, Tversky and Kahneman (1981) found that a high complexity of practical problems results in the unconscious exclusion of decision options. Other research shows that the decision process changes from a compensatory decision process while performing a low-complexity task to a non-compensatory process based on selective information while performing a high-complexity task (Payne 1976, Lussier/Olshavsky 1979, Kim/Khoury 1987). In the goal-setting field, task complexity was identified as a moderator of the goal-setting effect. More concretely, the positive effect of goal setting on task performance diminishes as task complexity increases (Wood et al. 1987, Campbell 1991). In the auditing field, task complexity was documented as interacting with report format, knowledge, and accountability to predict individuals' behavior and task outcome (Blocher et al. 1986, Tan et al. 2002).

Various experimental studies on task complexity focus on information-gathering (Puerta Melguizo et al. 2012, Walker/Janes 1999, Kim/Allen 2002).[8] Byström and Järvelin (1995) observed that the success rate of search tasks as a performance measure decreases when task complexity increases, whereas coincidently, the need for problem-solving information and the number of sources increases. Also, within the field of information-gathering, Singer et al. (2012) showed that performance is slightly positively influenced by previous experience. However, the positive effect of experience was more modest under complex search tasks compared to simple ones (Singer et al. 2012). Moreover, the results of previous studies showed that complex information-gathering tasks require more time spent on searching, time on search engine result pages, and reading time as compared to simple tasks. Thus, high performers need less time to complete the search (Singer et al. 2013, Jansen/Spink 2006, Walhout et al. 2015). Several other studies confirm that increased task complexity is accompanied by increased time spent on tasks (Borlund/Dreier 2014, Brennan et al. 2014, Kelly et al. 2015).

Further, as observed in the field of knowledge acquisition, the effect of task complexity seems to differ depending on the system type used. Based on performance data from an experiment, Lankton et al. (2012) suggest that quality in high-complex search tasks is higher under less restricted systems ("pull" systems such as Google search and web directories) compared to more restrictive systems ("push" systems such as listservs). In low-complexity tasks, performance, measured in quality and speed, was higher under predefined guidance than under participative guidance (Lankton et al. 2012).

Further, the effects on the task complexity-performance relation seems to be connected to hierarchical aspects. Ashish et al. conducted an experiment to investigate the impact of interruption frequency on task performance and perceived workload (Gupta et al. 2013). Hereby, interruption frequency via instant messenger served as a contributing factor to complexity. Results suggest that task performance depends on the hierarchical level of the message sender. On the one hand, interruptions from a superior reduced primary task completion time, but at the same time increased the negative effect of interruptions on task quality. On the other hand, interruptions from a peer increased primary task completion time (Gupta et al. 2013).

---

[8] Wildemuth and Freund (2012) and Willett et al. (2014) provide literature reviews on exploratory search behavior.

The interplay of task complexity and incentives is of special interest. For example, within two experiments, Glucksberg (1962) found incentives to positively influence performance in a task with low complexity but yielding a negative effect on performance in the complex task. Bonner et al. (2000) observed that with increasing task complexity, the positive effect of incentives on performance diminishes. This finding is consistent with observations from previous studies from Pelham/Neter (1995) and Wright/Abdoul-Ezz (1988) in which the positive incentive-performance relation was clearly evident in simple task versions but not in the complex ones. However, there are also studies observing a reserve effect, meaning that incentives had a greater positive effect in more complex compared to less complex settings (Libby/Lipe 1992, Ashton 1990). Further, Bonner and Sprinkle (2002, p. 323) suggest that task complexity might function as an incentive in some fields. Although a majority of studies suggest a decreased effect of incentives in complex as compared to simple tasks, it remains open under which conditions this relation might be negated.

In considering the literature, it becomes obvious that empirical studies on gamification predominantly implement gamified applications in low complexity tasks with a repetitive or mundane character (Seaborn/Fels 2015, Kim et al. 2018). In this context, studies in the field of pedagogy and education constitute an exception as they often gamify the process of learning (Landers/Landers 2014, Frost et al. 2015, Monterrat et al. 2017). However, there exists no study that examines the effects of gamification on different levels of task complexity.

3.4 Meta Analytical Findings on the Effects of Monetary Incentives

Several meta-analytical studies have been conducted that focus on the effects of financial incentives on motivation and performance (Cerasoli et al. 2014). In addition to the moderating factors mentioned in Bonner and Sprinkle's framework (2002), these studies suggest that the significance of the incentives-performance-relation depends on performance measures used and measurement.

Jenkins et al. (1998) provided a meta-analytical review of empirical research. They evaluate 39 studies, including laboratory studies, field studies, and experimental simulations. Findings suggest that incentives explain variances in performance quantity but do not significantly affect performance quality. Moreover, they identified theoretical frames (goal setting, expectancy-reinforcement, cognitive evaluation) and setting (laboratory, field, simulation) that served to moderate the relationship, though task type did not affect the incentive-performance relationship (Jenkins et al. 1998).

Moreover, Condly et al. (2003) conducted a meta-analytical study with a focus on the incentive-performance effect in the workplace. By examining 45 studies, they find that incentives in the workplace increased performance by 22% on average (Condly et al. 2003). In these studies, monetary incentives and long-term programs resulted in more dramatic performance increases when compared to non-monetary incentives and short-term programs. Also, team-directed incentives were more effective than individual-directed ones. Similar to Jenkins et al. (1998), they find that the effects of monetary incentives were moderated by measures of performance (e.g., outcome quantity, quality, or both). However, the moderating effect of such measures did not reach a significant level. The differences concerning the significance of the two studies might be traced back to the duration and setting of the included studies. Whereas Jenkins et al. (1998) included mainly laboratory studies, Condly et al. (2003) draw on studies that are more diverse concerning their setting (private business, public business, and university). Hereby, incentives in laboratory settings have a shorter application time compared to incentives in the field. From a theoretical perspective, time limitations within laboratory settings affect the effort-performance relation, as they restrict effort directed towards learning or strategy development (Bonner/Sprinkle 2002). Furthermore, Condly et al. (2003) find that neither the location of the study (business, government, school) nor competitive structure (only high performer versus everyone receive rewards), nor the type of study (laboratory, field study) moderates the effect on financial incentives significantly.

More recently, Garbers and Konradt (2014) and Cerasoli et al. (2014) have provided summative insights. Garbers and Konradt included 146 studies ($n = 31{,}861$) with a laboratory or a quasi-experimental field design to investigate the effects of financial incentives on performance, including individual and team-based incentives. They found the overall effect size of individual incentives to be positive ($g = 0.32$), whereby the effect size was larger for field studies ($g = 0.34$) compared to laboratory studies ($g = 0.29$).[9] Moreover, moderator analysis suggested that effect size differs depending on performance measures and level of task complexity. Concerning individual financial incentives, qualitative

[9] Garbers and Konradt (2014) used a comprehensive meta-analysis to calculate effect size estimates and moderator effects as described by Hedges and Olkin (1985). For significant effects ($p < .01$) Hedges's g was calculated to predict the effect size of financial incentives on overall, individual and team-based performance.

performance measures were associated with a larger effect (g = 0.39) as compared to quantitative performance measures (g = 0.28) (Garbers/Konradt 2014, p. 115). However, analyzing the effects of performance measures, the study of Garbers and Konradt (2014) refers to qualitative assessment (e.g., through a supervisor) when speaking about qualitative performance measures, while neglecting a differentiation between performance quantity and quality itself.

Concerning task complexity, the authors categorized tasks into four types: "generate tasks" and "execute tasks" are perceived as less complex, "negotiate tasks" as moderately complex, and "complex work situations (simulations)" as highly complex tasks (Garbers/Konradt 2014). In less complex tasks a smaller effect of financial incentives on individual performance was observable (g = 0.19) when compared to more complex ones (medium complex g = 0.36 and highly complex g = 0.37). Thus, results of the meta-analysis contradict previous models (Bonner/Sprinkle 2002, p. 321) as they suggest that financial incentives affect performance more effectively if the task is more complex (Garbers/Konradt 2014).

Within their study, Cerasoli et al. (2014) focus on the relations of extrinsic incentives, intrinsic motivation, and performance, considering performance type and incentive contingency as moderators. Their extensive meta-analysis includes 183 independent samples (n = 212,468) from various fields, including school, work, and physical activities (Cerasoli et al. 2014). Results suggest that intrinsic motivation predicts performance to a medium to strong degree (r = 0.21 to 0.45) (see Cerasoli et al. 2014, p. 995).[10] This effect was observable independent of the presence of incentives. Further, incentive contingency, which distinguishes whether incentives are directly performance-salient or indirectly performance-salient, affected the validity of predictions. If incentives were directly connected to performance, intrinsic motivation was less relevant to predict performance, and vice-versa. Regarding the performance type, Cerasoli et al. (2014) distinguish between quality and quantity of performance using three categories in the meta-analysis: performance quality, quantity, and both. Performance quality captured output variables that were assessed on "evaluative performance standard other than quantity," such as creativity, assembly quality, or quality of a research proposal. Performance quantity was used to code output measures that count discrete units such as the number of problems solved, the number of points, or the number of errors detected (Cerasoli et al. 2014). The category "both" represented all measures that could not be assigned to one of the categories mentioned above, such as

[10] R corresponds to the regression coefficient. To test for the moderating effects of categorical variables Garbers and Konradt (2014) used the procedure analogue to ANOVA proposed by Hedges (1982). Moderating effects of continuous variables were tested using the modified weighted multiple regression approach developed by Hedges and Olkin (1985).

"academic performance." The authors find intrinsic motivation to more accurately predict variances in quality of performance compared to extrinsic incentives; and extrinsic incentives to more accurately predict the quantity of performance when compared to intrinsic motivation (Cerasoli et al. 2014).

Results from a meta-analysis conducted by Stajkovic and Luthans show that incentives resulted in a stronger effect in manufacturing firms as compared to service firms (Stajkovic/Luthans 1997). Another meta-analysis focusing on performance effects of performance-contingent rewards reports an overall positive effect, and moreover, identifies the task type as a moderating factor (Weibel/Rost/Osterloh 2007). Here the overall effect (d = 0.23) originates mainly from simple and boring tasks (d = 0.42), while the effect for complex or interesting tasks was negative (d = -0.13).

In sum, these meta-analyses provide evidence for the effectiveness of financial incentives and the relation between compensation and other endogenous and exogenous factors. Thus, they confirm the theoretical framework developed by Bonner and Sprinkle (2002) and additionally identify the measures of performance as a moderator of the incentive-performance effect.

3.5 Interim Conclusion and Research Questions

Despite a rapidly growing body of publications and its practical relevance, gamification has received little to no attention in the field of management accounting and control so far. By reviewing the recent literature systematically, I identify at least three research gaps in this context.

First, it remains open whether the effectiveness of gamification is linked to a specific combination of, or the number of implemented game elements. In other words, it is an open issue whether there is a minimum number of game elements necessary to affect motivation, effort, and performance.

Second, it remains open how gamification and compensation interact concerning their effects on motivation, effort, and performance. Consistent with recent literature reviews (Seaborn/Fels 2015, Hamari et al. 2014), results from my systematic literature review show that studies provide a rather mixed picture on the effectiveness of gamification. Further analysis of the studies suggests that these mixed findings on the effectiveness of gamification are linked to different forms of compensation utilized in the empirical studies. Thus, understanding the interaction between gamification and compensation is critical for determining how to maximize the effectiveness of both incentive schemes.

Third, literature on gamification fails to investigate gamification at different levels of task complexity. Studies predominantly use mundane, repetitive task to examine the effects of gamification. However, task complexity moderates the effectiveness of monetary incentives (Bonner/Sprinkle 2002). Thus, gamification should be investigated at different levels of task complexity.

After having provided the theoretical foundations on monetary incentives and task complexity in this chapter, the remainder of this study focuses on addressing the above-mentioned gaps. To do so, I conduct two laboratory experiments on gamification.

My first experimental study (chapter 4) will address the research question related to the number of game elements needed. The examination of different levels of gamification provides insights into optimal gamification design for my second experiment.

The second experimental study (chapter 5) will shed light on the relationship between gamification, compensation, and task complexity. Thus, it adds to a limited number of studies that examine monetary and non-monetary incentives in a single setting.

First Experimental Study—Levels of Gamification

4

In practice, gamification has become a popular method to foster desired psychological and behavioral outcomes such as motivation, engagement, and performance. There has been increasing interest among companies and institutions in the use of non-monetary incentive schemes across different branches. The worldwide gamification market was valued at USD 6.33 billion in 2019 and is expected to be worth USD 37.00 billion in 2027 (Fortune Business Insight 2020). However, empirical research on gamification is still limited and shows a rather mixed picture of the effects of gamification on motivation and behavior (Seaborn/Fels 2015). Studies find positive (Cafazzo et al. 2012, Fernandes et al. 2012), no (Witt et al. 2011, Massung et al. 2013) or negative effects (Domínguez et al. 2013), whereby these studies differ widely in settings, form of implementation, designs of gamification, compensation and performance measures used. In this context, there is a disagreement on whether studies should examine the effects of gamification using a single game element or rather a variety of game elements. Despite these diverse approaches, two questions remain: how many elements are necessary to gamify a non-game context, and do more elements result in stronger effects on motivation and/or performance?

Within the existing research, a distinction between two methodical approaches can be observed. Either studies explore one specific element and analyze its psychological and behavioral effects (Attali/Arieli-Attali 2015, Landers/Landers

Electronic supplementary material The online version of this chapter (https://doi.org/10.1007/978-3-658-35195-3_4) contains supplementary material, which is available to authorized users.

A. Faust, *The Effects of Gamification on Motivation and Performance*,
https://doi.org/10.1007/978-3-658-35195-3_4

2014, Seaborn/Fels 2015), or studies implement several elements at once to investigate gamification as a holistic concept (Dias 2017, Harwood 2012, Buckley et al. 2019). Within the corresponding scientific discourse, Robertson (2010) and Bogost (2011) argue that the introduction of a single game element is insufficient to gamify a task or environment. Thus, investigating a single element does not capture the whole concept of gamification. Moreover, Werbach (2014) claims that it is inaccurate to refer to gamification based on the implementation of one game element because, consequently, every display of a progress bar would wrongly be classified as gamification. On the contrary, Perryer et al. (2016) criticize prior research as methodologically flawed if experiments investigate multiple game elements at once. Moreover, Seaborn and Fels (2015) call for research that specifically isolates particular game elements and investigate their usefulness.

To contribute to this stream of literature, I conduct a 1 × 4 between-subjects experiment with students as participants and manipulate the number of gamification elements (not gamified, low gamification, mid gamification, high gamification). Participants are asked to perform a real effort task. In this setting, I collect data on motivation, effort, and performance in the form of behavioral data and a post-experimental questionnaire. Based on the collected data, I analyze the effects of different levels of gamification on motivation and effort.

My study expands upon earlier research in at least two ways. First, I contribute to the debate on the number of elements necessary for gamification. Thus, I extend the theoretical perspective by examining evidence on psychological outcomes collected in a laboratory experiment. Second, I shed more light on the reasons for the partly contradictory results concerning the effectiveness of gamification on psychological and behavioral metrics. In order to examine these aspects, I designed four versions of a real effort task that were either not gamified or gamified using different levels of gamification. Here different levels of gamification were based on the number of implemented game elements. From the perspective of research, understanding the effects of gamification and underlying mechanics is critical for maximizing the effectiveness of non-monetary incentive schemes. This knowledge is also crucial for practitioners as designing, implementing, or restructuring a gamified system can be costly and ineffective, and inefficient incentive schemes should be avoided.

The study proceeds as follows. In the next section, I will present the theoretical background and develop hypotheses. Section 4.2 provides details on the experiment by providing information on implemented software, experimental design, procedures, and used measures. Section 4.3 reports the results of the experiment on different levels of gamification. Chapter six contains an integration of the findings of the three studies of this thesis and provides an integrated discussion of the implications of my findings for research and practice.

4.1 Theoretical Background and Development of Hypotheses

Gamification is commonly held to positively affect motivation. However, studies that investigate the effectiveness of gamification show a rather mixed picture of results, and the implementation of gamification differs considerably (Seaborn/Fels 2015). One reason for this can be found in the definition of gamification, which does not specify how many or what kind of game elements should be implemented. Despite a continuing theoretical discussion, there is still no prevailing view on how many elements are necessary for an effective gamification. This study will extend the ongoing debate by providing new theoretical arguments and behavioral insights. In the following chapter, I will merge theory and findings from previous studies to deduce my hypotheses.

First, I will refer to the effects of gamification on motivation from the perspective of self-determination theory and arousal theory. Next, I will rely on Bartle's classification of player types (Bartle 1996) and argue that gamification requires more than one game element.

Following self-determination theory, there exist five regulatory styles that differ in their locus of causality, ranging from a purely internal locus to a purely external locus (Deci/Ryan 2000). Thus, enjoyment-based motivation, integrated (norm-based) motivation, identified motivation, introjected motivation, and extrinsic motivation exist as psychological factors that provide a foundation for behavioral outcomes (Hamari et al. 2014). Behavior that stems from enjoyment-based motivation resides on an internal locus of causality (Kunz/Linder 2012). Motivation with an internal locus is associated with a feeling of interest and joy; and leads to natural and spontaneous activities in which individuals follow their inner interests (Deci/Ryan 2000, Lindenberg 2001). According to self-determination theory, enjoyment-based motivation is fostered by the satisfaction of three innate human needs: the need for autonomy, the need for competence, and the need for relatedness (Gagné/Deci 2005). In this taxonomy, the need for autonomy reflects the need to perceive one's own behavior as self-determined. Experiencing free choice and a sense of volition sustain feelings of autonomy (Kunz/Linder 2012). The need for competence describes "a propensity to have an effect on the environment as well as to attain valued outcomes within it" (Deci/Ryan 2000, p. 231). The need for relatedness is referred to as the desire to feel a sense of interconnection and familiarity with others (Deci/Ryan 2000).

The implementation of game elements has been seen as fostering a stronger perception of enjoyable aspects of a task or environment (Peng et al. 2012, Hamari et al. 2014, Sailer et al. 2017, Przybylski et al. 2010). Game elements provide feedback on progress (e.g., progress bar, level upgrade) and/or performance (e.g., high-score list) and thus, enhance the experience of competence (Mekler et al. 2017). Simultaneously, they induce a game-like experience of fun (Jung et al. 2010, Wang et al. 2012). Therefore, according to self-determination theory, gamification should positively interact with enjoyment-based motivation. Further, certain game elements and mechanics (e.g., multi-player modus, badges for helping others, badges for team achievements) foster the social character of a task or an environment. Thus, gamification can contribute to the satisfaction of an individual's need for relatedness.

However, previous research also suggests that gamification affects perceived pressure and tension. Studies have shown a rather mixed picture of results. In an educational setting, Ling (2018) finds that students in a gamified condition reported very low levels of pressure and tension. However, the study seems methodological flawed as it does not compare the reported levels of pressure and tension to a control group. Smeddinck et al. (2014) investigate the effects of a gamified training interface and find no significant differences in perceived pressure and tension between the gamified and control condition. Findings from the explorative study of Pedro et al. (2015) suggest that participants in a gamified virtual learning environment felt more pressure and tension in gamified conditions than those in non-gamified ones. Moreover, Hong and Masood (2014) investigate the effects of gamification on students' motivation and engagement. They find that participants that experienced a gamified teaching method showed higher means in perceived pressure and tension as compared to those that experienced a conventional teaching method. Authors assume that this significant difference may occur due to the collaborative and competitive nature of their setting. Thus, they conclude that gamification may contribute to negative experiences. However, they draw these conclusions without paying further attention to the absolute level of perceived pressure and tension. On a seven-point Likert scale, these means were 3.79 for the conventional teaching method and 3.85 for the gamified teaching method. Consequently, these results may also be interpreted as evidence that gamification increases perceived pressure and tension to a moderate degree. Following this interpretation, gamification would increase tension, starting from a level close to amotivation to a comfortable and productive level. This reasoning is in accordance with the arousal theory (Broadbent 1971, Easterbrook 1959,

Yerkes/Dodson 1908). Arousal theory posits an inverted-U relationship between arousal and effort: Increasing arousal first leads to higher levels of effort and performance. Later, as the level of arousal exceeds a moderate level, it hinders effort and instead induces anxiety.

Following self-determination theory, gamification can increase motivation as it contributes to the satisfaction of innate human needs. However, individuals differ in their needs, and gamified environments can be implemented in various designs, including different game elements and game mechanics. Thus, while a certain gamified environment might satisfy the needs of one individual, it might not affect another individual in the same way. For this reason, the spectrum of dispositions and characteristics of the target group must be kept in mind during the design of gamified environments (Werbach/Hunter 2012). To better understand this interactive relationship, previous research identified and classified different player types. Bartle (1996) identified four player types, classifying individuals according to their preferences for action and interaction and their orientation (world versus player). Thus, individuals can be classified as either killer, achiever, explorer, or socializer. Ferro et al. (2013) expanded the player type matrix by Bartle by adding a creative player type. The respective five player types are called dominant, objectivist, humanist, inquisitive, and creative. Fullerton (2014) presented a further approach of classification yielding in nine different player types: competitor, explorer, collector, achiever, joker, artist, storyteller, performer, and director. In this study, I chose to rely on Bartle's (1996) categorization of player types for three reasons. First, the classification presents the most fundamental categorization (Ferro et al. 2013, Kocadere/Özhan 2018). Second, the classification was developed based on observable behavior in a multiplayer video game, rather than just based on theoretical assumptions (Nicholson 2014). Third, Bartle's categorization of player types is the most commonly used categorization in the research community (Kocadere/Özhan 2018, Werbach/Hunter 2012).

Bartle (1996) states that players who are classified as *killers* aim to dominate other players. Thus, killers are not concerned about completing assignments or scoring points for themselves but strive to achieve scores that prove their dominance and are suitable to demonstrate superiority over others. Killers explore the environment with the objective of learning new possibilities to harm other players and use communication to humiliate opponents. *Achievers* aim to complete tasks successfully in order to win. Players that are classified as achievers exert effort towards reaching their goals (e.g., increase scoring). They tend to socialize to gain information on how to improve their performance and strategies or to gloat over their triumph (e.g., how quickly reached the next level). The possibility of earning points motivates this player type to explore environments. In general, achievers are focused on themselves and their own progress while showing no interest in other players. However, achievers may harm opponents to prevent them from earning the rewards they strive for. The *explorer* aims to discover the environment and experience new things. Earning points bores this player type, who is instead driven by identifying bugs and facilitators within the game environment. Explorers socialize with the ambition to learn about new aspects and harm opponents that hamper their need to explore. The final player type is called *socializer*. Players who are classified as such enjoy the interaction with other players and avail themselves of communication functions in the environment. Socializers aim to discover topics of conversation, experience stimulating dialogs, get to know new people, and develop friendships. In this context, they only exert effort towards gaining points or achievements to get access to new communities. Socializers only tend to harm players that attack their friends.

Individuals' behavior is sensitive to the perceived situation and environment. Thus, players can show varying player type characteristics in different situations and be classified as killer, achiever, explorer, or socializer depending on the context and environment (Ferro et al. 2013). Moreover, Bartle (2005) assumes that individuals' dominant player type might be complemented by an additional player type. Consistent with this finding, previous studies suggest that individuals show more than one player type characteristics (Herbert et al. 2014, Kocadere/Özhan 2018). Herbert et al. (2014) and Barata et al. (2014) clustered individuals in gamified learning environments and developed typologies, which included combined player types.

Ferro et al. (2013) categorized individuals into the player types suggested by Bartle (1996), examined personal traits and theoretically derived game elements and game mechanics that attract the respective player types. Thus, the environment of killers should contain leaderboards, progress bars, statuses, achievements, and points. Achievers should encounter badges, bonuses, combos, levels, progress bars, and reward schedules. Explorers prefer quests, rewards, and story elements, while a socializer's environment should include quest, customization, and story elements. Building upon the theoretical suggestions of Ferro et al. (2013), Kocadere and Özhan (2018) performed a seven-week experiment using a gamified learning environment to determine which game elements and mechanics attract respective player type or affect them negatively. Results suggest that the mechanics and game elements that attract players differ depending on the player type. Moreover, depending on the player type, an element can serve different mechanics. Thus, the competition mechanic triggered by a leaderboard allows the killer type to perceive the feeling of dominance, whereas it provides the achiever type with a competitive environment and information on progress. Table 4.1 gives an overview of the elements and mechanics that affect different player types positively or negatively.

Table 4.1 shows that game elements such as points, achievements, badges, gifting, and levels can trigger different mechanics depending on the player type. Moreover, it illustrates the complexity involved in designing gamified environments since elements, such as *team* and *gifting,* affect some players positively while affecting others negatively. In summary, from the perspective of self-determination theory, game elements can contribute to the satisfaction of innate human needs, whereby the needs of individuals vary depending on their disposition (Hamari et al. 2014, Sailer 2017). A suitable classification of dispositions in the context of gamification can be found in Bartle's player types (Bartle 1996, 2005). Depending on the player type, game elements trigger different mechanics, yielding in positive or negative effects (Kocadere/Özhan 2018).

Following this line of argumentation, a gamified environment should comprise more than one element to ensure that individuals with different dispositions experience respective mechanisms and to create positive effects across the spectrum of dispositions. In other words, to achieve positive effects through gamification, all individuals should receive game stimuli that are in accordance with their disposition. This argumentation explains some of the mixed results in previous studies (Seaborn/Fels 2015). Assuming that participants in an experiment present a random sample of the population, they would have different dispositions. Thus, previous studies that implemented gamification based solely on one element may not find positive effects, since the gamified environment lacked an appropriate stimulus to appeal to the whole spectrum of dispositions. Based on this reasoning, I make the following predictions.

H1a: Gamification, based on one element, is less effective to positively affect interest and enjoyment compared to gamification based on various game elements.

H1b: Gamification, based on one element, is less effective to increase perceived competence compared to gamification based on various game elements.

H1c: Gamification based on one element is less effective in increasing perceived pressure and tension towards a moderate level compared to gamification based on various game elements.

Further, psychological outcomes, such as increased motivation, lead to behavioral outcomes (Hamari et al. 2014, Suh et al. 2017). Thus, incentives lead to motivation, and motivation is presumed to lead to increased effort (Bonner/Sprinkle

Table 4.1 Overview of game elements and their effects on different player types[1]

	Killer		**Achiever**		**Explorer**		**Socializer**	
Mechanic	Positive	Negative	Positive	Negative	Positive	Negative	Positive	Negative
Competition	Leader-board, Points	Gifting	Leader-board					
Status	Leader-board, Level	Team						
Progression			Points, Level		Level			
Resource Acquisition			Achiev.					
Narrative					Story		Story, Badge, Achiev.	
Reward					Badge, Achiev.			
Cooperation				Team		Team	Team	
Transaction				Gifting			Gifting	

[1] Cf. Kocadere/Özhan (2018), p. 19.

2002). Several theories explain underlying cognitive and motivational mechanisms of the relationship between incentives, motivation, effort, and performance: agency theory (Baiman 1982), expectancy theory (Vroom 1964), goal-setting theory (Locke/Latham 1990), and self-efficacy theory (Bandura 1993). However, empirical evidence shows that motivation does not always translate into effort (Bonner/Sprinkle 2002).

In this context, arousal theory (Broadbent 1971, Easterbrook 1959) states that arousal can hinder the positive effects of incentives on effort. Following an inverted U-shape, incentives initially lead to decent arousal and increase effort. If the arousal level exceeds a moderate level, it induces anxiety that may decrease effort. However, as game elements foster the perception of a task as more game-like, excessive arousal levels are avoided.

Generally, incentives lead to increased effort (Bonner/Sprinkle 2002). However, previous studies have identified several factors that interfere and disrupt this relationship. Bonner and Sprinkle (2002) analyzed relevant literature and identified person variables, task variables, environmental variables, and incentive scheme variables that hinder the incentive-effort relation. Thus, disturbing environmental influences, lacking skills, or a task complexity that exceeds the abilities of individuals can diminish or annul the incentive-effort relation. Nevertheless, assuming that individuals are asked to perform a feasible task that does not require previous knowledge or skills within a calm and peaceful environment, gamification is expected to lead to increased effort. Furthermore, player types have different dispositions and implementing various game elements is seen as affecting different player types differently. In other words, a gamification based on various game elements is expected to affect a broader range of people as compared to gamification based on one element.

Based on the argumentation above, I expect that a single game element provides less stimulus and game affordance compared to diverse game elements. Thus, different levels of gamification lead to different motivational outcomes, which then transfer to different levels of effort.

Thus, I expect increased motivation due to gamification to translate into increased effort. This leads to the following hypothesis:

H2: Gamification based on one element is less effective in increasing perceived effort compared to gamification based on various game elements.

4.2 Method

To examine the hypotheses, I used a controlled laboratory experiment. The laboratory is located at the Technical University Berlin and consists of 25 workstations. I utilized a 1 × 4 between-subject design. The experimental task was administered computer-based using an application specifically designed to test gamification effects (Sailer et al. 2017). In the following, I will provide detailed information on the chosen research design, manipulations, and measures.

4.2.1 Alternative Experimental Methods

4.2.1.1 Advantages and Disadvantages of Experimental Research Design

Experiments allow a systematic manipulation of relevant variables and observation of related effects (Smith 2015). Deciding for a laboratory experiment, a field, or a quasi-experiment entails advantages and disadvantages (Gill/Johnson 2010). A laboratory setup is advantageous as it allows for specific interventions and precludes the influences of other extraneous variables. The intervention is conducted in the form of variable manipulation. Subsequently, the researcher can observe a dependent variable and evaluate how the manipulated independent/exploratory variables affect the subjects of interest. Assuring an effective intervention is crucial for an adequate experimental design. Overall, the probability of identifying causalities between the observed variables increases when deciding for a laboratory experiment (Blumberg et al. 2014). Another advantage of experiments is their organizational nature that allows for scheduling. Furthermore, experiments are replicable, which facilitates the evaluation of effects across time, demographics, and situations. Moreover, laboratory experiments are more advantageous in terms of costs and more convenient to carry out as compared to other research methods, such as field studies (Gill/Johnson 2010).

However, laboratory experiments also involve disadvantages. In a laboratory experiment, participants may perceive the situation as artificial and the intervention as controlled by the researcher (Gill/Johnson 2010, Smith 2015). Also, the inherent interest of voluntary participants in the investigated topic can affect results. Another disadvantage of experiments is the limited possibility for generalizable results (e.g., student vs. manager). Furthermore, studying causalities within an experiment can entail ethical issues (Blumberg et al. 2014). In other words, a laboratory setting ensures a greater degree of internal validity due to minimalized external influences; but at the same time, external validity diminishes due to the artificial nature of laboratory experiments and the exclusion of real-life factors (Gil/Johnson 2010, Blumberg et al. 2014).

4.2.1.2 Internal and External Validity of Experiments

In general, the validity of a study is, to a great extent, determined by the experimental design (Slack et al. 2001, Campbell 1986). Internal validity requires a valid cause-effect relationship between treatment and outcome. Thus, effects or results should solely occur due to manipulations and not be influenced by other factors or variables. External validity describes the extent to which results are generalizable to other groups or contexts outside of the experimental setting. An experimental design enables the researcher to control for threats to internal and external validity. Nonetheless, threats to validity should be examined for every experiment (Onwuegbuzie 2000).

Campbell and Stanley (2015) identified several threats to *internal validity*, namely history, maturation, testing, instrumentation, regression, selection, experimental mortality, and interaction. Moreover, threats to internal validity can arise due to the unintended flow of information or interactions. In this context, design contamination occurs when participants know or find out about their experimental group and associated expectations. Effects due to compensatory rivalry can occur when participants gain knowledge about the compensation of others and attempt to reduce others' expense allowances by adapting their own behavior. Also, along with knowing about less desired expense allowances, participants can develop feelings of resentment and demoralization (Cook/Campbell 1979).

While internal validity captures the degree to which a study establishes a cause-and-effect relationship, *external validity* refers to the degree to which results of a study can be generalized across individuals, settings, and times (Campbell/Stanley 1966). External validity includes population validity and ecological validity (Blumberg et al. 2014). Threats to external validity can arise due to the interaction effects of testing, selection biases and the experimental treatment, as well as the reactive effects of experimental arrangements, multiple-treatment interference, and experimenter effects (Cook/Campbell 1997).

4.2.1.3 Laboratory Experiment as the Selected Methodology

With respect to the research focus and hypotheses developed in this study, the advantages of a laboratory experiment outweigh the disadvantages. In previous research, laboratory studies were frequently used to examine the effects of incentive schemes in a cross-sectional research design.

Laboratory studies facilitate investigating the impact of incentives while coincidently avoid interfering events that do occur in field studies (Condly et al. 2003,

p. 49). A computer laboratory environment comes close to a desk job situation, which is an intended objective and therefore weakens the perception of a contrived environment. Also, the consistent set up of a computer-based laboratory experiment secures identical processes and minimizes the probability that other variables affect the dependent variable. Moreover, choosing a computer laboratory environment improves internal validity as it prevents changes in measuring instruments or observers. By randomly assigning participants to experimental conditions, I prevent selection issues that would otherwise lower the internal validity.

In the following sections, I will describe the implemented laboratory experiment in more detail. Each section will include corresponding procedures that were followed to minimize threats to internal and external validity.

4.2.2 Employed Software

To test my hypotheses, I relied on software that was designed to test the effects of gamification. Initially developed and used by Sailer et al. (2017), the software displays a virtual two-dimensional storage depot and offers virtual order picking assignments as a task. Within this environment, various game elements can be activated separately or at the same time. The software was programmed in Java and C#. Data were kept in SQL data banks.

I followed a software engineering process to further develop the software and implement new functionalities. First, the existing software was installed and explored. Second, requirements were analyzed, resulting in a software requirements specification. Examples of identified requirements include adjustments of algorithms, the inclusion of questionnaire functionalities, extension of implemented game elements, embedding visual effects, demarcation of a test round, and integration of time as a determinant element. The additional implementation of a time control allowed for the standardization of experimental procedures among participants and the more precise analysis of performance data. Third, in an iterative process, the software specifications were conceptualized, framed, and implemented. Fourth, the software was tested in two steps. Initially, specifications and functionalities were tested on one device. Later, a stress test was performed in the laboratory environment using 24 computers. Overall, six months were spent on the software development process.

4.2.3 Participants

Participants were recruited via the web-based recruiting database ORSEE (Greiner 2015). All participants were students from Technical University Berlin. This similar but not identical background of recruits increases the realistic quality of the study, as participants show similar abilities but are not completely homogenous (Knauer et al. 2017). As a proxy for employees, students were asked to perform virtual order picking assignments, a central process of internal material and supply handling. Students are a reasonable proxy for employees because the task did not require any previous knowledge. Moreover, the use of students as participants in experimental studies has been justified by several authors (Smith 2015). Prior research suggests that the performance of subjects with and without work experience does not differ in experiments using information data sets (MacKay/Villarreal 1987, Stock/Watson 1984). Further, reviewing studies from the fields of business and psychology, Ashton and Kramer (1980) find that the decision behavior of students does not differ from real-world decision-makers.

Interested students could apply to participate in an hour-long experimental session, for which they were informed they would earn 15 € fixed sum, irrespective of their performance. In total, 119 students participated in the experiment. The average age was 23.3 years, 51.3% were female.

4.2.4 Setting

To investigate the effects of gamification on motivation and performance, I conducted an experiment with a digital simulation setting. In this setting, the virtual context simulates order-picking as a central process of internal material and supply handling as used in actual production or delivery. Order-picking describes "the manual collection of delivery parts from a storage depot in response to a customer's order" (Sailer et al. 2017, p. 375). Within the simulation, participants had to collect listed items from a virtual storage depot consisting of several aisles and shelves. The context and task are considered suitable due to their repetitive character. Thus, the task naturally carries the potential for improvement. Moreover, order-picking does not require prerequisite knowledge, experiences, or special skills, which is essential, as the participants are students.

4.2.5 Experimental Task

The participants' task was to process order picking assignments within a given time. An overview of the virtual environment and an exemplary order picking list is shown in electronic supplementary material S8. The participants found themselves in a two-dimensional virtual environment of a storage depot. The storage was displayed in a top-down-view, presenting a printer, a conveyor belt, and 20 racks.

Racks were displayed in alphabetical order from left to right, labelled from A to E. A rack consists of eight shelves, each storing 30 items. Participants were asked to process order picking assignments. Commands were entered via a keyboard and/or mouse.

To process an order picking assignment, participants first need to get an order list from the printer. Thus, they have to move their token and click on the printer. Next, the list is displayed in the upper right of the screen, and participants must collect the items listed from the storage into a merchandise-basket. Besides the article description, the list contains information on the required quantity and the location of the items in the form of an alphabetical and numerical code that indicates the correct rack, shelf, and shelf space. Thus, participants have to move their token within the virtual storage depot to a respective rack. Clicking on a rack allows participants to change from a storage overview to a view of the desired shelf and its items (see electronic supplementary material 7). Items were collected in a virtual merchandise-basket by clicking on them. After collecting all items from the list, participants have to move their token to the virtual conveyor belt to drop the merchandise basket. This drop-off presents the last step of processing one order picking assignment. Overall, the design and structure of the task is based on real-world order-picking as a central process of internal material and supply handling as used in the context of production or delivery.

Participants were instructed to process six order picking assignments, each within a given time of 120 seconds. The remaining time was constantly visible for all participants. The time restriction was implemented for two reasons. First, it ensures that all participants end their experimental session within a similar time frame, allowing a scheduling of experimental sessions. Second, it ensures the comparability of data. With the exception of the test round, in which a 4-item list was displayed, the number of items was specified based on a pre-test of the software with ten researchers in the management accounting department. Results from the pre-test suggest that 18 items present a challenging but achievable goal.

4.2.6 Manipulations

Within this experiment, I manipulated the degree of gamification. Different levels of gamification were operationalized through an increasing number of implemented game elements. Table 4.2 gives an overview of the game elements implemented in the conditions.[2] Whereas the control condition included a time display and neutral presentation of the number of dispatched items, in the low gamification condition, points were also displayed. On the one hand, points present the most used game element in research (Seaborn/Fels 2015). On the other hand, previous studies criticized the mere implementation of points as "pointification" that neither increases motivation nor improves incited performance (Robertson 2010, Costa et al. 2020).

Table 4.2 Specification of elements in conditions

	Treatment Condition			
Game Elements	**Control**	**Low Game**	**Mid Game**	**High Game**
Time	remaining time	remaining time	remaining time	remaining time
Score	-	yes	yes	yes
High score list	-	-	yes	yes
Level	-	-	yes	yes
Progress bar	-	-	-	yes
Avatar	-	-	-	yes
Wording	Aufträge	Runden	Mission	Mission

With an increasing level of gamification, the game elements missions, levels, and a high-score list were included in the medium gamification condition. Game elements were chosen based on the finding that there exist at least four player types that differ in their orientation, focus and interaction preferences (Bartle 1996, Monterrat et al. 2017). Thus, the chosen elements present additional stimuli to attract different player types. Furthermore, Sailer et al. (2017) found that

[2] A high-score list, as included in the condition of medium and high gamification represents a form of RPI. However, the highly gamified condition also includes other elements as outlined in Table 4.5 (p. 83). The additional provision of an avatar and a progress bar allows the study to show that gamification as a holistic concept fosters more dynamics and affects motivation and performance differently compared to RPI.

the elements foster the satisfaction of different human needs. The next level of gamification (“high”) also contained a progress bar and an avatar. These elements trigger the same player types and motivational outcomes as the elements included in the level of medium gamification. However, they represent a visually more prominent stimulus compared to the elements used in the medium gamification condition (e.g., selecting an avatar is linked to a drop-down menu that requires confirmation) (Sailer et al. 2017). Figure 4.1 shows the user interface of participants in the highly gamified condition. Moreover, Table 4.3 provides an overview of game elements designed as pop-ups.

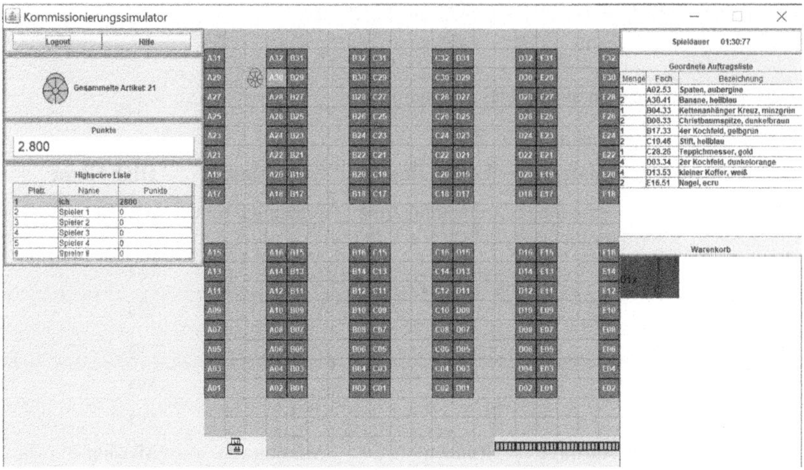

Figure 4.1 User interface for participants in highly gamified condition

Participants received fixed compensation in all conditions. Providing fixed pay to all participants prevents discriminating effects related to variable remuneration schemes. I decided to implement a fixed compensation scheme for two reasons. First, except for upper management levels, in real life, the largest proportion of the total compensation is covered by a base salary, which constitutes a fixed compensation scheme (Manthei/Mohnen 2013). Second, according to self-determination theory, performance-contingent monetary incentives cause pressure on individuals to exert effort and perform in the given task (Gagné/Deci 2005, Ryan/Deci 2000b). Implementing performance-contingent financial incentives would cause a

Table 4.3 Implemented game elements designed as pop-ups

Level upgrade	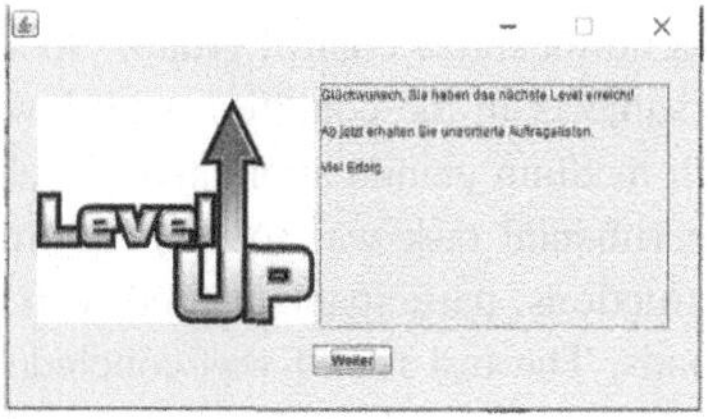
Progress bar	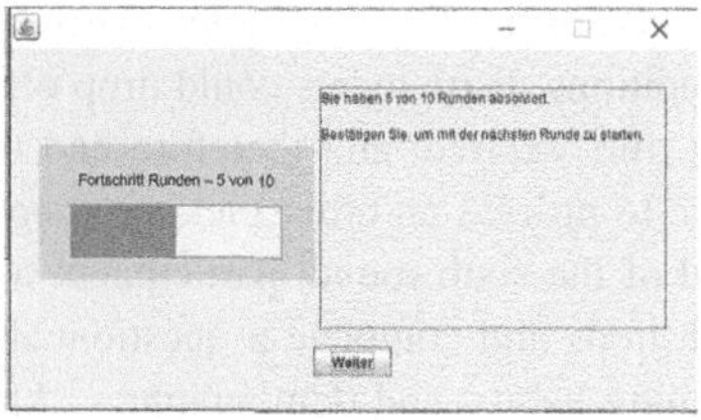
Selection box avatar	

shift of the perceived locus of causality towards an external locus. Previous literature shows that this shift undermines norm-based as well as enjoyment-based motivation and associated effects on effort (Gagné/Deci 2005, Kunz/Linder 2012). This study focuses on the effects of gamification on types of motivation that would be negatively affected by this shift. For these reasons, I decided to implement a fixed compensation scheme.

4.2.7 Experimental Procedures

When arriving at the experimental laboratory, participants identified themselves and took a seat at a workstation. The cubical designed workstations limited the participants' view outside of their own workstation, thus preventing unwanted communication and exchange of information. At the beginning of the experiment, participants were randomly assigned to one of the four conditions with different levels of gamification (low, medium, or high level of gamification, complemented by a no-incentive control group). 30 subjects were assigned in the control group, 29 subjects in the condition with low gamification, 33 subjects in the condition with medium gamification, and 27 subjects in the highly gamified condition. The experimental task was to process order picking assignments. After reading the instructions, participants started with an explanatory test round followed by five rounds. The test round was concluded with control questions to ensure participants understood the task. Each round (with the exception of the explanatory test round) consisted of 2 minutes, whereby time was displayed as a countdown in all conditions. Participants could drop off collected items at the conveyor belt before the time expired, and therefore end the round. Not spending all the time available to process an order picking assignment had no further consequences. At the end of the sixth round, participants were required to answer manipulation check questions and complete a questionnaire section evaluating perceived motivation, gaming habits, and demographics. After filling in the questionnaire, participants had to wait until all other participants had finished the experiment before they were dismissed.

4.2.8 Measures

To test my hypotheses, I collected data on perceived motivation through a post-experimental questionnaire. Within this section, the scales used in the questionnaire are described in more detail.

4.2.8.1 Measures of Motivation

After completing the experimental task, participants were asked to complete a questionnaire. The post-experimental questionnaire collected data on perceived motivation in the form of four scales. All scales originate from the Intrinsic Motivation Inventory (IMI) that was derived from self-determination theory. The IMI was designed for laboratory experiments. As a multidimensional measure, it assesses individuals' perceived motivation and self-regulation (Ryan 1982, Ryan et al. 1983). The initial version offers six subscales with 37 items: an interest and enjoyment scale and scales for perceived competence, effort and importance, perceived pressure and tension, perceived choice, values, and usefulness. A later version was supplemented by a seventh subscale with eight items, namely the relatedness subscale. In previous research, subscales and their items have proven to be factor analytically coherent and stable in experiments with different settings, tasks, and conditions (Plant/Ryan 1985, Ryan et al. 1990, Ryan et al. 1991, Deci et al. 1994).

For this study, I constructed a questionnaire with 18 items selected from four of the subscales and used a 7-point Likert scale with response alternatives ranging from strongly disagree (1), to neither agree nor disagree (4), to strongly agree (7). The scales used capture perceived interest and enjoyment, perceived competence, perceived effort and importance, as well as perceived pressure and tension. Subscales and items were selected based on relevance for my research question and fit with the experimental setting. An integration or non-inclusion of subscales of the IMI is reported to have no effect on the response behavior of participants (Deci et al. 1994). For my study, original items were slightly modified for reasons of adjustment to the experimental task. The 18 selected items of the four scales were randomly ordered in the questionnaire to limit the effects of question order bias. Further, four items were formulated in reverse. Electronic supplementary material S3 gives an overview of the questionnaire.

The scale for interest and enjoyment consists of seven items and is considered a self-reported measure of intrinsic motivation. Exemplary items of the scale are: "I enjoyed doing this activity very much," and "I would describe this activity as very interesting." Within reliability analysis, Cronbach's alpha was calculated to assess the internal consistency of the scale. Cronbach's alpha was .86, which indicates a high level of internal consistency (Bortz/Döring 2006).

The scale for perceived competence consists of four items. Perceived competence is theorized to be a positive predictor of motivation and of behavioral measures such as performance (Deci et al. 1994). An exemplary item of the scale is: "I think I am pretty good at this activity." Based on a Cronbach's alpha of .86, the internal consistency of the scale can be rated as high (Bortz/Döring 2006).

Moreover, the scale that captured perceived effort and importance consists of three items. The construct of effort is related to motivation and performance (Bonner/Sprinkle 2002). In this portion, participants were asked to what extent they agree with statements such as "I tried very hard on this activity." Cronbach's alpha to the scale of perceived effort and importance was .78, indicating a good internal consistency.

Finally, the scale for perceived pressure and tension consists of four items. Pressure and tension are theorized to be negative predictors of motivation. However, arousal theory (Broadbent 1971, Yerkes/Dodson 1908) posits that the relationship between tension and performance follows an inverted-U function. Thus, arousal initially increases effort and performance, but once arousal exceeds a moderate level, it begins to cause a decrease in effort and performance and induces anxiety (Bonner/Sprinkle 2002). For the evaluation of pressure and tension, participants were asked to specify their level of agreement with statements such as: "I felt very tense while doing this activity." Based on Cronbach's alpha of .74, the internal consistency of the scale can be rated as good. Besides the measures on motivation, the questionnaire collects additional data of interest, which will be described in the next section.

4.2.8.2 Additional Measures

The software automatically collects data in the form of time spent on the task and diverse performance indicators (e.g., quantity of collected items and errors).[3] Since Siemens et al. (2015) have argued that video game habits might correlate with participants' perception and motivation, I measured participants' video game experience. Thus, participants were asked to report their frequency of video gaming on a 7-point scale ranging from "never" to "over 20 hours per week." Moreover, demographic data in the form of gender, age, and education level were collected.[4] Table 4.4 shows the descriptive statistics of demographic data.

4.3 Results—levels of Gamification

The following chapter presents the results of my research. I begin by describing the implemented manipulation checks and the corresponding drop in experimental subjects. Afterward, results linked to my hypotheses are presented. The final section of this chapter provides a summary of the results.

[3] This experiment focuses on effects of gamification on motivation. Thus, no hypotheses were formulated on the relationship of gamification and performance. Effects of gamification on performance and effort duration will be examined within the second experiment (chapter 5). However, as data on performance and time spent on task were collected, it is worth mentioning that based on an ANOVA there were no significant main effects of gamification on time spent on the task or performance measures.

[4] Participants were randomly assigned to one of four experimental groups. Based on a Chi-squared test and an ANOVA I find no significant differences between groups considering the age, gender and the frequency of gaming. Thus, data suggest that the randomization of participants was successful. The electronic supplementary material S4 presents the results of the randomization tests.

Table 4.4 Descriptive Statistics—Participants Experiment 1

Age	Mean		23
	n		119
		n	%
Gender	female	61	51.3%
	male	58	48.7%
	other	0	0.0%
Educational level	Bachelor	86	72.3%
	Master	25	21.0%
	Diploma	1	0.8%
	Ph.D.	4	3.4%
	other	3	2.5%
Frequency of gaming	never	69	58.0%
	1 to 7 h per week	29	24.4%
	8 to 14 h per week	16	13.4%
	15 to 21 h per week	4	3.4%
	>21 hours per week	1	0.8%

4.3.1 Manipulation Checks

The experiment included manipulation checks. Manipulation check questions were inserted at the end of the questionnaire to prevent negative effects on validity due to the chronological order of testing. In this subsection, more details on the relevant questions will be provided.

4.3.1.1 Manipulation Check of Gamification

Within my study, I manipulated gamification to create four conditions that contain different levels of gamification (no gamification, low gamification, mid gamification, high gamification). Participants were asked to answer three questions to determine the effectiveness of the conducted manipulation: 1) Did you have the chance to choose an avatar? 2) Did you receive information about reaching a higher level? 3) Did the screen display your current score in the course of the experiment? For participants in the non-gamified condition, the correct answer was no to all of the above-mentioned questions. Participants in the condition of low gamification would recall game elements correctly if they denied the choice of an avatar, denied information about a level upgrade, and confirmed the display of their score. In the condition of mid gamification, participants' correct answers to manipulation check questions would consist of confirmations of displayed points and information about a level upgrade while not having had the option of an avatar. Participants in the highly gamified condition would answer correctly by confirming the presence of all three game elements.

Of the 119 participants, 52.1% of participants answered all the nominal scaled manipulation check questions correctly. 29.4% of participants gave a wrong answer concerning the avatar, whereby 20.1% should have confirmed the choice of avatar as they participated in the highly gamified condition. The reasons for the increased incidence of wrong answers might be found in a low level of concentration within the situation or confusion about the terminology itself. 7.6% of participants did not perceive the manipulation in the form of a level upgrade correctly. Further, 27.7% of participants failed to correctly recall the display of their score, whereby 10.1% of them belong to the condition with a low level of gamification; 6.7% of participants belong to the condition of mid gamification; 6.7% of them participated in the condition with a high level of gamification. One reason for this might be that after spending time on the questionnaire, participants might have wrongly recalled the displayed number of collected items as points. Table 4.5 provides an overview of the manipulation check questions and participants' answers.

4.3.1.2 Drop of Experimental Subjects

Some participants were unable to answer the manipulation check questions correctly. In line with previous literature, I exclude those subjects who failed the second and third manipulation check questions to ensure that the results are restricted to a population of subjects that correctly perceived the experimental stimuli (Wilson et al. 2010, p. 66). However, I decided to include subjects that failed to answer the first manipulation check question for two reasons. First, 24 of 27 subjects in the condition with high gamification were unable to correctly recall the choice of an avatar; the remaining three subjects who answered correctly would provide no sufficient basis for statistical analysis. Second, in contrast with the other experimental conditions, the condition with high gamification also provided a continuous display of a performance graph. Due to its end-to-end display, this element is salient and, in combination with the other implemented game elements, ensures that participants received stimulus in a highly gamified environment. In fact, all participants that answered the manipulation check questions two and three (level and points) correctly were included in the further analysis (see Table 4.5).

Moreover, I controlled collected data for response bias (Furnham 1986). Due to extreme responses, I excluded one more participant who only answered "strongly

Table 4.5 Results of manipulation check questions—Experiment 1

	MC1 Avatar	MC2 Level	MC3 Points	Combined MC2 and MC3
Control	27 [3]	27 [3]	25 [5]	24 [6]
Low Game	26 [3]	26 [3]	17 [12]	16 [13]
Med Game	28 [5]	31 [2]	25 [8]	24 [9]
High Game	3 [24]	26 [1]	19 [8]	18 [9]
Total	84 [35]	110 [9]	86 [33]	82 [37]

a) Total number of participants was 119.
b) Number of participants that answered correct and [incorrect].

disagree" throughout the whole questionnaire on motivation. As the questionnaire included reversed items, this presents contradictory statements.

In sum, 38 of the 119 participants were excluded.[5] Thus, the data from 81 participants were included in further analysis, with the following distribution of conditions: 24 participants in the control condition, 16 participants in the condition with low gamification, 24 participants in condition with medium gamification, and 17 participants in the condition with high gamification. For statistical reasons, each treatment should include 10 to 30 subjects per treatment condition, as this presents a good basis for further analysis (Campbell/Stanley 2015).[6]

4.3.2 Hypotheses Test

This study investigates the effects of gamification on motivation. Therefore, the level of gamification was manipulated between subjects resulting in four conditions (no gamification, low gamification, mid gamification, high gamification). Quantitative data on four different types of motivation was collected via a post-experimental questionnaire. The four types of motivation were: interest

[5] To ensure robustness of results all analysis was additionally performed with the complete data set. Differing results are outlined in the respective sections below.

[6] Since there are no significant differences in age and gender across conditions, these variables are not included in the further analysis.

and enjoyment, perceived competence, perceived effort and importance, and perceived pressure and tension. Thus, an ANOVA was chosen to analyze the effects of gamification on motivation. All analyses were performed with IBM SPSS Statistics.

Before the respective hypothesis tests, assumptions concerning normal distribution and homogeneity of variances were tested. The Shapiro-Wilk test revealed that data on interest and enjoyment, on perceived competence, and on perceived pressure and tension was distributed normally in all groups. Data on effort and importance was distributed normally in three groups, while in the medium game condition, the data showed a distribution close to normal. Further, Levene's test showed that for data on the respective measures of motivation, all variances were equal for the four groups.

In the following, I use a univariate ANOVA to test my hypotheses on the effect of gamification on motivation. The ANOVA has a normal distribution assumption that is violated for the data on effort and importance in one group. However, an ANOVA is considered robust against violations of the normal distribution assumption and is therefore considered an appropriate analysis (Schmider et al. 2010).

I conducted an ANOVA to evaluate the overall effect of gamification. Table 4.6 provides the descriptive statistics; Table 4.7 (p. 95) shows the ANOVA with the four motivational constructs as dependent variables. I find that neither interest and enjoyment, nor perceived competence, nor effort and importance, nor pressure and tension were significantly affected by gamification. Thus, the overall effect of gamification on motivation was not significant.

Further, I conducted planned comparisons and therefore implemented six contrasts to test: (1) whether the low game condition was different from the medium and high game conditions, (2) whether the low game condition was different from the high game condition, (3) whether the low game condition was different from the medium game condition, (4) whether the control group was different from the low game condition, (5) whether the control group was different to the condition of mid gamification and (6) whether the control group was different from the high game condition with regard to the effects of gamification on motivation. Table 4.8 gives an overview of applied contrast coefficients.

Hypothesis **H1a** predicts that gamification based on one element is less effective to positively affect interest and enjoyment compared to gamification based on various game elements. Support for this hypothesis would consist of a significant difference between the means in the low gamified condition when compared to the two other gamification conditions (medium gamified, highly gamified).

Table 4.6 Descriptive statistics—Motivation Experiment 1

	Experimental Condition							
	Control (n = 24)		Low Game (n = 16)		Mid Game (n = 24)		High Game (n = 17)	
	Mean	SD	Mean	SD	Mean	SD	Mean	SD
Interest and enjoyment	4.10	1.34	3.87	1.24	4.27	1.34	4.57	1.33
Perceived competence	3.51	1.41	3.20	0.93	4.07	1.20	4.04	1.34
Effort and importance	4.79	1.14	4.46	1.20	4.89	1.57	5.37	1.24
Pressure and tension	4.05	1.27	3.78	1.18	4.09	1.38	4.50	1.05

Table 4.7 ANOVA—The Effects of Gamification on Motivation

		Sum of Squares	df	Mean Square	F	Sig.
Interest and enjoyment	Between Groups	4.503	3	1.501	0.865	0.463
	Total	138.195	80			
Perceived competence	Between Groups	10.098	3	3.366	2.141	0.102
	Total	131.150	80			
Perceived effort	Between Groups	7.157	3	2.386	1.384	0.254
	Total	139.877	80			
Pressure and tension	Between Groups	4.400	3	1.467	0.945	0.423
	Total	123.858	80			

Table 4.9 shows the outputs of the contrast analysis. Concerning the scale of interest and enjoyment, neither of the contrasts yielded significant results.[7] Thus,

[7] Performing planned contrast analysis with the complete data set resulted in a significant contrast one (low versus medium and high gamification), $t(115) = 2.13$, $p = .04$. This may suggest that participants did not consciously perceive all game elements, but nonetheless the medium gamified and highly gamified condition lead to higher levels of interest and enjoyment based on an unconscious perception.

Table 4.8 Contrast Coefficients

	Treatment condition			
Contrast	Control	low Game	mid Game	high Game
1) Low vs. Mid & High	0	−2	1	1
2) Low vs. High	0	−1	0	1
3) Low vs. Mid	0	−1	1	0
4) Control vs. Low	−1	1	0	0
5) Control vs. Mid	−1	0	1	0
6) Control vs. High	−1	0	0	1

the comparison between conditions showed that increasing levels of gamification did not result in significant differences in perceived interest and enjoyment. Figure 4.2 shows the effect of gamification on interest and enjoyment graphically. The biggest difference in perceived interest and enjoyment is observable between the low gamified condition and the high gamified condition. Whereas the highest level of interest and enjoyment occurs in the highly gamified environment, a gamification with just one element yielded decreased interest and enjoyment compared to the control condition.

However, results from contrast two (low versus high gamification) reveal that this difference is not significant, $t\ (77) = 1.54$, $p = 0.13$. In sum, ANOVA and contrast analysis show that gamification did not significantly affect interest and enjoyment. Thus, the expectation expressed in H1a must be rejected. Neither gamification based on one element nor based on various elements significantly affected interest and enjoyment.

Within the hypothesis **H1b,** I predict that gamification based on one element is less effective to increase perceived competence compared to gamification based on various game elements. Support for this hypothesis would come from a significant main effect of gamification on perceived competence in the ANOVA and significantly lower means in the low gamified condition compared to the two other gamification conditions (medium gamified, highly gamified) as coded in contrast one. Results from the ANOVA (see Table 4.7, p. 95) show no significant effect of gamification on perceived competence $F\ (3, 80) = 2.14$, $p = .10$. However, results from contrast analysis show that the high and medium level of gamification leads to a significantly higher perceived competence compared to a low level of gamification, $t\ (77) = 2.31$, $p = .02$. Figure 4.3 shows the effect of different levels

Table 4.9 Contrast Tests—Effects of Gamification

Panel A: Interest and Enjoyment					
Contrast	Value of Contrast	Std. Error	t	df	Sig. (2-tailed)
1	1.107	0.780	1.419	77	0.160
2	0.705	0.459	1.537	77	0.128
3	0.402	0.425	0.945	77	0.348
4	−0.229	0.425	−0.539	77	0.592
5	0.173	0.380	0.454	77	0.651
6	0.476	0.418	1.140	77	0.258
Panel B: Perceived Competence					
Contrast	Value of Contrast	Std. Error	t	df	Sig. (2-tailed)
1	1.711	0.742	2.305	77	0.024
2	0.841	0.437	1.926	77	0.058
3	0.870	0.405	2.149	77	0.035
4	−0.307	0.405	−0.759	77	0.450
5	0.563	0.362	1.554	77	0.124
6	0.534	0.397	1.343	77	0.183
Panel C: Pressure and Tension					
Contrast	Value of Contrast	Std. Error	T	df	Sig. (2-tailed)
1	1.031	0.737	1.399	77	0.166
2	0.719	0.457	1.657	77	0.049
3	0.313	0.424	0.777	77	0.313
4	−0.271	0.424	−0.674	77	0.434
5	0.042	0.379	0.116	77	0.798
6	0.448	0.416	1.134	77	0.167
Panel D: Effort and Importance					
Contrast	Value of Contrast	Std. Error	t	df	Sig. (2-tailed)
1	1.345	0.777	1.730	77	0.088
2	0.914	0.434	1.999	77	0.102
3	0.431	0.402	1.016	77	0.439
4	−0.333	0.402	−0.787	77	0.503
5	0.097	0.360	0.257	77	0.908
6	0.581	0.395	1.396	77	0.260

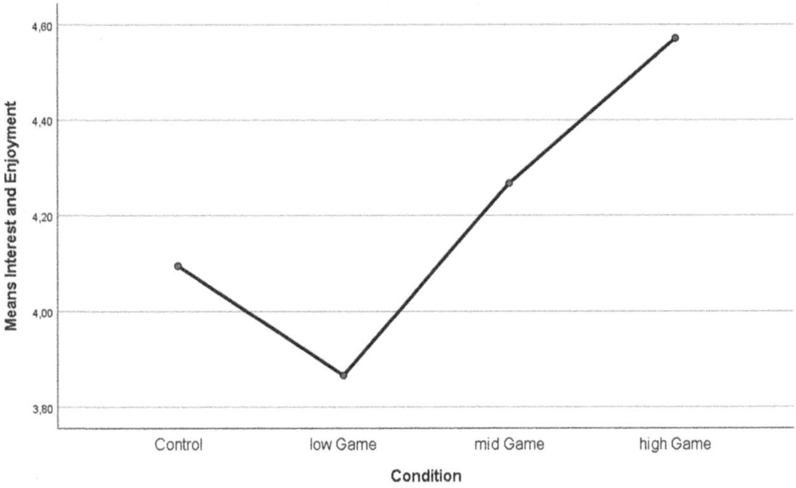

Figure 4.2 Effect of gamification on interest and enjoyment

of gamification on perceived competence graphically and illustrates that gamification based on one game element leads to a lower level of perceived competence when compared to the control condition.

The highest level of perceived competence is obtained in the condition with a moderate level of gamification, closely followed by the condition with a high level of gamification. Contrast three reveals that perceived competence in the condition with moderate gamification (medium game) is significantly higher compared to perceived competence in the condition with low gamification, $t\ (77) = 2.15$, $p = .04$. However, as the ANOVA did not show significant effects of gamification on the perceived competence hypothesis, H1b is only partly supported.

Hypothesis **H1c** predicts that gamification based on one element is less effective in increasing perceived pressure and tension towards a moderate level compared to gamification based on various game elements. Support for this hypothesis would consist of a significant main effect of gamification on perceived pressure and tension detected in the ANOVA and a significant difference between perceived pressure and tension in the condition with low gamification and the conditions with moderate or high gamification. Hereby, the level of perceived pressure and tension should not exceed an intermediate level. Planned contrasts reveal that perceived pressure and tension was significantly higher in the condition of high gamification compared to the condition of low gamification, $t\ (77) = 1.66$, $p =$

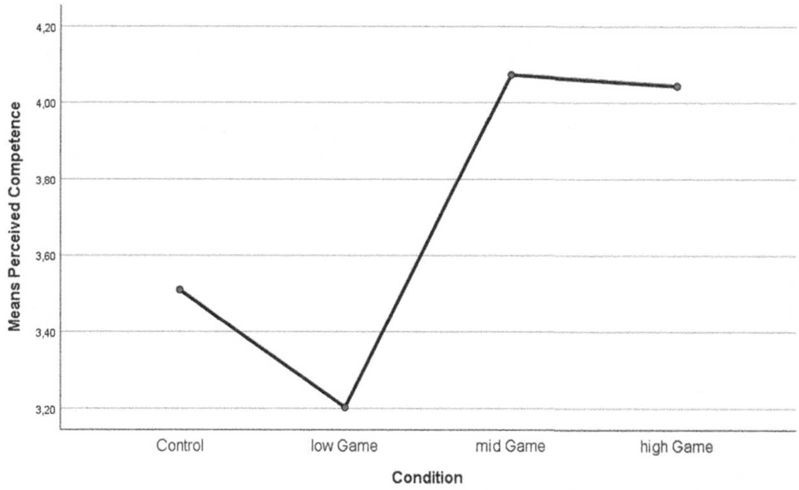

Figure 4.3 Effect of gamification on perceived competence

.05[8]. Further, against the background of the seven-point Likert scale, the mean of 4.5 in the highly gamified condition can be interpreted as a moderate level of perceived pressure and tension. Figure 4.4 shows the effect of gamification on pressure and tension graphically.

Thus, we can see that gamification based on one element leads to a lower level of perceived pressure and tension compared to a non-gamified environment. Gamification based on various game elements leads to the highest level of perceived pressure and tension, whereby this effect remains at an intermediate level. In sum, planned contrast analysis provides support for the hypothesis; however, based on the insignificant results from the ANOVA, H1c is only partly supported.

Within hypothesis **H2,** I predict that gamification based on one element is less effective in increasing perceived effort and importance compared to gamification based on various game elements. Support for this hypothesis would consist of a significant main effect of gamification on perceived effort and importance, complemented by significant differences between the self-reported effort in the

[8] Performing planned contrast analysis with the whole data set shows no significant differences between perceived pressure and tension in the low gamified condition and the high gamified condition, $t(115) = 1.26$,

$p = .10$. Thus, perceived pressure and tension of participants did not change if participants did not consciously perceived implemented game elements that trigger tension.

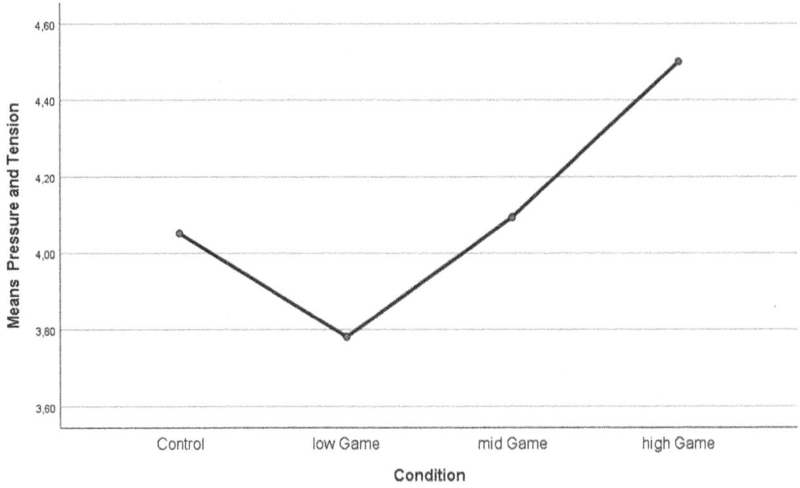

Figure 4.4 Effect of gamification on pressure and tension

condition with low gamification and the conditions with a medium or highly gamified environment.

Results from the ANOVA show no significant effect of gamification on perceived effort and importance, $F(3, 80) = 1.38$, $p = .25$. The conducted contrast analysis shows that self-reported effort in the low condition (gamification based on one game element) was lower compared to the effort reported in the conditions with a high and medium level of gamification.

However, with $t(77) = 1.73$, $p = .09$, this relationship was not significant. Figure 4.5 plots the effect of gamification on self-reported effort. Although the relationship is not significant, it becomes obvious that gamification based on one game element leads to a lower level of effort compared to the control condition. Participants in the highly gamified condition reported the highest level of effort exerted towards the task. However, results provide no support to confirm H2.

Moreover, even though no hypotheses were formulated on the comparison between the motivation of participants that experienced a non-gamified environment and those that experienced a low level of gamification, it is worth mentioning that contrast four did not show significant differences for any type of motivation.

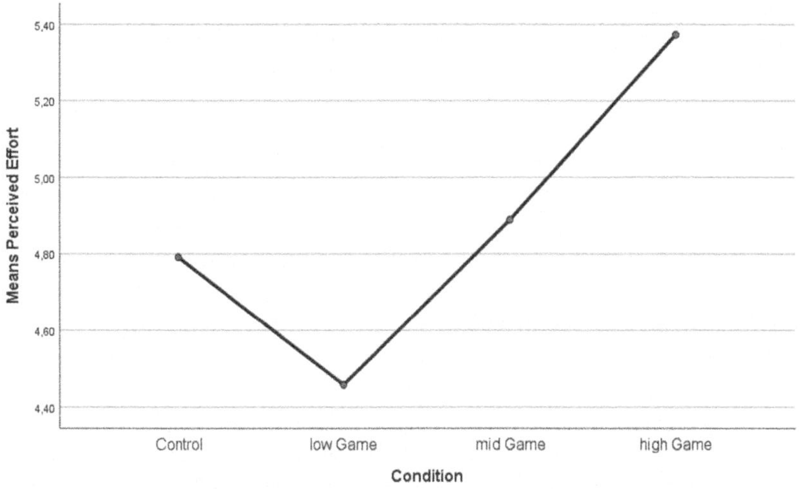

Figure 4.5 Effect of gamification on effort

4.3.3 Summary—Levels of Gamification

In practice, an increasing use of gamification can be observed. The implementation of gamified systems aims to increase employees' motivation and performance. However, previous studies present a rather mixed picture of the effectiveness of gamification, including no, positive and negative results (Seaborn/Fels 2015). Causes for the varying effects of gamification are still unclear. One reason may be found in the different operationalization of gamification. From a theoretical point of view, there exists a scientific discourse on the number of elements used to create a gamified environment. Scholars either call for an isolated examination of game elements (Perryer et al. 2016) or demand a variety of elements as they consider one element as insufficient manipulation in terms of creating a gamified environment (Robertson 2010, Bogost 2011). Up until now, this theoretical dispute remains unsolved.

My first experiment addresses the issue of the number of game elements, as it investigated how the number of game elements affects the influence of gamification on motivation and performance. In order to do so, I conducted a laboratory experiment in which participants worked on a real effort task. For the manipulation of gamification, a 1×4 between-subject design was utilized; next to a control condition, three different levels of gamification (low, medium, high) were operationalized through an increasing number of implemented game elements. The effect of the different levels was examined based on scales measuring motivation and perceived effort.

Results from contrast analysis indicate that gamification based on one game element led to a significantly lower level of perceived competence compared to the medium and highly gamified condition ($t(77) = 2.31$, $p = .02$). In addition, perceived pressure and tension was significantly higher, but still remained at a moderate level in the condition of high gamification compared to the condition of low gamification ($t(77) = -1.66$, $p = .05$). Further, participants in a highly gamified environment reported higher levels of interest and enjoyment as well as higher levels of effort compared to participants in the condition with a low level of gamification. However, these differences were not significant.

In the context of the above-mentioned scientific discourse, these results strengthen the position that the implementation of one game element is insufficient to create a meaningful gamification that positively affects motivation, effort, and performance (Robertson 2010, Bogost 2011). Thus, in line with the hypothesis, gamification based on various game elements seems more effective at inducing positive motivation than gamification based on one game element.

However, results also show that gamification based on one game element decreased interest and enjoyment, perceived competence, perceived pressure and tension, and perceived effort compared to the control condition, though not at a significant level. Thus, contrary to the hypothesized association and argumentation that the implementation of game elements in general yields in positive effects on motivation, a low level of gamification was proven to decrease motivation and effort.

Explanation for this might come from the argument that simply adding points to a system yields in meaningless pointification that is associated with no effect or even aversive effects on motivation (van Roy/Zamann 2017). A similar conclusion is drawn by Domínguez et al. (2013), who finds that a flawed design of gamification can lead to undesirable results. Thus, based on fixed compensation, participants might feel demotivated and unwilling to exert effort in a badly designed gamification application.

Moreover, despite the significant differences in motivation between the low and high level of gamification found via contrast analysis, which support stated expectations, no significant main effect of gamification on any of the scales of motivation was observable in the ANOVA. Thus, this experimental study falls into the category of studies that report neutral results concerning the effectiveness of gamification on psychological measures (Kwon et al. 2015, Hamari/Koivisto 2015, Leclercq et al. 2017, Attali/Arieli-Attali 2015).

These results indicate that the manipulation in the form of levels of gamification provided limited incentives beyond what was already provided by compensation. In sum, these results demonstrate the complexity of designing an effective gamified system. Chapter 6 provides an integrated discussion of these results as well as the results of the other two studies.

5 Second Experimental Study—Moderating Effects of Gamification and Task Complexity

Monetary incentives present a standard method to motivate individuals and improve their performance (Bonner/Sprinkle 2002). However, previous research shows a mixed picture on the effectiveness of monetary incentives on effort and performance, including positive, neutral, and negative effects (Bonner et al. 2000; Camerer/Hogarth 1999, Jenkins et al. 1998). These seemingly contrary results can partially be explained by taking environmental variables (nature of the task, individuals' abilities and attitude towards task) and task characteristics (such as task complexity) into account (Bailey/Fessler 2011). In other words, task characteristics are supposed to interact with the compensation-performance relation, which results in varying degrees of effectiveness of incentive pay on motivation, effort, and performance.

Further, a growing body of literature draws attention to the phenomena of gamification, while results provide a rather mixed picture of the effectiveness of gamification on affecting motivation and performance (Seaborn/Fels 2015). However, previous attempts to explain the partially conflicting results neglect the influence of compensation schemes.

Thus, to contribute to the existing body of literature, this experiment sheds light on the reasons for conflicting results with respect to the effects of monetary incentives and the effects of gamification. To do so, I conduct a laboratory experiment that investigates the joint effects of compensation, task complexity, and gamification on motivation, effort, and performance. The experiment will utilize

---

Electronic supplementary material The online version of this chapter (https://doi.org/10.1007/978-3-658-35195-3_5) contains supplementary material, which is available to authorized users.

A. Faust, *The Effects of Gamification on Motivation and Performance*, https://doi.org/10.1007/978-3-658-35195-3_5

a 2 × 2 × 2 mixed factorial design, manipulating gamification between subjects (absent vs. present), compensation scheme between subject (fix vs. piece-rate), and task complexity within-subject (less complex vs. complex). Participants are asked to perform a real effort task. The effects of the manipulations on motivation, effort, and performance are analyzed based on collected behavioral and motivational data.

The remainder of this chapter is organized as follows: in the following section, I develop hypotheses on the relation of gamification and monetary compensation. In the next section, I will describe the experimental design, and in the final section of this chapter, I will offer a description of the data analysis and results.

5.1 Hypotheses Development

As stated above, my hypotheses addresses the joint effects of three independent variables. The independent variables are monetary compensation (fixed-wage versus piece rate), task complexity (less complex versus complex), and gamification as a non-monetary incentive scheme (absent versus present). The theoretical basis draws on the framework of Bonner and Sprinkle (2002) and self-determination theory (Deci/Ryan 1985, Deci/Ryan 2000). My hypotheses are organized in blocks. The organization of blocks is organized along the line of arguments provided by the underlying theories, whereby my study will focus on three categories of dependent variables in the following order: motivation, effort duration, and performance. Hence, I will start with my predictions on the effects of gamification on motivation.

5.1.1 Predictions on the Effects of Gamification on Motivation

Relying on prior literature, I argue that gamification as a non-monetary incentive scheme leads to higher motivation. In doing so, I merge literature from the field of psychology and management control and predict that gamification will affect various types of motivation differently. While most researchers focus on the effects on extrinsic and intrinsic motivation, I will expand this focus to include effects on all types of motivation and the index of relative autonomy. Gamification is expected to affect motivation (Seaborn/Fels 2015). Corresponding effects result primarily from two factors: First, gamifying a task affects the corresponding task's characteristics, which leads to a different stimulus of work. Second, from the individual's perspective, gamification is expected to contribute to the satisfaction of psychological needs. Both perspectives are elaborated in the following.

Hackman and Lawler (1971) state that every job offers specific characteristics that add up to a stimulus of work. They identify five core job dimensions that determine the stimuli of work: skill variety, task identity, task significance, autonomy, and feedback. Gamifying a task can affect all these dimensions, whereby the effect depends on the implemented game element(s) (Siemens et al. 2015, Seaborn/Fels 2015, Suh et al. 2017). Affordance theory states that every stimulus affords the opportunity to react and perform actions (Gibson 1977). The changed stimulus of work is associated with an increased perception of meaningfulness and responsibility, and thus yields in increased motivation and performance (Hackman/Oldham 1976). Implementing game elements creates a game-like task character and is associated with increased enjoyment in performing the task (Seaborn/Fels 2015). Consequently, implementing game elements affords the opportunity to play and can lead to an increased stimulus of work, which in turn is expected to lead to increased motivation and performance. Further, the stimuli are seen as fostering psychological states that lead to a desired action and outcome (Hackman/Oldham 1976).

Following self-determination theory, individuals can be distinguished by dispositional differences (Ryan/Deci 2000a). Their innate psychological needs, namely the need for competence, autonomy, and relatedness, vary within a lifespan and between cultures (Gagné/Deci 2005). According to self-determination theory, the satisfaction of the three needs positively affects motivation and leads to self-regulated behavior and well-being (Ryan et al. 1997, Ryan/Deci 2000b).

Gamification entails modifying the environment in a way that fosters the satisfaction of needs and, therefore, leads to increases in motivation and positively influences behavior (Vansteenkiste et al. 2010, Sailer 2016). The satisfaction of the three needs is a prerequisite for the emergence of intrinsic motivation. Previous research suggests that certain game elements can contribute to enhance feelings of competence, relatedness, and autonomy (Mekler et al. 2017, Sailer et al. 2017). For example, gamification includes the provision of informational performance feedback (e.g., leaderboards and points), allowing individuals to record, assess and compare their performance.

Further, game elements offer goals (e.g., missions and level) and visualization of made progress and gained knowledge/experience (e.g., badges and progress bars) (Nacke/Deterding 2017). Tracking their own performance enables individuals to experience personal growth (Suh et al. 2017). According to self-determination theory, informational feedback positively affects the feeling of competence, which in turn increases intrinsic motivation (Deci/Ryan 2012). Therefore, gamification is believed to foster intrinsic motivation, self-regulation, and well-being (Baard et al. 2004, Ryan/Deci 2000a). In line with expected increases in intrinsic motivation, amotivation should decrease.[1] Further, game elements do not provide explicit external rewards (such as money or grades) and, thus, are expected to have no effect on extrinsic motivation. Consistent with the theoretical argumentation, previous findings show that game elements can foster the satisfaction of needs and catalyze a stronger perception of the enjoyable aspects of a task (Francisco-Aparicio et al. 2013, Jung et al. 2010, Przybylski et al. 2010). This leads to the following hypotheses:

H1a: Gamification leads to increased intrinsic motivation.

H1b: Gamification does not affect extrinsic motivation.

H1c: Gamification leads to decreased amotivation

Theorizing the effects of gamification on the satisfaction of the need for autonomy is more complex. On the one hand, game elements that offer choices (e.g., choosing an avatar) are argued to foster the feeling of autonomy (Sailer et al. 2017, Annetta 2010). On the other hand, several game elements (e.g., points, leaderboards) provide immediate performance feedback or information (e.g., countdown), which can induce a feeling of being controlled. Empirical research that evaluates the effects of game elements on the satisfaction of psychological needs is still limited and contradictory (Sailer et al. 2017). Against this background, one could suspect that while some elements contribute to the satisfaction of the need for autonomy, other elements hinder its satisfaction. Thus, the net effect on need satisfaction is counterbalanced depending on implemented game elements. This reasoning leads to the following null hypothesis for a gamified environment that includes diverse game elements:

H1d: Gamification does not affect the ratio of autonomous motivation to controlled motivation.

[1] As outlined in section 3.1, intrinsic motivation refers to "doing something because it is inherently interesting or enjoyable," and extrinsic motivation refers to "doing something because it leads to a separable outcome" (Ryan/Deci 2000a, p. 55). On the other hand, amotivation describes a state of lacking an intention or willingness to act (Ryan/Deci 2000a, p. 61).

5.1.2 Predictions on the Effects of Gamification on Effort

Following the above-mentioned reasoning, implementing game element(s) is expected to foster the feeling of competence, autonomy, and relatedness, which leads to increases in intrinsic motivation (Mekler et al. 2017, Sailer et al. 2017). According to self-determination theory, intrinsic motivation translates into behavioral effects such as increased effort and performance (Deci/Ryan 2012). Consistent with this theory, scholars from the field of computer science claim that objects and systems should satisfy basic psychological needs, as they find that a system positively influences individuals' user frequency as well as the system's effectiveness (Jung et al. 2010, Zhang 2008). Moreover, in a longitudinal field study, Venkatesh and Johnson (2002) show that the modification of a system in the form of enhanced social richness and presence leads to increased motivation and sustained use of the system. In other words, effort duration, which is defined as the amount of time an individual invests cognitive and physical resources towards a task or activity, increases (Bonner/Sprinkle 2002). In the workplace, Webster and Martocchio (1992) show that computer playfulness positively influences individuals' attitudes, involvement, and training outcomes/ competence. Following self-determination theory and previous findings, increased motivation as a psychological outcome would transfer into increased effort duration as a behavioral outcome (Hamari et al. 2014). Based on this reasoning, I make the following prediction for the effects of gamification on effort duration:

H2: Effort duration is higher in a gamified task compared to a non-gamified task.

5.1.3 Predictions on Effects on Performance

Conceptual frameworks from the field of management accounting suggest a two-step process. First, cognitive and motivational mechanisms lead to increased effort, which, in a second step, leads to increased performance (Bonner/Sprinkle 2002). Hereby, effort can either be directed towards current performance or strategy development and learning, which yields improvements in future performance (Bonner/Sprinkle 2002). Thus, performance in a repetitive task can be broken down into initial performance, subsequent improvement rate, and performance after learning ceases (Bailey et al. 1998). Previous studies show that incentives affect these performance parameters differently.

Within their study that operationalized a single routine task, Bailey et al. (1998) observe that monetary incentives improved overall and initial performance while at the same time having no effect on improvement rate. Bailey and Fessler (2011) documented similar findings for a repetitive skill-based task. The missing effects on improvement rate can be ascribed to at least two factors. First, individuals prefer to allocate effort towards improving initial performance because it might seem simpler than improving subsequent performance. Against the background of limited cognitive and physical resources of individuals, spending effort on initial performance seems more promising as compared to potential later performance increases. Second, a piece rate does not incite the improvement rate directly. Therefore, the improvement rate is a less salient objective that stays unaffected by performance-contingent monetary incentives (Bailey et al. 1998).

In contrast to Bailey and Fessler (2011), Sprinkle (2000) finds that monetary incentives increase the rate of performance improvement if the design of the incentive contract is optimal, and learning plays an important role. He used an experiment with a multi-period decision task in which participants could use feedback to adjust decisions and, thus, optimize their output decisions. Results suggest that incentive-based compensation enhances performance and the performance improvement rate through increases in time spent on the task and use of feedback. However, one could argue that Sprinkle's experiment required learning to maximize participants' profit, and the provision of feedback made learning a more salient objective. Thus, I posit the following hypothesis for a task that does not directly incite learning:

H3: In a repetitive task, monetary incentives that positively affect performance, do not affect the rate of performance improvement.

5.1.4 Predictions on the Moderating Effects of Gamification and Task Complexity

The incentive-performance relation is affected by several factors (Bailey/Fessler 2011). Bonner and Sprinkle (2002) provide a conceptual framework that explains the effects of performance-contingent monetary incentives on effort and task performance, while also including moderating effects of numerous other factors, such as task variables and person variables. Within the next block of hypotheses, I first focus on a more detailed view of the moderating effects of task complexity, and second, I expand the abovementioned framework by proposing gamification as a hitherto unknown moderator of the incentive-effort-performance relation. Thus, I am the first to test the interaction effects among compensation and gamification.

The relationship between monetary incentives and individual performance can be moderated by various factors, of which task complexity is one (Bailey/Fessler 2011, p. 191). Task complexity can be caused by an increase in the amount of information or a decrease in clarity of information affecting the three components of general information processing, namely the input, processing, and output components (Bonner 1994, Bonner/Sprinkle 2002, Ashton 1990). Increasing task complexity can be achieved by involving a larger number of components, involving higher level dynamics, and/or requiring more coordinated actions as opposed to less complex tasks (Wood 1986). Thus, task complexity affects the cognitive load, information processing, individuals' intrinsic motivation, perceived satisfaction, as well as their decision strategy and total performance (Liu/Li 2012, Bonner/Sprinkle 2002, Ashton 1990). With increasing task complexity, performance becomes more difficult and is accompanied by the need for more individual effort in complexity management (Liu/Li 2012, p. 559). Complex tasks require strategy development or additional cognitive effort because otherwise subjects are unable to achieve desired performance and rewards (Locke/Latham 1990). Bonner et al. even call for "complex, task-specific strategies for proper completion" of complex tasks (Bonner et al. 2000, p. 22).

According to previous research, the performance increasing effect of piece-rate as compared to fixed wages decreases with increasing task complexity (Bonner/Sprinkle 2002, p. 321). Referring to the two-step process from the framework by Bonner and Sprinkle (2002), task complexity is suggested to moderate both steps, meaning that the incentive-effort relation, as well as the effort-performance relation, is moderated. For the first step, Bonner and Sprinkle (2002) argue that increased task complexity decreases effort duration. Their expectation is based on utility theory, which states that individuals counterbalance the costs of performing a task against the benefits of that task. Assuming identical benefits, task complexity shifts this ratio towards the cost side. This shift will yield a reduction in effort and performance. However, they expect that benefits can still outweigh expected costs for complex tasks if individuals believe in their ability to perform well by exerting additional effort (Bonner/Sprinkle 2002). Thus, the attenuating effect of task complexity depends on individuals' estimates concerning expected costs and benefits. These costs and benefits are linked to an individual's skills. From the perspective of objective task complexity, the perception of complexity at the input stage is independent of personal attributes such as skill or motivation. However, in the processing stage, skills do affect performance differently depending on the levels of task complexity (Bonner 1994). With increasing task complexity, the effects of skill on performance increases (Campbell, 1988). Assuming a complex, skill-sensitive task[2] (e.g., auditing tasks), increased motivation would not transfer into improved performance due to a lack of skills. If a task is low in complexity (skill-insensitive such as a sorting task), variances in skill do not affect performance (Bonner 1994). Thus, the importance of skill increases with the increasing complexity of a task.

From another perspective, increasing task complexity can also be interpreted as setting more challenging goals. Following the argumentation of Bandura (1993), setting goals positively affects performance in three ways. First, a challenging goal leads to higher expectations, which in turn yields in increased performance. Second, assigned goals foster self-efficacy. Third, accomplishing goals is associated with increasing satisfaction, which in turn leads to higher performance in the future. These effects are particularly strong for goals that are context-related and immediate, which is the case in gamified tasks (Hamari 2017). Goal-setting theory (Locke/Latham 1990) states that specific and challenging goals and an additional provision of feedback foster increases in effort and task performance. In general, exerting additional effort in tasks that require perceptual abilities can translate into increased attention or concentration, which is often associated with longer deliberation (Awasthi/Pratt 1990). Accordingly, assuming a feasible task, task complexity would increase effort duration. Therefore, I propose the following hypothesis:

H4a: For a feasible task that does not require previous knowledge or skills, increased task complexity leads to increased effort duration.

As mentioned before, performance on a repetitive task consists of three components: initial performance, subsequent improvement rate, and performance after learning ceases. Especially higher initial performance adds up to higher total performance over the course of a repetitive experiment (Bailey et al. 1998). In the following, I address the moderating effect of task complexity on the incentive-performance relation induced by monetary incentives. In this context, this dissertation adds to a limited number of studies that examine not only initial/total performance but also the performance improvement rate. Moreover, I am the first to propose gamification as a moderator of the incentive-effort-performance relation. In the following hypothesis development, I begin with my predictions on the moderating effect of task complexity. I then move on to address the moderating effect of gamification.

---

[2] Skill-sensitive refers to tasks that requires relevant skills or previous knowledge to carry out the task (Bonner 1994).

Theoretical frameworks suggest that monetary incentive's effect on initial performance is mediated by effort (Bonner/Sprinkle 2002). Bailey and Fessler (2011) give an example by comparing a routine production task with a puzzle. Apparently, a puzzle brings a higher level of task complexity than a routine production task. This becomes obvious when faster processing is requested, which can be achieved in a production task by executing specific work steps faster but is harder to achieve in a puzzle task. As a result, variable compensation is less likely to influence performance in a puzzle task. Other scholars argue that task complexity influences individuals' mental workload, which results in a reduced performance effect (Jacko/Ward 1996, Zhao 1994). Another argument for the weakened link between compensation and performance in complex tasks stems from the different need for tacit versus explicit knowledge. Complex tasks require more tacit knowledge, which refers to an individual's skill in performing a task that is not easily explained, such as executing movement patterns in sports (Cianciolo et al. 2006). Using financial incentives to draw attention to activities that are based on tacit knowledge will decrease the effectiveness of the effort-performance relation (Kleiman-Weiner/Berger 2006).

In contrast to the above-mentioned moderating effect of task complexity concerning total performance, I do not expect a moderation effect of task complexity on the effort-performance improvement-relation. This prediction is driven by two arguments. Firstly, as mentioned before, performance improvement is not affected by monetary incentives unless learning is directly incited (Bailey/Fessler 2011, Sprinkle 2000). It follows that a non-existent effect cannot be moderated. However, a moderator can facilitate the appearance of effects. Thus, the second argument is based on factors linked to an experimental laboratory setting. Bonner and Sprinkle (2002) argue that task complexity can increase or decrease effort directed towards strategy development. On the one hand, an increase in effort directed towards strategy development requires participants to recognize the need for a complex strategy to achieve desired performance (Locke/Latham 1990). On the other hand, in time-restricted situations, as in a laboratory experiment, participants may not have enough opportunity to acquire needed skills or test new strategies that are not immediately called for (Bonner et al. 2000, Campbell 1988, Naylor/Clark 1968). So secondly, if participants become aware of the need for a complex strategy, time restrictions within a laboratory experiment are likely to hinder the occurrence of effects on performance improvement based on strategy development. Therefore, I state the following hypothesis:

H4b: The moderating effect of task complexity on the incentive-performance relation is limited to total performance, leaving performance improvement rate unaffected.

Next, I will focus on the moderating effects of gamification on the incentive-effort-performance relation. Previous findings suggest that intrinsic motivation is not the only mediator accounting for the effort and performance effects of gamification. Mekler et al. (2017) systematically examined the effects of diverse game elements in an online experiment in which participants performed an image annotation task. They found that game elements did not significantly affect perceived competence or intrinsic motivation, but nonetheless, the performance quantity of participants in the gamified conditions was significantly higher compared to the control group. Whereas these findings are not in line with self-determination theory, the framework by Bonner and Sprinkle (2002) offers an explanation by theorizing task characteristics that moderate the incentive-performance relation. Thus, I argue that gamification may serve as a moderator of the incentive-performance relation.

On the one hand, monetary incentives lead to higher total performance, whereby the overall effect is caused by increased initial performance that persists through the entire observation period. On the other hand, studies on the effects of gamification on performance provide mixed results, whereby positive effects were frequently observable when depending variables capture learning performance (Seaborn/Fels 2015). Game elements simultaneously offer the occasion of fun and simplify entering a state of flow while learning, which is associated with faster learning and increased learning outcomes (Bitrián et al. 2020). Flow refers to a state characterized by intense concentration in which time becomes distorted (Csikszentmihalyi 2000).

From a theoretical perspective, learning curve models refer to parameters as initial performance and learning (Bailey et al. 1998, Bailey/Fessler 2011). Hereby, the body of literature that investigates learning differentiates at least two types of outcomes: the absolute learning outcome and the pace of learning. These two types of outcomes are closely linked as learning flow is positively related to perceived learning and actual learning in the form of acquired skills (Bitrián et al. 2020). Previous studies that focus on the effects of gamification on learning collect data either on absolute performance outcomes (e.g., academic grades, acquired knowledge and efficacy), on perceived motivation in learning, or other behavioral effects of gamified training (nutrition and consumer behavior) (Berger/Schrader 2016, Berger et al. 2014, Su/Cheng 2015, Barata et al. 2014, Domínguez et al. 2013). To the best knowledge of the author, no study exists that examines the effects of gamification on the pace of learning (performance improvement rate). Against this backdrop, I propose gamification to be a moderator of the incentive-effort-performance relation. There exist several reasons to expect the moderating effect of gamification.

The first reason relates to the amount of effort. On the one hand, performance-contingent monetary incentives create pressure and motivation that influence effort direction and lead to increases in effort duration and effort intensity exerted on a task. Accordingly, increased effort leads to higher performance (Bonner/Sprinkle 2002). However, monetary incentives in the form of a constant piece-rate affect effort up until a certain point, but not any further. Yet gamification is assumed to positively influence motivation to learn and increase engagement (Domínguez et al. 2013). Thus, gamifying a task causes an additional stimulus that can further increase motivation and overall effort (Hamari et al. 2015). From a theoretical perspective, there is very little stimulus under fixed wages, whereas, under piece-rate compensation, there is a comparable high stimulus (Hackman/Oldham 1976, Vroom 1964). In this context, I expect to observe different effects of the additional stimulus through gamification. Whereas fixed wages allow for the observation of the effects of additional stimuli through gamification, piece-rate wages provide less scope for further stimulation due to the a priori higher level of stimulation.

The second reason can be found in the direction of effort. Previous findings suggest that monetary incentives increase effort towards initial performance while at the same time having no effect on learning/ performance improvement rate (Bailey et al. 1998, Bailey/Fessler 2011). Results from the multidisciplinary literature review of Seaborn and Fels (2015) suggest that gamification increases effort directed towards learning. Positive effects of gamification were more frequently observed when dependent variables measured effects in the form of learning or total performance related to learning (Foster et al. 2012, Li et al. 2012, Musthag et al. 2011, Rapp et al. 2012). In accordance with this argumentation, gamification is associated with increases in time spent on tasks (Annetta et al. 2009). Concentration and time-on-task are related to increased learning outcomes (Landers/Landers 2014). Based on a higher level of concentration, perceived fun, and time on task, I reason that gamification improves the pace of learning (performance improvement rate).

The third reason stems from the effectiveness of effort distributed towards learning and performance improvement. Theory suggests that for learning to occur, two necessary requirements must be fulfilled. First, individuals must be able to use feedback on previous performance to question and adapt their behavior and, thus, improve their future performance (Sprinkle 2000). Game elements provide a broad range of feedback mechanisms, amongst others, points, badges, leaderboards, and progress bars. Additional feedback that comes with game elements facilitates a reflection and adaption of behavior and, thus, fosters learning and performance improvement. Further, I presume that game elements, with their fun affording character, increase the attention spent on a given task. Previous research shows that individuals who keep their attention focused upon a task learn more than those who do not (Kanfer/Ackerman 1989). Thus, effort that is directed towards learning would result in faster and increased performance improvements in a gamified setting compared to a non-gamified one. A second prerequisite for learning is the existence of incentives that motivate exertion and the allocation of effort towards learning (Sprinkle 2000). Performance-contingent monetary incentives only indirectly motivate performance improvement, whereas gamification is expected to foster performance improvement. Accordingly, we can assume that game elements establish a basis for learning and make learning a more salient objective. This reasoning leads to the following hypotheses:

H5b: The effect of monetary incentives on effort duration is moderated by gamification, whereby the positive stimulus of gamification is higher under fixed compensation compared to variable compensation.

H5b: he effect of monetary incentives on performance improvement is moderated by gamification, with piece-rate compensation being more effective in increasing the performance improvement rate in a gamified task compared to a non-gamified task.

H5c: The effect of monetary incentives on performance improvement is moderated by gamification, with fixed compensation being more effective in increasing the performance improvement rate in a gamified task compared to a non-gamified task.

In summary, the predictions developed in this chapter can be clustered into four blocks. The first block of hypotheses deals with the effect of gamification on different constructs of motivation. The second block of hypotheses focuses on the effects of gamification on effort duration. The third block of hypotheses elaborates on the effects of financial incentives on performance while distinguishing between the total performance and the rate of performance improvement. Finally, the fourth block of hypotheses concentrates on the moderating effects of task complexity and gamification on the incentive-effort-performance relation. Figure 5.1 gives an overview of all hypotheses and the expected relationships. In the next chapter, I describe the method used to test my hypotheses in detail. Each section includes corresponding procedures that were followed to minimize threats to internal and external validity. More precisely, I present information on the chosen research design, the setting, the design of the experimental task and manipulations, as well as information on the participants, procedures, and measures.

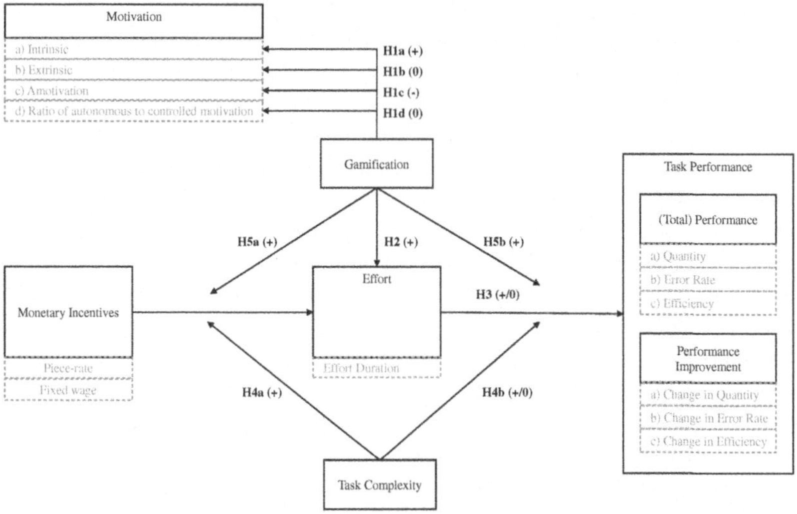

Figure 5.1 Overview Hypotheses

5.2 Method

This chapter presents details on the method used for the third investigation in my thesis. Based on the reasoning provided in section 4.2.1, I choose to conduct a laboratory experiment. In the following sections, I introduce detailed information on data collection and analysis. Therefore, I provide information on the research design and used measures.

5.2.1 Research Design

This section provides detailed information on the implemented laboratory experiment. In doing so, it reveals the general approach for investigating predicted effects and relationships. In the following, I provide information on the software employed, the implemented setting, and the experimental task. Moreover, information on participants, manipulations, and experimental procedures is presented.

5.2.1.1 Software, Setting and Experimental Task

To investigate the effects of the triad of gamification, task complexity, and compensation on motivation and performance, I conduct an experiment within a digital simulation setting. In this experiment, the employed software and the experimental setting are identical to the one used in the first experiment, as outlined in section 4.2.2 and 4.2.4. Just as in the first experiment, participants were requested to process order picking assignments within the virtual storage depot (see section 4.2.5 for the description of the experimental task). However, the experiments differ with regard to the design of the order lists. With the exception of the test round, in which a 4-items list was displayed, the length of order lists in the following ten rounds was consistently 20 items. The number of items was chosen according to a pretest and presents a feasible yet challenging goal. An overview of the virtual environment is shown in the electronic supplementary material S8. Thus, while most research on the effect of gamification on performance and performance improvement (e.g., learning) stems from the field of pedagogy and is associated with an evaluation of knowledge acquisition, I evaluate the effects of gamification in a real effort task that captures a sub-process of internal material handling.

5.2.1.2 Participants

In total, 119 students from Technical University Berlin took part in the experiment. For the recruitment of participants, the web-based recruiting database ORSEE was used (Greiner 2015). The database lists more than 3,000 students from various fields of study. Interested students could apply to participate in a 40-minute long experiment session, for which they could earn 13 € on average. A similar but not identical background among recruits increases realism as participants show similar abilities but are not completely homogenous (Knauer et al. 2017). A total of 119 students participated in the experiment; 67.2% of them were undergraduates. The average age of participants was 24.9%, while 48.7% of them were female.[3] Table 5.1 provides information on the descriptive statistics of participants.

[3] Within the experiment participants were randomly assigned to one of four experimental groups. Based on a Chi-squared test and an ANOVA I find no significant differences between groups with regard to age, gender and the frequency of gaming. Thus, data suggest that the randomization of participants was successful. The electronic supplementary material S9 presents the results of the randomization tests.

Table 5.1 Descriptive statistics—Participants Experiment 2

Age	Mean	25	
	n	119	
		n	%
Gender	female	58	48.7
	male	61	51.3
	other	0	0
Educational level	Bachelor	80	67.2
	Master	28	23.5
	Diploma	2	1.7
	Ph.D.	1	0.8
	other	8	6.7
Frequency of gaming	never	51	42.9
	1 to 7 h per week	36	30.3
	8 to 14 h per week	23	19.3
	15 to 21 h per week	3	2.5
	>21 hours per week	6	5

5.2.1.3 Manipulations

This thesis includes three dichotomous manipulated factors: compensation, gamification as a non-monetary incentive scheme, and task complexity. The manipulations are specified in the following sections, beginning with the manipulation of compensation.

5.2.1.3.1 Manipulation of Compensation

Compensation was implemented as between-group manipulation, whereby the pay scheme provided either a fixed wage or piece rate. Participants under the fixed-wage received 13 € independent of their performance. The piece-rates were calculated after each experimental run to ensure the total compensation would average 13 € in piece-rate and fixed-wage compensation conditions. Participants receiving variable compensation were informed that they would earn lira, which was later converted into euros, whereby no further information on the rate of exchange was given. After each experimental run, the exchange rate was calculated. Participants in the piece-rate condition received 10.3 cents per correctly processed item on average. Correctly processed refers to successfully collecting items in the merchandise basket in accordance with the list of articles and dropping it at the conveyor belt within the allotted time.

5.2.1.3.2 Gamification Manipulation

In the experiment, gamification was manipulated between groups so that gamification was either implemented (present/ gamified task) or not implemented (absent/ non-gamified task). Several game elements were utilized to implement gamification. A variety of game elements was chosen for two reasons. First, as argued before, a single game element is insufficient to create a gamified environment. Second, using different game elements ensures adequate stimuli for different player types.[4] In the experiment, the following game elements were implemented: points, high-score list, avatar, progress bar, level, and game-like wording. In the following, the design of elements is described more concretely. Further, Table 4.3 (p. 84) and Figure 4.1 (p. 83) present a graphic overview of implemented game elements.

Points were displayed on the left of the computer screen. Participants received points for dropping correctly collected items at the conveyor belt within the allotted time. Collecting wrong items or the wrong number of items resulted in a deduction of points. After each round, points were added up, except for the test round. The high-score list was displayed continuously on the right side of the screen showing six positions, whereby participants were ranked by points. Only participants within the same condition of the respective experimental run were ranked to avoid effects due to negative feedback and unfair comparisons. Thus, in the case of the worst-performer, the participant was ranked sixth. Furthermore, participants had the opportunity to choose an avatar after round three and after round eight. Specifically, they could choose one of five avatars. In order to provide a gender-neutral environment, options include female, male and gender-neutral characters.

Further, a progress bar was displayed after each round. It showed progress in terms of completed rounds in relation to total numbers of rounds. After the fifth round, participants in the gamified condition were moreover informed that they had reached the next level. Here, the first level (rounds one to five) corresponds to the less complex tasks and the second level (rounds six to ten) to the more complex ones. Additionally, wording in the gamified condition was adapted to "rounds" and "missions" (instead of "tasks" and "assignments" in the non-gamified condition).[5]

---

[4] According to Bartle, there are four player types which differ in orientation focus and interaction preferences (1996). Monterrat et al. 2017 found that participants have different player profiles and different preferences for gaming features.

[5] Original as implemented in the experiment rounds („Runden") and missions ("Missionen") in the gamified condition and orders ("Aufträge") and tasks ("Aufgabe") in the non-gamified one.

5.2.1.3.3 Manipulation of Task Complexity

Concerning task complexity in an experimental setting, I followed the common approach in the literature and manipulated objective task complexity (Byström 1999, Liu/Li 2012, Schwab/Cummings 1976). Following Bonner's model, task complexity is determined by the amount and further the clarity of input, processing, and output (Bonner 1994). For the operationalization of task complexity within the experiment, input clarity was manipulated (structured versus ill-structured order picking lists), and at the same time, the input and output was kept at a constant level. The complexity of processing increased as a consequence of the manipulated input.

Task complexity was implemented as within-group manipulation, whereby the task was either less or more complex. All participants had to process ten order-picking lists. Each list contains ten positions with varying quantities of goods, with a total of 20 items per list. Lists one to five were designed to be easy while lists six to ten were designed more complex. The lists in the easy task displayed items arranged in the same order as aisles and shelves in the virtual storage depot. In other words, by following the list, participants automatically took the shortest way to collect all items, which is essential under given time constraints. The more complex task presented items in an unsorted list. Under increased task complexity in the form of unsorted order lists, the previous working method of processing order lists from top to button would result in substantially longer pathways and consume more time. Under the given time restrictions, this would lead to decreased performance. Nevertheless, individuals can exert additional cognitive effort to transform the information (Speier 2006). By mentally reordering items on the order list, participants were able to optimize their path and collect more items within the given time. Following Campbell (1988), operationalization, as stated above, can be categorized as task complexity due to path multiplicity to a single desired outcome. Path multiplicity includes conflicting interdependence among paths, whereby outcome multiplicity is irrelevant (Campbell 1988, p. 47). Based on a pre-test, all lists were designed to be feasible but challenging under given time restrictions.[6]

5.2.1.4 Experimental Procedures

The experiment was conducted in six sessions. At the start of each session, each participant took a seat in front of a computer terminal and was provided with instructions (see electronic supplementary material S1 and S2). Instructions were

[6] The pre-test was performed with 9 colleagues from the department. Results show that several but not all participants were able to collect all items on the list in time.

read out loud by the supervisor of the experiment. Afterward, participants had the opportunity to ask questions. Participants then individually started the experiment at their respective workstations, whereby the software randomly assigned participants to one of the four conditions.

After completing a practice round, participants completed ten performance rounds in which they process virtual order picking assignments. At the end of the experiment, participants completed a post-experiment questionnaire. After the experiment, participants were directed to the next room and privately received their compensation in cash. Each session took approximately 40 minutes. Participants received 13€ on average.

In the following section, I provide detailed information on the measurement and calculation of the dependent variables.

5.2.2 Measures

To test my hypotheses, I collected data on perceived motivation through a post-experimental questionnaire. Moreover, I collected behavioral data in the form of individuals' effort and performance throughout the experiment. Within this section, the measures used are described in greater detail, starting with measures of motivation. Next, measures of effort and performance are defined.

5.2.2.1 Measurement of Motivation

In order to assess effects on motivation, I collected data on perceived amotivation, intrinsic and extrinsic motivation. Furthermore, based on these data, I calculated the relative autonomy index. All measures of motivation were collected via a post-experimental questionnaire using a Likert scale. The electronic supplementary material S5 provides an overview of questions asked and their corresponding sources. For reasons of improved readability, the 23 questions on motivation were presented on four pages, followed by a page of manipulation check questions and questions on demographics, respectively. The electronic supplementary material S6 and S7 provide an overview of all questions regarding demographics and manipulation checks.

5.2.2.1.1 Intrinsic Motivation

To measure the level of intrinsic motivation, I rely on self-reported measures. Used items were largely adopted from the Intrinsic Motivation Inventory developed by Ryan et al. (1991) and the Multidimensional Work Motivation Scale by Gagné et al. (2015) with minor changes to the wording. Both have been used and validated in several laboratory experiments (Tsigilis/ Theodosiou 2003, Ryan et al. 1991, Deci et al. 1994). Participants were asked to indicate their level of agreement to eight statements on a seven-point Likert scale ranging from "strongly agree" to "strongly disagree." Within these options, three subscales can be distinguished. The first subscale included three items and assessed the level of intrinsic motivation. The second subscale consisted of three items and assessed participants' perception of pressure and tension. Pressure and tension are theorized to be negative predictors of intrinsic motivation. Finally, the two items of the third subscale assessed the willingness to exert additional work effort and motivation, which was adopted from Kunz and Linder (2012) and Schwering (2016).[7] The willingness to exert additional work effort is a positive predictor of intrinsic motivation. Exemplary items of the scales are: "I felt very tense while doing this activity," "It was important to me to do well at this task" and "I would spend additional time on these tasks."

For reliability analysis, Cronbach's alpha was calculated to assess the internal consistency of the scale. Cronbach's alpha of the complete scale of intrinsic motivation was .78. After excluding one item that assessed perceived pressure and tension,[8] Cronbach's alpha for the scale of intrinsic motivation improved to .80, which indicates a high level of internal consistency (Field 2009).

5.2.2.1.2 Extrinsic Motivation

Following the self-determination continuum by Deci and Ryan (2012), extrinsic motivation includes three regulatory styles, namely: external regulation, identified regulation, and introjected regulation. All three regulatory styles were included in the questionnaire relying on items already used and validated in the literature to capture extrinsic motivation in its full spectrum. More concretely, for each regulatory style, I used three relevant items from either the Multidimensional Work Motivation Scale (Gagné et al. 2015), Motivation at Work Scale (Gagné et al. 2010) or a scale to measure motivation developed by Kunz and Linder (2012), which resulted in a total of nine items for the scale of extrinsic motivation. Minor changes of wording have been used to ensure association with the experimental task. The overarching question was: "Why do you or would you put effort into

[7] I consciously decided to query the "willingness to exert additional work effort and motivation" as a measure of intrinsic motivation instead of effort itself. Effort is a separate variable and as a self-reported measure would be biased. Measures of effort will be described in section 5.3.2.

[8] The excluded item is „Beim Bearbeiten der Aufgabe fühlte ich mich unter Druck"/ "I felt pressured while doing the task.")

your current job?" Participants were asked to report their agreement with statements such as "Because I personally consider it important to put efforts in this job." on a seven-point Likert scale. Cronbach's alpha of this scale was .76, which indicates good reliability (Field 2009).

5.2.2.1.3 Amotivation

To evaluate the level of amotivation, participants answered the corresponding three-item scale taken out of the Multidimensional Work Motivation Scale (Gagné et al. 2015). As before, minor changes in wording were used to better correspond to the context. The questionnaire is based on the conceptualization of motivation according to self-determination theory. Evidence for the scale's factorial validity exists for seven languages across nine different country samples (Gagné et al. 2015). On a seven-point Likert scale, participants indicate the degree to which they agree to presented statements answering the question, "Why do you or would you put efforts into your current job?" A sample item was "I do little because I don't think this work is worth putting efforts into." Cronbach's alpha of the scale on amotivation was .79, which indicates good reliability.

5.2.2.1.4 The Relative Autonomy Index

The relative autonomy index (RAI) was derived within the self-determination theory literature and measures the strength of autonomous motivation relative to controlled motivation (Grolnick/Ryan 1987, Sheldon/Kasser 1998, Sheldon/Elliot 1998). RAI is considered as the most common measure of autonomous vs. controlled motivation in the self-determination theory literature (Grolnick/Ryan 1987). The index is calculated as a linear function. At this, the first two components represent controlled types of motivation and the latter two autonomous motivation:

$$RAI = (-2) * external\ regualtion + (-1) * introjected\ regulation + (1) * identified\ regulation + (2) * intrinsic\ regulation$$

The corresponding scores for the regulation types were measured on the aforementioned motivation scales derived within self-determination theory. Participants indicated on each of the four seven-point Likert subscales the extent to which they agree with certain statements. For instance, the response "Because I will be financially compensated only if I put enough effort in this task," serves as an example of external regulation, while "Because I have to prove to myself that I can," represents introjected regulation. The response "Because I personally consider it important to put effort in this task," displays identified regulation while "Because I enjoy this work very much," exhibits intrinsic regulation.

5.2.2.2 Measurement of Effort

The effort construct distinguishes between various components, including direction, duration, intensity, and strategy development (Bonner/Sprinkle 2002, p. 304). Some components immediately affect performance. Strategy development and increased effort directed towards learning aims at delayed performance improvement (Bonner/Sprinkle 2002, p. 306). Measuring effort in a laboratory setting requires three criteria to be fulfilled by proxy (Baiman 1982; Knauer et al. 2017). First, the proxy measuring effort must be controlled by the individual. Second, proxy and performance must be correlated. Third, the proxy must be costly.

Within my study, I followed the approach of Sprinkle (2000) and measured effort in the form of effort duration as the amount of time a participant spent on the task in each round. Effort duration fulfills the required criteria stated by Baiman (1982): Individuals control the time they spend on the task as they may choose to hand in collected items early or even end the experiment early by clicking-through the rounds without collecting items. The time spent on the task is correlated to performance, as collecting items is a time-consuming activity. The more time an individual invests, the more items can be collected, which, depending on the compensation scheme, results in an increased financial reward. On the other hand, rounds are time-restricted and, therefore, costly. Effort duration is measured as stated below:

$$Effort\,duration = time\,used\,to\,process\,order\,picking$$

5.2.2.3 Measurement of Performance and Performance Improvement

Previous research suggests that monetary incentives vary in their effectiveness on performance measures, whereby performance quality and quantity are affected differently (Jenkins et al. 1998, Camerer/Hogarth 1999). Further, literature in accounting and management control focuses on measuring initial and total performance while mostly ignoring performance improvement measures.[9] To evaluate effects on performance, I used measures of total performance and performance

[9] Exceptions that include performance improvement measures can be found in Bailey and Fessler (2011) and Bailey et al. (1998)

improvement. Total performance was captured in absolute and relative parameters, more concrete as output quantity, output quality, and efficiency of working. Moreover, performance improvement gathered changes in the abovementioned performance variables over the course of time. In the following, more details on implemented performance measures are provided.

Performance quantity as an absolute indicator is measured as the number of items that are both, picked correctly (according to the order list) and submitted to the conveyor belt within the given time.

$$Quantity = number\ of\ correct\ items\ picked\ and\ submitted$$

Performance quality is captured by the error rate, whereby error rate is measured as a ratio between the number of performance errors and the number of items on the list (consistently 20 items in all rounds). Specifically, there are three types of performance errors that were captured. First, participants can collect too much of an item (e.g., two red pencils on the order list, three red pencils put in the basket). Second, participants can collect the wrong items (e.g., two red pencils on the order list, two blue pencils put in the basket). Third, participants can fail to collect an item (e.g., two red pencils on the order list, one red pencil in the basket). Error rate is displayed as a percentage:

$$Error\ rate = \frac{number\ of\ performance\ errors}{number\ of\ items\ on\ list} * 100$$

Further, efficiency is measured as the number of items correctly picked and submitted per time used. Participants have a limited time frame of 120 seconds per round and order list but can decide how much of that time they dedicate to solving the task. Two aspects might come into play here: Time dedicated to the task can represent the level of effort duration, but time use can also indicate strategic decisions by an individual. Thus, participants can choose to play it safe and offload the collected items well before the time elapses, or they can keep on collecting items until shortly before the end of time at risk of not being able to offload them.

$$Efficiency = \frac{number\ of\ correct\ items\ submitted}{time\ used}$$

Furthermore, to evaluate performance improvement, I used the abovementioned measures to calculate changes in performance. Here, changes in performance were calculated separately for both rounds that were low on task complexity (rounds 1–5) and rounds with high task complexity (rounds 6–10). I compare the first round and the last round of these two levels of task complexity, respectively. Thus, changes in output quantity, output quality, and efficiency of working were calculated as follows:

$$Change\,in\,quantity\,I = quantity\,in\,round\,5 - quantity\,in\,round\,1$$

$$Change\,in\,quantity\,II = quantity\,in\,round\,10 - quantity\,in\,round\,6$$

$$Change\,in\,error\,rate\,I = error\,rate\,in\,round\,5 - error\,rate\,in\,round\,1$$

$$Change\,in\,error\,rate\,II = error\,rate\,in\,round\,10 - error\,rate\,in\,round\,6$$

$$Change\,in\,efficiency\,I = efficiency\,in\,round\,5 - efficiency\,in\,round\,1$$

$$Change\,in\,efficiency\,II = efficiency\,in\,round\,10 - efficiency\,in\,round\,6$$

5.3 Results—The Moderating Effects of Gamification and Task Complexity

In this section, the results of the conducted experiment are presented. First, I describe the implemented manipulation checks and corresponding drop of experimental subjects. Second, I present the results of my hypotheses organized by blocks. I start with the first block, which comprises hypotheses on the effects of gamification on motivation, followed by the second block of hypotheses, which focus on the effect of gamification on effort duration. The third block focuses on incentive effects on various performance measures. In the last hypotheses block, I present the result linked to my hypotheses on the moderating effects of gamification and task complexity. The chapter finishes with a summary of the results.

5.3.1 Manipulation Checks

In order to determine the effectiveness of manipulations, I implemented manipulation checks. The manipulations of gamification, as a non-monetary incentive scheme, and compensation were evaluated through manipulation check questions. The manipulation of task complexity was evaluated based on a comparison of performance measures. Manipulation check questions were inserted at the end of the questionnaire to prevent negative effects on validity due to the chronological order of testing. The following subsections provide more details on the relevant manipulation checks.

5.3.1.1 Task Complexity

Increasing task complexity is expected to negatively influence task performance (Liu/Li 2012, p. 560). As objective task complexity yields in subjective task complexity, subjective task complexity can be used to verify objective task complexity. Therefore, manipulation of objective task complexity requires a validation of subjective task complexity (Liu/Li 2012). The performance quantity in rounds five (structured list) and six (ill-structured list) were compared to evaluate whether the manipulation of input (structured versus ill-structured order picking lists) resulted in increased complexity. A successful manipulation of task complexity would yield significant differences in performance between these two rounds. Results show a significant different output between the less and more complex tasks. On average, participants' output[10] under low complexity ($M = 16.03$, $SE = .47$) significantly exceeds output under high complexity ($M = 14.36$, $SE = .42$), $t\ (118) = 5.8$, $p<.01$, $r = .47$[11]. Thus, task complexity was manipulated successfully.

5.3.1.2 Gamification

Three questions captured participants' perception of the non-monetary incentive scheme. I first asked participants to recall whether they received information on points, progress, and levels in the course of the experiment. For participants in a gamified condition, the correct answer was yes, while for participants in a non-gamified condition, the correct answer was no. Of the 119 participants, 100 answered this nominal scaled question correctly. Hence, 16% failed the manipulation check, whereby most of them (15 of 19) participated in a condition without game elements. A reason for this might be that after spending time on the questionnaire, participants wrongly recalled the displayed number of collected items

[10] Performance output measured as correctly collected items.

[11] I compared means using a dependent t-test.

as points. A second question asked participants to recall if they had the chance to choose an avatar. Again, for participants in a gamified condition, the correct answer was yes, while for participants in a non-gamified condition, the correct answer was no. Of the 119 participants, 109 answered this normal scaled question correctly. The remaining 8.4% that answered incorrectly were mainly participating in the non-gamified condition with flat wage (8 out of 10 participants). A reason for the increased incidence of wrong answers might be found in a low level of concentration within the condition, as the fixed-wage provides no further incentives to foster engagement with the questionnaire.

5.3.1.3 Compensation

To determine whether participants perceived the manipulation of compensation, they were asked to recall their assigned compensation scheme as either "fixed and therefore independent from the performance" or "variable and therefore dependent on performance." Of the 119 participants, 102 answered this nominal scaled question correctly. The 14.3% that failed to recall the correct compensation scheme mainly belong to either the condition that offered a gamified environment combined with variable compensation (7 participants) or the condition without game elements that provided fixed compensation (6 participants). Reasons for false answers might come from two sources. A lack of sufficient language skills might prevent comprehension of the information provided on the compensation scheme in the first place, and therefore, participants are unable to recall this correctly. Additionally, decreasing motivation and engagement at the end of the experimental activity might lead to a careless click-through.

5.3.1.4 Fatigue and Boredom

As the experiment is based on a repetitive task, participants' performance may change over time due to boredom or fatigue (Friedman et al. 1994). With this in mind, Friedman et al. (1994, p. 30) recommend experimental sessions of at most two hours. With a duration of 40 minutes per session, the experiment followed this recommendation. However, to exclude effects of boredom or fatigue, the development of performance quantity over the ten rounds was evaluated. Except for round six, in which task complexity was increased, data show a constant increase in performance quantity. Thus, data suggest that participants did not show effects of boredom or fatigue.

5.3.1.5 Drop of Experimental Subjects

Some participants were unable to answer manipulation check questions correctly. In line with previous literature, I exclude those subjects who failed the manipulation check questions. Removing subjects aims to ensure that estimates are restricted to the population of subjects that understood the experiment correctly (Wilson et al. 2010, p. 66).

Concerning the manipulation of a non-monetary incentive scheme (in the form of gamification), I exclude only those subjects that answered both questions incorrectly. I decided to include those that answered one of the questions incorrectly because even the correct recall of just one of the implemented game elements shows a perception of gamification. Concerning the manipulation of compensation, I exclude all subjects that failed to recall the correct compensation scheme.

Lastly, participants who did not collect at least two items over the course of the experiment were excluded from further analysis. I decided to do so, as these participants obviously did not understand the given task. I set the limit at two items because this demonstrates an understanding of the task—in the test round, participants received a list with four items. At the same time, the limit of two items still includes participants that understood the task and performed in the test round but decided not to perform the task after being informed about a fixed wage. In sum, 22 of the 119 participants were excluded. Thus, data from 97 participants were included in further analysis. Table 5.2 provides information on the drop of participants in conditions. This presents a good basis for further analysis, as for statistical reasons, each treatment should include 10 to 30 subjects per treatment condition (Campbell/Stanley 2015).[12]

Table 5.2 Drop of participant

	nonGamified_Fix	Gamified_Fix	nonGamified_Var	Gamified_Var
Participants [excluded]	25 [7]	28 [2]	24 [4]	20 [9]

[12] To ensure robustness of results, all analyses were additionally performed with the complete data set. Differing results are outlined in the relevant sections.

5.3.2 Hypotheses Test

In the following, hypotheses will be tested by blocks. The first block of hypotheses tests focuses on gamification's effects on motivation. The second block will then focus on gamification's effect on effort duration. In the third hypotheses block, predictions on the effects of monetary incentives on total performance and on performance improvement are examined. In the last block, I focus on the moderating effects of task complexity and gamification on the incentive-effort-performance relation

5.3.2.1 Hypotheses on the Effects of Gamification on Motivation

Table 5.3 (p. 134) presents descriptive statistics related to variables of motivation. It shows that intrinsic motivation is highest in the condition with gamification and variable compensation, while the lowest level is observable in the condition without game elements and fixed compensation. Extrinsic motivation and the relative autonomy index are mainly affected by the compensation scheme, with variable compensation yielding in an increased level of extrinsic motivation and a decreased level of RAI compared to fixed compensation. The highest level of amotivation was observed in the condition without game elements under fixed compensation, while the level of amotivation was lowest in the condition with performance-contingent compensation without gamification.

Before the respective hypothesis tests, assumptions concerning normal distribution and homogeneity of variances were checked. Results of the Shapiro-Wilk test showed that data on motivation in most of the groups were distributed normally. However, data on intrinsic motivation in the group with game elements and variable compensation, and RAI in the group without game elements under variable compensation was significantly different from the normal distribution. Also, data on amotivation were significantly different from the normal distribution across groups. Further, Levene's test showed that for intrinsic motivation, extrinsic motivation and RAI variances were equal for groups, but for amotivation, the variances were significantly different in the groups $F(3, 93) = 2.71$, $p<.05$. In accordance with Field (2009), I transformed the data on amotivation using a natural logarithm, which resulted in the homogeneity of variances. I use a two-way independent ANOVA to test my hypotheses on the effects of gamification on motivation. The Shapiro-Wilk test revealed that the assumption of normally distributed data is violated. However, an ANOVA is considered robust against violations of the normal distribution assumption and is therefore considered an appropriate analysis (Schmider et al. 2010).

My hypotheses **H1 (a-c)** predict that the gamification of a task results in lower amotivation, higher intrinsic motivation, while not affecting extrinsic motivation. Support for these hypotheses would comprise a significant main effect of game elements on perceived amotivation as well as on intrinsic motivation reported by participants, but no main effect of gamification on extrinsic motivation. As expected, Table 5.4 (p. 135) shows no significant main effect of gamification on extrinsic motivation, $F(1, 93) = .12$, $p = .72$. Contrary to my prediction, no significant main effects of gamification on neither intrinsic motivation ($F(1, 93) = .41$, $p = .52$) nor amotivation ($F(1, 93) = .04$, $p = .83$) were observable. In fact, gamification had no effect on any type of motivation. Thus, I can support my hypotheses H1b, but must reject my hypotheses H1a and H1c.

Within my hypotheses **H1d,** I predict that gamification, contrary to performance-contingent monetary rewards, does not affect the ratio of autonomous motivation to controlled motivation. Support for this hypothesis would consist of no main effect of gamification on the RAI. Panel D in Table 5.4 (p. 135) provides the results of the corresponding analysis. Consistent with H1d there was no significant main effect of gamification on the RAI ($F(1, 93) = .12$, $p = .72$). Consequently, I find support for my hypotheses H1d.

Furthermore, though no hypotheses were formulated on the effects of performance-contingent monetary incentives on motivation and the potential interaction of gamification and compensation concerning motivation, the respective results should be mentioned. Following the theory and state of research, piece-rate compensation is expected to increase extrinsic motivation. Further, performance-contingent monetary rewards lead to lower levels of autonomous motivation while increasing controlled motivation, which would result in a significantly lower RAI. Consistent with previous research, results show a significant effect of compensation on extrinsic motivation ($F(1, 93) = 8.32$, $p = .005$) and RAI ($F(1, 93) = 10.89$, $p = .001$). These significant main effects support a successful manipulation of the factor. However, no interaction effects between compensation and gamification were observable concerning motivation.

5.3.2.2 Hypotheses on the Effect of Gamification on Effort Duration

As in the first experiment, I explored collected data on effort duration to check if assumptions for parametric tests were met. Whereas Levene's test shows that assumptions concerning homogeneity of variances were met, the Shapiro-Wilk test reveals that the assumption of normally distributed data is violated. However, as an ANOVA is considered robust against violations of the normal distribution assumption, I use a three-way mixed ANOVA to test the respective hypotheses (Schmider et al. 2010).

Table 5.3 Descriptive Statistics—Motivation

		Intrinsic Motivation		Extrinsic Motivation[13]		Amotivation		RAI	
Experimental Condition	n	Mean	SD	Mean	SD	Mean	SD	Mean	SD
Gamified_Fix	28	4.09	1.10	4.57	0.97	2.37	1.01	4.29	3.57
Non-Gamified_Fix	25	3.89	1.08	4.43	1.02	2.49	1.59	3.37	3.84
Gami-fied_Var	20	4.11	1.40	5.07	1.14	2.00	1.37	0.88	4.70
Non-Gamified_Var	24	3.99	1.34	5.07	0.72	1.88	0.93	1.19	4.52
Experimental Manipulation									
Non-Gamified	49	3.94	1.21	4.74	0.94	2.19	1.33	2.31	4.29
Gamified	48	4.10	1.22	4.78	1.06	2.22	1.17	2.87	4.37
Fix	53	3.99	1.09	4.50	0.99	2.43	1.30	3.86	3.70
Var	44	4.05	1.35	5.07	0.92	1.93	1.14	1.05	4.55

Pay Scheme was either fixed-wage (Fix) compensation or piece-rate (Var) compensation.
Gamification was manipulated as either present (Gamified) or absent (Non-Gamified).
Intrinsic Motivation was measured in a post-experimental questionnaire based on a seven-item scale.
Extrinsic Motivation was measured in a post-experimental questionnaire based on a nine-item scale.
Amotivation was measured in a post-experimental questionnaire based on a three-item scale.
Relative Autonomy Index (RAI) was calculated as outlined in section 5.2.2.1.4.

[13] Descriptive statistics of the underlying subscales are displayed in the electronic supplementary material S10.

Table 5.4 ANOVA—Effect of Compensation and Gamification on Motivation

Panel A: Intrinsic Motivation

	Sum of Squares	df	Mean Square	F-Statistic	p-value
Gamification (Game)	0.617	1	0.617	0.411	0.523
Compensation (Comp)	0.110	1	0.110	0.073	0.787
Game X Comp	0.039	1	0.039	0.026	0.872
Error	139.691	93	1.502		

Panel B: Extrinsic Motivation

	Sum of Squares	df	Mean Square	F-Statistic	p-value
Gamification (Game)	0.114	1	0.114	0.122	0.728
Compensation (Comp)	7.791	1	7.791	8.325	0.005
Game X Comp	0.123	1	0.123	0.132	0.718
Error	87.043	93	0.936		

Panel C: Amotivation a)

	Sum of Squares	df	Mean Square	F-Statistic	p-value
Gamification (Game)	0.005	1	0.005	0.043	0.836
Compensation (Comp)	0.496	1	0.496	4.092	0.046
Game X Comp	0.001	1	0.001	0.012	0.912
Error	11.270	93	0.121		

Panel D: Relative Autonomy Index

	Sum of Squares	df	Mean Square	F-Statistic	p-value
Gamification (Game)	2.160	1	2.160	0.126	0.723
Compensation (Comp)	186.106	1	186.106	10.888	0.001
Game X Comp	8.943	1	8.943	0.523	0.471
Error	1589.606	93	17.093		

a) To meet the assumption of homogeneity of variances, I transformed the data on amotivation using a natural log.

Table 5.5 shows descriptive statistics for the dependent variables of performance and effort duration. Thus, participants receiving fixed compensation spent more time on the task when the task was gamified, whereas participants receiving variable compensation spent less time on the task when the task was gamified. Overall, the highest and lowest level of effort duration was observable under variable compensation. Most time was spent on the non-gamified task, whereas the least time was spent on the task in the gamified condition

In my hypothesis H2, I argue that effort duration is expected to be higher in a gamified task compared to a non-gamified task. Support for this hypothesis would consist of a significant main effect of gamification on effort duration. Table 5.6 (p. 138) provides the results of the corresponding analysis. Contrary to the prediction in H2, I found no significant main effect of gamification on effort duration ($F(1, 93) = .39$, $p = .53$). This indicates that gamification does not directly affect effort duration. Thus, I reject the hypothesis H2.

5.3.2.3 Hypothesis on the Effects on Performance

Previous literature on effects on performance frequently relies on a limited number of measures that capture either performance quantity or performance quality. Meta-analysis shows that the effects of compensation differ depending on the chosen measure (Jenkins et al. 1998). Thus, in contrast to previous studies, I investigate effects on performance using both: measures of performance quantity and performance quality.

Before analyzing the data, I explore collected data on performance to check if assumptions for parametric tests were met. Whereas Levene's test shows that assumptions concerning homogeneity of variances were met, the Shapiro-Wilk test reveals that the assumption of normally distributed data is violated. However, as an ANOVA is considered robust against violations of the normal distribution assumption, I again use a three-way mixed ANOVA to test the respective hypotheses (Schmider et al. 2010).

Descriptive statistics of performance variables are provided in Table 5.5 (p. 137). Noteworthy, the performance of participants receiving fixed compensation was good, and no serious slacking occurred. Participants in this compensation scheme could have stopped exerting the task at any time and still would have received full payment. However, there is no evidence of such behavior. The best performance in the form of total output quantity (mean = 145), error rate (mean = 17.4), and efficiency (mean = 0.14) was observable in the condition with gamification and variable compensation. Efficiency was lowest under fixed compensation, independent of whether the task included game elements (mean = 0.11). The highest error rate was observable in the non-gamified condition with

Table 5.5 Descriptive Statistics—Performance and Effort Duration

	Experimental Condition							
	Gamified_Fix		Non-Gamified_Fix		Gamified_Var		Non-Gamified_Var	
	Mean	SD	Mean	SD	Mean	SD	Mean	SD
Quantity Round 1–5	62	34	59	23	75	28	75	29
Quantity Round 6–10	59	35	63	26	69	32	68	27
Total Quantity a)	**121**	**66**	**122**	**44**	**145**	**59**	**143**	**51**
Error Rate Round 1–5	25.93	22.54	33.00	22.75	16.40	18.52	20.75	22.33
Error Rate Round 6–10	25.36	20.23	25.84	18.58	18.40	16.66	21.46	17.11
Error Rate b)	**25.64**	**20.50**	**29.42**	**19.29**	**17.40**	**16.50**	**21.10**	**18.67**
Avg Efficiency Round 1–5	0.12	0.07	0.11	0.04	0.15	0.06	0.14	0.06
Avg Efficiency Round 6–10	0.11	0.07	0.12	0.05	0.13	0.06	0.13	0.05
Avg Efficiency c)	**0.11**	**0.06**	**0.11**	**0.04**	**0.14**	**0.06**	**0.13**	**0.05**
Avg Effort Duration Round 1–5	108.36	8.79	106.76	7.96	105.60	8.56	109.38	6.38
Avg Effort Duration Round 6–10	111.81	6.64	110.06	6.77	107.90	7.37	110.95	5.37
Avg Effort Duration d)	**110.09**	**7.27**	**108.41**	**6.91**	**106.75**	**7.67**	**110.16**	**5.16**

Task Complexity was manipulated as less complex (round 1–5) and complex (round 6–10)
a) Quantity was measured as number of correct items submitted per round.
b) Avg Error rate was measured as number of performance errors per number of items on list per round in percentage.
c) Avg Efficiency was measured as number of correct items submitted per used time per round.
d) Avg Effort Duration was measured in seconds used per round.

Table 5.6 The Effect of Gamification, Compensation and Task Complexity on Effort Duration

Source of Variation	SS	df	MS	F	p
Between Subjects					
Gamification	18.06	1	18.06	0.39	0.53
Compensation	15.01	1	15.01	0.33	0.57
Gamification*Compensation	154.56	1	154.56	3.34	0.07
Error	4301.79	93	46.26		
Within Subjects					
Task Complexity	337.93	1	337.93	23.72	0.000
Task Complexity * Gamification	2.30	1	2.30	0.16	0.69
Task Complexity * Compensation	24.88	1	24.88	1.75	0.19
Error	66249.58	93	14.25		

fixed compensation. In general, error rates for both forms of compensation were lower when the task was gamified (fixed compensation: 25.4 versus 29.4/ variable compensation: 17.4 versus 21.1).

Further, Table 5.7 (p. 141) provides the means and standard deviations for the three dependent variables that capture performance improvement. Data on change in error rate show that variable compensation leads to less improvement compared to fixed compensation (in gamified task −13.8 versus −9.1/ in non-gamified task −15.2 versus −13.96). However, the effects of compensation on change in quantity and change in efficiency seem more complex. If the task was not gamified, variable compensation led to lower levels of improvement compared to fixed compensation (change in quantity 5.36 versus 2.02/ change in efficiency .05 versus .02). If the task was gamified, variable compensation led to higher levels of improvement compared to fixed compensation (change in quantity 3.52 versus 4.08/ change in efficiency .03 versus .05).

Hypotheses **H3** predicts that in a repetitive task, monetary incentives that positively affect performance do not affect the rate of performance improvement. This hypothesis would find support in a significant main effect of piece-rate compensation on output quantity, on quality of performance, and on performance efficiency, but no main effect of piece-rate compensation on performance improvement rates. Findings are consistent with these predictions and can be found in Table 5.8 (p. 140) and Table 5.9 (p. 142). On the one hand, I find significant main effects of compensation on output quantity ($F(1, 93) = 3.67$, $p = .06$), on quality of performance ($F(1,93) = 4.55$, $p = .04$)[14] and on performance efficiency ($F(1, 93) = 3.74$, $p = .06$.). On the other hand, I find no significant effects on the performance improvement rate concerning improvement in quantity ($F(1, 93) = 1.74$, $p = .19$), improvement in quality ($F(1, 93) = 1.05$, $p = .31$) and changes in efficiency ($F(1, 93) = .79$, $p = .38$). Consequently, I find support for my hypotheses H3.[15]

5.3.2.4 Hypotheses on the Moderating Effects of Gamification and Task Complexity

Finally, within the last block of hypotheses, I focus on the interaction effects among compensation and task complexity (H4a and H4b) and among compensation and gamification (H5a, H5b and H5c).

Hypothesis **H4a** predicts that for a feasible task that does not require specific knowledge or skills, increased task complexity leads to increased effort duration. Consistent with this prediction, the descriptive statistics provided in Table 5.5 (p. 137) show that participants in all conditions spent less time in rounds one through five (less complex task) compared to round six through ten (more complex task). Furthermore, support for this hypothesis would come from a significant main effect of task complexity on effort duration. Table 5.6 (p. 138) shows the results of the respective ANOVA with effort duration as the dependent variable. There was a highly significant main effect of task complexity on effort duration, $F(1, 93), = 23.72$, $p<.001$. Further, estimated marginal means show that participants spent more time on tasks with high complexity ($M = 110.18$, $SE = .67$) than on tasks with low complexity ($M = 107.52$, $SE = .82$), providing support for H4a.

Hypothesis **H4b** predicts that the moderating effect of task complexity on the incentive-performance relation is limited to total performance, leaving performance improvement rate unaffected. Support for this hypothesis would consist of significant interaction effects between task complexity and compensation scheme on performance measures (quantity, quality, and efficiency), but no significant interaction effects between task complexity and compensation on performance improvement measures (change in quantity, change in quality and change in efficiency). Table 5.8 (p. 140) and Table 5.9 (p. 142) provide results of the

[14] Performing the ANOVA with the complete data set yielded a non-significant main effect of compensation on the quality of performance, $F(1, 115) = 1.63$, $p>.05$.

[15] Analyzing performance and performance improvement based on the complete data partly no significant effects were found. This is a logical consequence of including participants that did not understood the task (collected less than two items). Those subjects represent performance outliers and, since the ANOVA is sensitive to outliers, yield partly non-significant effects.

Table 5.7 The Effect of Gamification, Compensation Scheme and Task Complexity on Performance

Panel A: Quantity					
Source of Variation	*SS*	*df*	*MS*	*F*	*p*
Between Subjects					
Gamification	1.59	1	1.59	0.002	0.96
Compensation	2869.15	1	2869.15	3.67	0.06
Gamification*Compensation	13.31	1	13.31	0.02	0.90
Error	72621.24	93	780.87		
Within Subjects					
Task Complexity	902.57	1	902.57	2.40	0.12
Task Complexity*Gamification	180.37	1	180.37	0.48	0.49
Task Complexity * Compensation	1192.07	1	1192.07	3.17	0.08
Error	35011.30	93	376.47		
Panel B: Quality (error rate)					
Between Subjects					
Gamification	334.39	1	334.39	0.93	0.34
Compensation	1638.12	1	1638.12	4.55	0.04
Gamification*Compensation	0.03	1	0.03	0.00	0.99
Error	33461.56	93	359.80		
Within Subjects					
Task Complexity	150.74	1	150.74	0.82	0.37
Task Complexity*Gamification	371.00	1	371.00	2.02	0.16
Task Complexity * Compensation	651.14	1	651.14	3.54	0.06
Error	17101.18	93	183.88		
Panel C: Efficiency					
Between Subjects					
Gamification	0.000	1	0.000	0.10	0.75
Compensation	0.011	1	0.011	3.74	0.06
Gamification*Compensation	0.000	1	0.000	0.13	0.72
Error	0.274	93	0.003		
Within Subjects					
Task Complexity	0.007	1	0.007	5.48	0.02
Task Complexity*Gamification	0.001	1	0.001	0.90	0.35
Task Complexity * Compensation	0.004	1	0.004	2.92	0.09
Error	0.119	93	0.001		

Table 5.8 Descriptive Statistics—Performance Improvement

	Experimental Condition							
	Gamified Fix		Non-Gamified Fix		Gamified Var		Non-Gamified Var	
	Mean	SD	Mean	SD	Mean	SD	Mean	SD
Change in Quantity a)	**3.52**	**4.46**	**5.36**	**4.84**	**4.08**	**6.40**	**2.02**	**5.04**
Round1—Round 5	3.79	7.42	5.68	6.02	5.20	8.08	2.88	6.33
Round 6—Round 10	3.25	5.38	5.04	7.53	2.95	7.01	1.17	7.72
Change in Error Rate b)	**−13.84**	**12.52**	**−15.20**	**15.78**	**−9.13**	**11.13**	**−13.96**	**16.38**
Round1—Round 5	−18.39	20.77	−18.20	24.49	−14.25	17.11	−16.67	27.09
Round 6—Round 10	−9.29	14.76	−12.20	17.68	−4.00	11.88	−11.25	18.31
Change in Efficiency c)	**0.03**	**0.04**	**0.05**	**0.05**	**0.05**	**0.06**	**0.02**	**0.05**
Round1—Round 5	0.04	0.07	0.06	0.06	0.06	0.07	0.03	0.06
Round 6—Round 10	0.03	0.05	0.05	0.07	0.04	0.07	0.02	0.08

Task Complexity was manipulated as less complex (round 1–5) and more complex (round 6–10)
a) Change in Quantity was measured as differential value for quantity in round 5 and quantity in round 1, or rather, quantity in round 10 and quantity in round 6
b) Change in Error Rate was measured as differential value for error rate in round 5 and error rate in round 1, or rather, error rate in round 10 and error rate in round 6
c) Change in Efficiency was measured as differential value for efficiency in round 5 and efficiency in round 1, or rather, efficiency in round 10 and efficiency in round 6

Table 5.9 The Effect of Gamification, Compensation Scheme and Task Complexity on Performance Improvement

Panel A: Change in Quantity					
Source of Variation	*SS*	*df*	*MS*	*F*	*p*
Between Subjects					
Gamification	0.27	1	0.27	0.01	0.92
Compensation	46.24	1	46.24	1.74	0.19
Gamification*Compensation	90.70	1	90.70	3.42	0.07
Error	2464.38	93	26.50		
Within Subjects					
Task Complexity	157.48	1	157.48	1.82	0.18
Task Complexity*Gamification	1.14	1	1.14	0.01	0.91
Task Complexity * Compensation	46.26	1	46.26	0.53	0.47
Error	8067.43	93	86.75		
Panel B: Change in Quality (change in error rate)					
Between Subjects					
Gamification	229.22	1	229.22	1.14	0.29
Compensation	211.93	1	211.93	1.05	0.31
Gamification*Compensation	72.05	1	72.05	0.36	0.55
Error	18732.42	93	201.42		
Within Subjects					
Task Complexity	5657.92	1	5657.92	7.56	0.01
Task Complexity*Gamification	376.69	1	376.69	0.50	0.48
Task Complexity * Compensation	1.87	1	1.87	0.00	0.96
Error	69622.26	93	748.63		
Panel C: Change in Efficiency					
Between Subjects					
Gamification	0.00	1	0.00	0.01	0.93
Compensation	0.00	1	0.00	0.79	0.38
Gamification*Compensation	0.01	1	0.01	4.55	0.04
Error	0.22	93	0.00		
Within Subjects					
Task Complexity	0.01	1	0.01	1.45	0.23
Task Complexity*Gamification	0.00	1	0.00	0.03	0.86
Task Complexity * Compensation	0.00	1	0.00	0.63	0.43
Error	0.71	93	0.01		

corresponding ANOVAs. Consistent with my predictions, I observe significant interaction effects between task complexity and compensation on output quantity ($F (1, 93) = 3.17$, $p = .08$)[16]; on output quality ($F (1, 93) = 3.54$, $p = .06$), and on efficiency ($F (1, 93) = 2.92$, $p = .09$. Further, I find no significant interaction effects between task complexity and monetary incentives on the performance improvement measures change in quantity ($F (1, 93) = .53$, $p = .47$), change in error rate ($F (1, 93) = .00$, $p = .96$), and change in efficiency ($F (1, 93) = .63$, $p = .43$). This indicates that the effectiveness of performance-contingent monetary incentives on total performance differs between less and more complex tasks, but this moderation effect does not occur with regard to performance improvement rates. Contrasts were performed comparing the two levels of task complexity across the piece-rate and flat wage compensation to gain a better understanding of the significant interaction. These revealed significant interactions when comparing performance in less complex task to performance in more complex task: output quantity $F (1, 93) = 3.17$, $p = .07$, output quality $F(1, 93) = 3.54$, $p = .06$ and efficiency $F (1, 93) = 2.92$, $p = .09$. These results therefore support hypothesis H4b.

Further, hypotheses H5a and H5b predict that the effect of performance-contingent monetary incentives on the incentive-effort-performance relation is moderated by gamification.

More concretely, in **H5a,** I propose that the effect of monetary incentives on effort duration is moderated by gamification, whereby the positive stimulus of gamification is higher under fixed compensation compared to variable compensation. Support for this hypothesis would consist of significant two-way interaction among compensation and gamification on effort duration. Table 5.6 (p. 138) shows the respective ANOVA with time spent on the task as the dependent variable. Consistent with H5a, I observe a significant interaction effect between gamification and compensation $F (1, 93) = 3.34$, $p = .07$.[17] This indicates that the effectiveness of monetary incentives differed in gamified and non-gamified tasks. Looking at the interaction graph in Figure 5.2, this suggests that gamification increased time on task under fixed-wage compensation while decreasing time on task under piece-rate compensation. Thus, the decrease is more pronounced than the increase, suggesting that piece-rate compensation is more influenced by gamification than fixed compensation. In sum, these results provide support for hypothesis H5a.

[16] Cohen suggests using a higher alpha level for interaction effects; he recommends 0.10 instead of 0.05 (Cohen 1988, p. 375).

[17] Again, I follow Cohen's recommendation to use an alpha of .10 instead of .05 for interaction effects (Cohen 1988, p. 375).

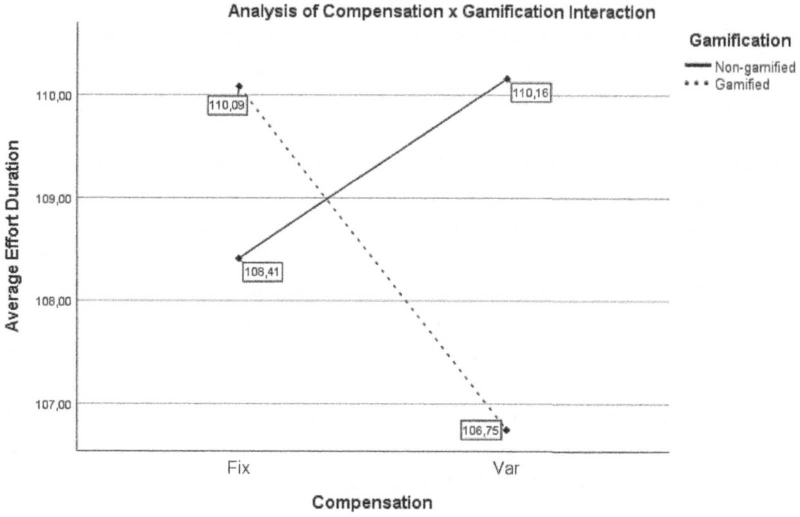

Figure 5.2 Analysis of compensation scheme x gamification on effort duration

Within **H5b,** I expect that the effect of monetary incentives on performance improvement is moderated by gamification, with a piece-rate compensation scheme being more effective in increasing the performance improvement rate in a gamified task compared to a non-gamified task. Moreover, within **H5c**, I expect that the effect of monetary incentives on performance improvement is moderated by gamification, with fixed compensation being more effective in increasing the performance improvement rate in a gamified task than a non-gamified task. Support for these hypotheses would come from a significant two-way interaction among compensation and gamification. As shown in Table 5.9 (p. 142), there was a significant interaction effect between the compensation scheme and gamification on the performance improvement rate in terms of change in efficiency, $F(1, 93) = 4.55$, $p = .04$. Further, I find a significant interaction effect on the performance improvement rate in terms of change in quantity, $F(1, 93) = 3.42$, $p = .07$.[18] The interaction effect is not significant for performance improvement concerning performance quality (error rate).

[18] As mentioned above, Cohen recommends using a higher alpha level for interaction effects, suggesting .10 instead of .05 (Cohen 1988, p. 375).

Figure 5.3 (p. 147) shows the significant two-way interaction graphically. The interaction indicates that participants in gamified conditions were affected differently by compensation than those in non-gamified conditions. Specifically, the improvement rate, in the form of change in efficiency, in non-gamified conditions is lower under piece-rate compensation compared to fixed compensation. However, for the gamified conditions, efficiency improvement was significantly higher under piece-rate compensation compared to fixed compensation. Under fixed compensation, efficiency improvement was lower in the gamified task compared to the non-gamified task. This suggests that gamification results in a superior performance improvement rate, in the form of a change in efficiency, under performance-contingent monetary incentives, but hinders performance improvement, in the form of change in efficiency, under fixed compensation.

A similar observation can be found for the improvement rate in the form of output quantity (change in quantity). Again, the improvement rate in non-gamified conditions is lower under piece-rate compensation compared to fixed compensation, whereas in gamified conditions, quantitative improvement is higher under piece-rate compensation compared to fixed compensation. This suggests that gamification encourages the performance improvement rate, in the form of output quantity, under monetary incentives, but slows down performance improvement rate under fixed compensation.

In summary, the expectation expressed in hypothesis H5b is supported: piece-rate compensation results in higher performance improvement rates (in the form of change in quantity and change in efficiency) in a gamified task compared to a non-gamified task. Coincidently, the expectations expressed in hypotheses H5c are not supported, as, under fixed compensation, the performance improvement rates are lower in gamified conditions compared to non-gamified conditions.

5.3.3 Summary—The Moderating Effects of Gamification and Task Complexity

Monetary incentives are frequently used to incite desired behavior and reward employees. However, research in accounting and management shows that performance-contingent compensation does not always affect performance as expected (Bonner et al. 2000). These findings emphasize the importance of understanding which specific factors influence the incentive-effort-performance relation and consequently lead to positive (Libby/Lipe 1992, Sprinkle 2000) no

Panel A: Change in Efficiency

Panel B: Change in Quantity

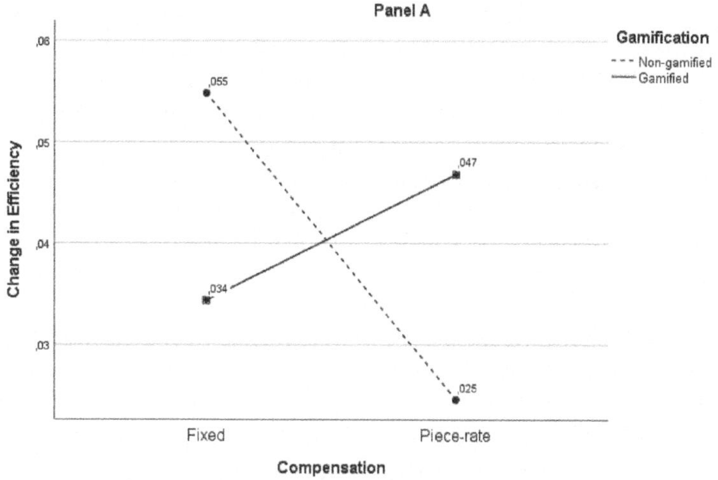

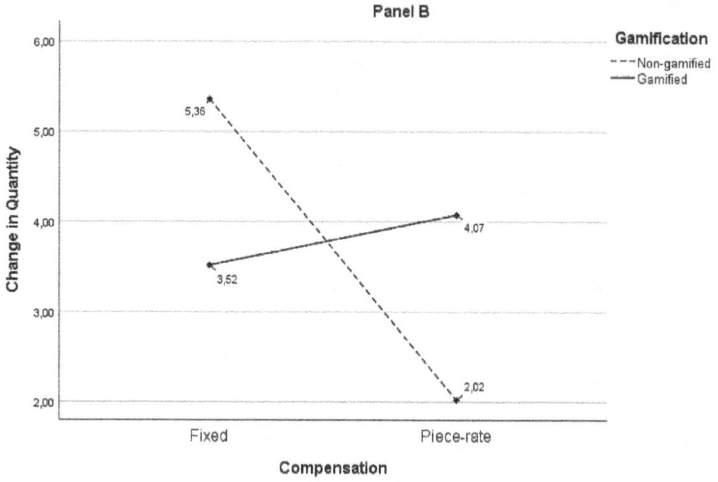

Figure 5.3 Analysis of Interaction of Compensation x Gamification. Panel A: Change in Efficiency, Panel B: Change in Quantity

(Awasthi/Pratt 1990) or even negative effects of monetary incentives on total performance (Ashton 1990, Fessler 2003). In this context, task characteristics play an important role as they can influence the effectiveness of incentive compensation (Bonner/Sprinkle 2002).

Within this experiment, I examined two task characteristics: gamification (absent/non-gamified vs. present/gamified) and task complexity (less complex vs. more complex). To the best knowledge of the author, this study is the first to combine both factors in an experiment. Further, it is the first study that formulates hypotheses on the interaction between compensation and gamification.

Theory and past research indicate that performance-contingent compensation will interact with task complexity, such that the effectiveness of monetary incentives will be greater for less complex tasks. For a general understanding of the effects of monetary incentives and task characteristics in a repetitive task, it is crucial to have a detailed look at the components of performance. Following Bailey et al. (1998), I broke down performance into two components: (1) total performance, and (2) performance improvement rate.

Thus, I extend the literature by predicting that both, the effect of monetary incentives as well as the moderating effect of task complexity, are limited to total performance, while these factors have no facilitating effect on performance improvement rate. I find support for these predictions as piece-rate compensation effectively increased total performance while having no effect on the performance improvement rate. At the same time, the effectiveness of compensation was mitigated by increased task complexity.

Further, I contribute to the body of literature that examines the effect of gamification on motivation, effort duration, and performance. Thus, I shed light on the conflicting results of previous studies and offer possible explanations.

All in all, the combination of performance-contingent compensation and gamification led to the highest total output quantity and output quality (lowest error rate), while at the same time, participants in this condition spent less time on the task. In other words, the combination of gamification and performance-contingent pay led to the highest total performance and highest level of efficiency.

Moreover, statistical analysis provides support for my predictions on the two-way interaction between gamification and compensation. I find that the effect of monetary incentives on effort duration is moderated by gamification. The effort duration under piece-rate was lower for a gamified task, whereas effort duration under fixed-wage was higher when the task was gamified.

Findings also show that the effect of monetary incentives on performance improvement is moderated by gamification. Results suggest that a piece-rate compensation is more effective in increasing the performance improvement rate in a gamified task compared to a non-gamified task, whereas under fix compensation, a gamification of the task results in a lower performance improvement rate compared to the non-gamified version.

From a theoretical perspective, these results suggest that the framework on the effects of monetary incentives (Bonner/Sprinkle 2002) can be extended by including gamification as a task variable that moderates the incentive-effort-performance relation.

These results should be taken into account when designing gamified applications for the field or research purposes. Assuming a fixed compensation scheme, gamifying a task will likely increase time spent on the task and decrease the pace of performance improvement, whereas, under variable compensation, gamification will likely positively affect performance and learning.

Results show no main effect of gamification on indicators of total performance or performance improvement, yet moderating effects on the monetary incentive-effort-performance relation. However, this study utilized a cross-sectional design, and the effects of learning on total performance would only show at a later point. Thus, further analysis of these moderating effects of gamification should utilize a longitudinal study design.

Moreover, relying on a broad spectrum of measures, this study provides an overview of the effects of gamification on different performance parameters. Findings show that the choice of measures (or key performance indicators) can be crucial when it comes to the evaluation of the effects of gamification. Goals and measures should be carefully considered before implementing and researching gamified applications.

Further, the identification of these moderating effects might provide an explanation for the mixed findings in previous studies (Seaborn/Fels 2015). In the field of education, gamification is often reported as having positive effects on performance (Landers/Landers 2014, Sailer/Sailer 2020). Measures of performance often capture aspects of learning, which might explain the frequency of positive results in this field.

In partial contrast to my predictions, I find no main effects of gamification on motivation. In this respect, this study adds to a number of studies that reported no significant effects of gamification on motivation (Seaborn/Fels 2015, Hamari et al. 2014). Furthermore, I expected effort duration to be higher in a gamified task. Surprisingly, results showed no main effect of gamification on effort duration.

In summary, results suggest that gamification fosters performance improvement under performance-contingent compensation and leads to increased work efficiency. The following chapter provides an integrated discussion of all three studies of this thesis.

6 Summary and Concluding Discussion

This thesis investigated the effects of gamification on motivation, effort, and performance and provides a number of new insights and findings. Within this chapter, I will integrate and discuss the results of the three conducted studies. Moreover, I will point out implications for researchers and practitioners. This chapter is organized as follows: In the first section, I will draw on findings of the three conducted studies and explain how each contributes to the existing literature. Next, I will derive implications for future research and practitioners. After pointing out the limitations of the studies, the last section will provide several directions for future research.

6.1 Integration and Discussion of Findings

In this thesis, I present three studies on gamification that (1) shed more light on the current state of research on gamification, (2) examine the effects of different designs of gamification on motivation and effort, and (3) investigate the interactive effects of gamification and task complexity on the effectiveness of performance-contingent monetary incentives in promoting effort and task performance.

Findings from the systematic review of literature on gamification show that the majority of previous studies on gamification focuses on analyzing psychological effects; only a small number of studies also include behavioral measures. Thus, it can be said that many studies lack to provide theoretical underpinnings and give information on the compensation used in their study. With that, my literature review on the second wave of studies on gamification identifies similar points of criticism as former literature reviews (Seaborn/Fels 2015, Hamari et al. 2014).

A. Faust, *The Effects of Gamification on Motivation and Performance*,
https://doi.org/10.1007/978-3-658-35195-3_6

Further, the literature review shows a rather mixed picture concerning the effects of gamification on motivation and performance, whereby overall positive and neutral effects prevail. These mixed results can partly be explained by a combination of measures and compensation schemes. Psychological measures (motivation, perception of usability, amongst others) predominantly resulted in positive and neutral results independent of the compensation scheme implemented. Behavioral measures (performance and time spent on task, among others) showed positive/neutral effects of gamification under non-monetary compensation and without compensation, but negative/neutral effects under monetary compensation.

Thus, the systematic literature review contributes to the existing literature in at least three ways. First, it provides a multidisciplinary review of the second wave of empirical research on gamification. Second, the study identifies the shortcomings of previous papers, especially their lack of theoretical underpinning and a lack of information about compensation schemes. Third, findings provide an explanation for the mixed results in previous empirical research.

The first laboratory experiment, which focused on the different levels of gamification, addresses an ongoing scientific discourse on the number of elements necessary to gamify an environment and affect psychological and behavioral measures (Perryer et al. 2016, Robertson 2010). In doing so, my study is the first that expands the previous theoretical discourse by providing psychological data collected in a laboratory experiment.

Results from the ANOVA suggest that gamification had no significant main effect on motivation and perceived effort. However, contrast analysis revealed significant differences in perceived competence as well as in pressure and tension between the condition with a low level of gamification and the condition with a high/medium level of gamification. It is worth noting that gamification based on one game element decreased motivation and effort compared to the control condition, while a medium and high level of gamification increase motivation and effort.

Thus, despite the non-significant main effect of gamification on motivation, contrast analysis provides partial support for the expectation that one game element is not sufficient to create effective gamification. Moreover, these findings strengthen the argumentation of Robertson (2010) and Bogost (2011). In contrast to Perryer et al. (2016), they claim that gamification should be implemented based on various game elements. Results suggest that one game element does not produce enough stimulus to qualify as gamification, and a flawed or insufficient implementation might cause undesired effects.

Additionally, these findings provide an additional explanation for the mixed results of previous findings. Thus, gamification based on one element or more generally, gamification that provides an insufficient game stimulus, might fail to affect psychological and behavioral measures as expected (e.g., Armstrong and Landers (2017) found that gamification based on game narratives did not increase but instead partly decreased performance in the form of knowledge acquisition).

The second laboratory experiment focused on the interactions of gamification, task complexity, and monetary incentives. In doing so, it is the first study to combine gamification, compensation, and task complexity in an experiment. Further, the study has a pioneering role as it is the first to evaluate gamification as a moderator of the relation between performance-contingent monetary incentives, effort, and performance.

Overall, the combination of performance-contingent compensation and gamification presented the most beneficial condition with respect to absolute and relative performance. Participants in this condition spent less time on the task while performing considerably better in terms of output quantity and quality.

Further, results suggest that the effect of monetary incentives on effort duration and performance is moderated by gamification. Findings show that under financial incentives, gamification led to lower levels of effort duration as compared to the non-gamified setting.

Moreover, results show that gamifying a task facilitates performance improvement under performance-contingent monetary incentives. Consistent with previous research, the positive effects of performance-contingent monetary incentives are limited to initial and total performance in a non-gamified environment (Bailey/Fessler 2011), whereas in a gamified environment performance-contingent monetary incentives are effective in increasing the performance improvement rate.

Thus, my second experiment contributes to the extant literature in multiple ways. First, it adds to a limited number of studies that examine the effects of gamification based on psychological and behavioral outcomes. Second, it addresses the call for more research that examines the effects of monetary and non-monetary incentives together (Kunz/Linder 2012). Third, it provides further explanation for the mixed results concerning the effects of gamification on motivation and performance. Fourth, it considers different types of performance (total performance, initial performance, and performance improvement rate) and demonstrated that under certain circumstances, monetary incentives could affect more types of performance than previously assumed.

Considering the results of the three conducted studies as a whole provides further insights. The literature review finds that gamification in previous studies mostly led to positive or neutral effects on motivation and performance. The two laboratory experiments conducted find no significant main effect of gamification on motivation or performance measures.

This suggests that game elements do not satisfy innate psychological needs as expected. Two reasons might account for this finding: First, implemented game elements might not offer enough game affordance or stimulus. Support for this interpretation comes from the first experimental study that shows a trend of increased levels of motivation leading to increased perceived motivation. Moreover, individuals come with different dispositions and can be categorized as one of several player types (Bartle 1996). Accordingly, game elements differ in their ability to satisfy the needs of certain player types. However, implementing more than one game element does not guarantee that the utilized elements trigger different types. Thus, an implementation of four elements could result in the satisfaction of four different player types as well as the satisfaction of a single player type depending on the choice of game elements. In fact, an increased level of gamification should not be confused with an increased number of game elements; instead it refers to the increased game stimuli perceived by individuals. Second, although the control condition did not include game elements, participants found themselves in the same virtual environment as participants in the gamified conditions and moved their token within this environment to perform the task. It cannot be ruled out that this environment itself presents a form of gamification from the perspective of participants. Thus, significant main effects of gamification on motivation might only occur when comparing effects to a raw and more pared down version.

Further, findings from the literature review suggest that there exists an interaction between gamification, monetary incentive scheme, and utilized measures. Indeed, in my second experiment, I find that gamification moderates the effect of performance-contingent monetary incentives on the performance improvement rate.

Despite the lack of significant motivational effects, the second study found interaction effects that affected behavioral measures (effort and performance). This observation is quite surprising as it conflicts with the assumption that in a first step, incentives lead to psychological outcomes (e.g., motivation), and in a second step, these psychological outcomes transfer into behavioral outcomes (e.g., effort and performance) (Hamari et al. 2014). However, my study is not the first to observe these seemingly contradictory effects. Similarly, Mekler et al. (2017) examined the effects of game elements and found that game elements did not significantly affect perceived competence or intrinsic motivation, but nonetheless, the performance quantity of participants in the gamified conditions was significantly higher compared to the control group.

Reasons for these seemingly contradictory findings come from three directions. First, although results show no significant effect of gamification on perceived motivation, gamification might affect motivation on a more unconscious level. Measuring motivation through a questionnaire does not capture potential effects on more unconscious changes of motivation. Second, there might exist other constructs aside from motivation that mediate effort and performance. Thus, game elements might provide feedback that increases participants' self-efficacy and thus affects effort and performance. Third, gamification might instead be considered a moderator instead of a mediator. Consistent with this approach, gamification does not mediate motivation and performance but moderates the relationship between monetary incentives, effort, and performance. Thus, from the perspective of the framework developed by Bonner and Sprinkle (2002), gamification could be considered as a moderating task variable.

Together, the three studies contribute to the existing literature as they provide a theoretical underpinning based on theories from the field of psychology and the field of management control and, based on these, introduce and embed the concept of gamification in the field of managerial accounting and control.

Further, my studies add to a limited number of studies that examine the effects of monetary and non-monetary incentives in one setting. Kunz and Linder (2012) criticize the narrow research focus on monetary rewards at the expense of non-monetary incentives. Whereas the effects of monetary incentives have been studied widely, yielding partly mixed results, there is a relatively small body of literature that is concerned with non-monetary incentive schemes (Bonner/Sprinkle 2002; Fessler 2003). My studies address this research gap and provide insights on the effects of gamification as a non-monetary incentive scheme in combination with a piece-rate compensation and a fixed compensation. Findings on the interaction effects of gamification and compensation align with and expand the framework by Bonner and Sprinkle (2002) that identifies diverse task characteristics that moderate the incentive-effort-performance relation.

In sum, the results of the three studies show that the effects of gamification on motivation, effort, and performance are more complex than previously assumed, and more research is needed to fully understand underlying relationships. An overview of the hypotheses and results of the two experiments is shown in Table 6.1 (p. 150).

Table 6.1 Overview Results Experiment 1 and Experiment 2

Experiment 1		
No.	Hypothesis	Supported
H1a	Gamification based on one element is less effective to positively affect interest and enjoyment compared to gamification based on various game elements.	no
H1b	Gamification based on one element is less effective to increase perceived competence compared to gamification based on various game elements.	partly
H1c	Gamification based on one element is less effective to increase perceived pressure and tension towards a moderate level compared to gamification based on various game elements.	partly
H2	Gamification based on one element is less effective to increase perceived effort compared to gamification based on various game elements.	no
Experiment 2		
No.	Hypothesis	Supported
H1a	Gamification leads to increased intrinsic motivation.	no
H1b	Gamification does not affect extrinsic motivation.	yes
H1c	Gamification leads to decreased amotivation.	no
H1d	Gamification does not affect the ratio of autonomous motivation to controlled motivation.	yes
H2	Effort duration is higher in a gamified task compared to a non-gamified task.	no
H3	In a repetitive task, monetary incentives, that positively affect performance, do not affect the rate of performance improvement.	yes
H4a	For a feasible task that does not require previous knowledge or skills, increased task complexity leads to increased effort duration.	yes
H4b	The moderating effect of task complexity on the incentive-performance relation is limited to total performance, leaving performance improvement rate unaffected.	yes
H5a	The effect of monetary incentives on effort duration is moderated by gamification, whereby the positive stimulus of gamification is higher under fixed compensation compared to variable compensation.	yes

(continued)

Table 6.1 (continued)

Experiment 2		
No.	Hypothesis	Supported
H5b	The effect of monetary incentives on performance improvement is moderated by gamification, whereas a piece-rate compensation will be more effective in increasing the performance improvement rate in a gamified task compared to a non-gamified task.	yes
H5c	The effect of monetary incentives on performance improvement is moderated by gamification, with a fixed compensation to be more effective in increasing the performance improvement rate in a gamified task compared to a non-gamified task.	no

6.2 Implications for Research and Practitioners

In practice, gamification is a widespread phenomenon with a respective market size of USD 6.33 billion in 2019 (Fortune Business Insight 2020). In research, the concept has attracted increasing attention over the last ten years, which has in turn lead to a continuously growing body of scientific contributions. However, the systematic literature review showed that gamification did not receive adequate attention in the management-related literature so far. In the future, scholars from this field will need to give enhanced attention to gamification as an object of research.

In this context, my results have implications for researchers that employ gamification in experimental studies. My study shows that the effect of gamification on motivation, effort, and performance is inextricably linked to the type of financial incentive scheme. Future research on gamification can benefit from these findings and consciously include them when designing experiments. Thus, results from my second experimental study suggest that investigating the effects of gamification differences between groups become most visible based on a variable compensation scheme. Further, future studies could examine and compare the effects of gamification in combination with diverse other forms of compensation (non-monetary and monetary, tournaments, compensation based on group performance, lotteries).

In general, future studies on gamification can overcome the shortcomings identified in previous studies by providing theoretical underpinnings.

Findings also highlight the need for a more detailed look at the components of performance. Whereas previous studies in the field of management accounting and management control focus on total and initial performance, they fail to examine the effects on performance improvement. However, the pace of performance improvement is strongly linked to long-term performance. Accordingly, future studies can be improved by considering all components of performance and choosing a time frame that allows improvement effects to occur. In this context, future studies should also examine the moderating effect of gamification on different performance measures.

Further, results from the second experimental study suggest that gamification moderates the effects of monetary incentives on performance improvement. Thus, future research in the field of management accounting should reevaluate the assumption that monetary incentives do not affect performance improvement (Bailey/Fessler 2011). Hereby, they could focus on the moderating effects of gamification and other moderators of the incentive-effort-performance relation (e.g., task variables and environmental variables) (Bonner/Sprinkle 2002).

Moreover, my findings have implications for practitioners and the design of incentive schemes. Before implementing an incentive scheme, practitioners should be aware of the moderating effect of gamification and consider whether the potential effects match their objectives under the given circumstances. In this context, monetary incentives are a frequently used incentive to increase employee's motivation and performance (Kunz/Linder 2012, Bonner/Sprinkle 2002). My findings highlight that gamification moderates the effectiveness of monetary incentives. In particular, the potential additional benefit of gamification seems to be related to at least two factors: 1) the objective and 2) the compensation scheme. Thus, an implementation of gamification can bring benefits when the objective is to accelerate the pace of learning under variable pay, whereas gamification can decelerate the pace of learning under fixed pay.

More generally, firms may restructure incentive schemes and implement gamified systems with the objective of increasing certain performance measures. However, if new incentives fail to affect cognitive processes that lead to increases in motivation, effort, and performance, then the restructuring will not be effective but rather present a waste of resources.

Moreover, findings highlight the importance of an appropriate design of gamified incentive systems. In this context, applications that rely on a multitude of game elements, which trigger different player types, appear to be a promising approach.

The relevance of these implications concerning the design of gamified incentive systems becomes obvious when one considers the disenchantment forecast that predicts 80% of gamified applications fail to meet their objectives (Kumar 2013). In conclusion, a recommendation cannot be made either for or against the implementation of gamification, but practitioners should analyze the given circumstances, consider objectives, and be aware of interactive effects between pay and gamification.

In conclusion, the effects of gamification as a non-monetary incentive scheme are more complex than previously assumed, and more research on this non-monetary incentive scheme is needed to fully understand effects on motivation, effort, and performance; and to understand underlying mechanisms and interactions with other monetary and non-monetary incentives. In the following section, I provide suggestions for future research and describe the limitations of the three studies.

6.3 Limitations and Suggestions for Future Research

My first study provides an explanation for the mixed results in previous literature. Findings from the systematic literature review suggest that results differ depending on the combination of measures used and the compensation scheme implemented. However, more than half of the reviewed papers failed to provide information on the utilized compensation scheme in the first place. Thus, the findings are based on a limited number of studies and have to be interpreted with caution.

Moreover, the choice of method involves limitations. A laboratory experiment is subject to time restrictions. Thus, the effects of cross-sectional manipulations may differ from effects observable in longitudinal studies. One reason for this can be found in the novelty factor, which refers to new or unusual experiences. From the perspective of participants, an experiment or/and a gamified task may present a novelty. Thus, psychological and behavioral effects in a novel environment may differ from those that are observable in a standard situation.

In general, laboratory experiments are associated with lower external validity as compared to other research methods. Based on the selection process of participants, it is questionable whether results can be extrapolated to the population without constraints. Participants of the experiments were recruited by laboratory staff using the web-based recruiting database ORSEE (Greiner 2015). The software ensured that participants from the first experiment were not able to also participate in the second experiment. This regimentation prevents distortions of performance data due to different levels of previous knowledge or strategy development. Nonetheless, all participants of the study were students of German universities. Previous research suggests that the attitude towards gamification varies when variables such as sex, age, and prior experience with games come into effect (Landers/Armstrong 2017, Landers/Callan 2012). As participants' age and level of education differ substantially from the population, results cannot be generalized without some degree of caution.

Further limitations of the study emerge based on the design of manipulations. For the manipulation of gamification, I selected commonly used game elements. Next to the chosen elements, there exists a multitude of other game elements that may affect motivation and performance differently. Moreover, to prevent effects stemming from interactions, I did not include game elements that allow direct communication between participants (e.g., gifting, sharing). According to Bartle (1996), different player types exist with different needs and orientations. The game elements chosen for the experiments in this study only contribute to the satisfaction of the needs of three of four player types, whereby no element triggers the player type "socializer" that is characterized by the need for communication (Kocadere/Özhan 2018).

Further, my study is limited to two types of financial compensation schemes (fixed pay and piece-rate) and therefore does not give insights on the effects under quota, tournament, profit-sharing, or budget-based and other schemes.

Another limitation arises due to the implemented task in both experiments. I utilized a repetitive real effort task that required no previous knowledge or expertise. However, practitioners and academics are interested in effects in a variety of tasks. It remains open whether manipulations would yield similar findings in other types of tasks (such as decision tasks, memory tasks, puzzles, decoding, physical challenges, or task related to creativity) or tasks that require specific knowledge.

Moreover, limitations stem from measures used in the first experiment. Within the first experiment (levels of gamification), I relied on participants answers from a post-experimental questionnaire evaluating perceived effort exerted towards the task to investigate the effect of gamification on effort. This method of collecting data carries two drawbacks. First, the implemented scale on perceived effort does not allow a distinction between different types of effort. Thus, it remains open whether additional effort caused by gamification is directed towards effort intensity, effort duration, or strategy development. Based on results from the second experiment, it can be suspected that gamification may influence effort direction. The second drawback relates to the construct of effort itself. The construct of effort represents a bridge between motivation and performance. Thus, effort can be characterized as psychological and behavioral in its nature. Examining effects on effort based on participants perception only covers its psychological manifestations. Thus, due to the measurement chosen in the first experiment, it remains unclear how different levels of gamification affect effort duration and effort direction.

Concerning the measures of motivation, I implemented a post-test only questionnaire. On the one hand, this prevents negative effects on validity, as a pre-test can change consciousness and influence reactions. On the other hand, this prevents the collection of other comparative values for post-test motivation besides the control group, in which participants received fixed compensation and experienced no gamification. Thus, it is not possible to control for external influences on individuals' motivation. Nevertheless, it is assumed that due to the random assignment of participants to conditions, the design prevented distorting effects.

Finally, participants performed the task as individuals, and thus, motivation and performance were measured at an individual level. Research in accounting and managerial control, however, is also interested in the determinants of motivation and performance in teams.

The above-mentioned limitations highlight that future research should continue to examine the effects of gamification. In the following, I will outline possible directions for future research.

First, further research on gamification with alternative study designs (such as field studies) is needed. A large proportion of studies on gamification draw on laboratory experiments. Previous research shows that results from laboratory studies or meta-analysis based on these studies cannot be easily extrapolated to the organizational field (Gagné/Forest 2008). For example, in a meta-analysis, Deci and colleagues investigated the effects of extrinsic rewards on intrinsic motivation (Deci et al. 1999). They found that performance-contingent rewards significantly undermined intrinsic motivation. Later, Fang and Gerhart (2012) failed to replicate these findings in their field study, as they observed a higher intrinsic motivation of employees in a pay-for-performance system compared to a base pay system. Apparently, the effects of compensation schemes in real life differ considerably from effects in laboratory settings (Gagné/Forest 2008). These contradicting results may occur due to differences in importance, size, and time frame of the task (Rynes et al. 2005). Thus, future research on gamification should focus on examining the functioning of gamification in the field. Further, to the best knowledge of the author, there exists no study that examines the effects of gamification in a multi-task setting. Conducting studies in the directions outlined above would provide new insights on the effects of gamification on effort direction.

Second, future research should investigate the effect of gamification on behavioral outcomes based on a more differentiated view. Future studies might focus on how gamification affects different components of effort (effort direction, effort intensity, effort duration, and strategy development).

A third important research question that needs to be addressed is how the removal of game elements affects motivation and performance. In this context, future experimental research may manipulate gamification in a within-group design and investigate effects linked to a removal of the non-monetary incentive scheme based on repeated measures.

Fourth, future research should continue to examine the functioning of gamification and its relationship with monetary incentives and task characteristics. Previous research has shown that gamification can increase intrinsic motivation (Seaborn/Fels 2015). Another stream of literature that originates from the fields of economics, accounting, and management control draws attention to the phenomenon of crowding out. Crowding-out refers to the process by which monetary incentives can have a detrimental effect on motivation and performance. Based on my literature review, I find that gamification often leads to increased motivation. However, the two experimental studies find no effect of gamification on motivation. Thus, it remains open whether gamification can decrease or even revoke the negative effects of performance-contingent compensation by inducing motivation. Future research could address this topic by investigating the effects of gamification with two different approaches: First, by exploring whether implementing both (financial incentives and gamification) together prevents the negative effects of financial incentives in the first place. Second, researchers might study whether implementing gamification after observing motivational crowding can reconstitute intrinsic motivation.

A fifth direction for research stems from the relation of task type and the design of gamification. There remains the unresolved question of whether the effects observed in this study would also occur when participants face a task that requires expertise or knowledge. To put this differently, future studies could probe whether, depending on the type of task, specific game elements are more suitable to affect motivation and performance. Finally, future research can focus on the design of gamification. At this point, it would be interesting to investigate the effects of diverse combinations of game elements in a structured approach.

With the knowledge that gamification shows no main effect on motivation, and gamification moderates the incentive-effort-performance relationship, one could suspect that gamification and monetary incentives might be considered as complements. However, my literature review shows that studies find gamification to have a main effect on motivation and performance, even in the absence of monetary incentives (Liu et al. 2018, Seiffert-Brockamnn et al. 2018). Thus, further research might focus on the question of whether gamification and monetary incentives are complements or substitutes.

References

Adler, Paul S.; Chen, Clara Xiaoling (2011): Combining creativity and control. Understanding individual motivation in large-scale collaborative creativity. In: Accounting, Organizations and Society 36 (2), p. 63–85. DOI: https://doi.org/10.1016/j.aos.2011.02.002.

Agogué, Marine; Levillain, Kevin; Hooge, Sophie (2015): Gamification of Creativity. Exploring the Usefulness of Serious Games for Ideation. In: Creativity and Innovation Management 24 (3), p. 415–429. DOI: https://doi.org/10.1111/caim.12138.

Ahn, Luis von; Dabbish, Laura (2008): Designing games with a purpose. In: Commun. ACM 51 (8), p. 58–67. DOI: https://doi.org/10.1145/1378704.1378719.

Amabile, Teresa M. (1998): How to kill creativity: Harvard Business School Publishing Boston, MA.

Annetta, Leonard A. (2010): The "I's" Have It. A Framework for Serious Educational Game Design. In: Review of General Psychology 14 (2), p. 105–113. DOI: https://doi.org/10.1037/a0018985.

Annetta, Leonard A.; Minogue, James; Holmes, Shawn Y.; Cheng, Meng-Tzu (2009): Investigating the impact of video games on high school students' engagement and learning about genetics. In: Computers & Education 53 (1), p. 74–85.

Aparicio, Andrés Francisco; Vela, Francisco Luis Gutiérrez; Sánchez, José Luis González; Montes, José Luis Isla (2012): Analysis and application of gamification. In: INTERACCION '12: Proceedings of the 13th International Conference on Interacción Persona-Ordenador, p. 1–2. DOI: https://doi.org/10.1145/2379636.2379653.

Armstrong, Michael B.; Landers, Richard N. (2017): An Evaluation of Gamified Training. Using Narrative to Improve Reactions and Learning. In: Simulation & Gaming 48 (4), p. 513–538. DOI: https://doi.org/10.1177/1046878117703749.

Ashton, Robert H. (1990): Pressure and performance in accounting decision settings. Paradoxical effects of incentives, feedback, and justification. In: Journal of accounting research 28, p. 148–180.

Ashton, R.H., Kramer, S.S., (1980): Students as surrogates in behavioral accounting research: Some evidence. Journal of Accounting Research, 1–15.

A. Faust, *The Effects of Gamification on Motivation and Performance*,
https://doi.org/10.1007/978-3-658-35195-3

Attali, Yigal; Arieli-Attali, Meirav (2015): Gamification in assessment. Do points affect test performance? In: Computers & Education 83, p. 57–63. DOI: https://doi.org/10.1016/j.compedu.2014.12.012.

Awasthi, Vidya; Pratt, Jamie (1990): The effects of monetary incentives on effort and decision performance. The role of cognitive characteristics. In: The Accounting Review, p. 797–811.

Baard, Paul P.; Deci, Edward L.; Ryan, Richard M. (2004): Intrinsic need satisfaction. A motivational basis of performance and well-being in two work settings 1. In: Journal of applied social psychology 34 (10), p. 2045–2068.

Bagley, Keith S. (2012): Conceptual mile markers to improve time-to-value for exploratory search sessions. University of Massachusetts Lowell.

Bailey, Charles D.; Brown, Lawrence D.; Cocco, Anthony F. (1998): The effects of monetary incentives on worker learning and performance in an assembly task. In: Journal of Management Accounting Research.

Bailey, Charles D.; Fessler, Nicholas J. (2011): The Moderating Effects of Task Complexity and Task Attractiveness on the Impact of Monetary Incentives in Repeated Tasks. In: Journal of Management Accounting Research 23 (1), p. 189–210. DOI: https://doi.org/10.2308/jmar-10104.

Bailey, Pippa; Pritchard, Gareth; Kernohan, Hollie (2015): Gamification in Market Research. In: International Journal of Market Research 57 (1), p. 17–28. DOI: https://doi.org/10.2501/IJMR-2015-003.

Baiman, Stanley (1982): Agency research in management accounting. A survey. In: Journal of accounting literature 1 (1), p. 154–210.

Baiman, Stanley (1990): Agency research in managerial accounting. A second look. In: Accounting, Organizations and Society 15 (4), p. 341–371.

Bandura, Albert (1977): Self-efficacy. Toward a unifying theory of behavioral change. In: Psychological review 84 (2), p. 191.

Bandura, Albert (1993): Perceived self-efficacy in cognitive development and functioning. In: Educational psychologist 28 (2), p. 117–148.

Barata, Gabriel; Gama, Sandra; Jorge, Joaquim A. P.; Gonçalves, Daniel J. V. (Hg.) (2014): Relating gaming habits with student performance in a gamified learning experience. CHI PLAY '14: Proceedings of the first ACM SIGCHI annual symposium on Computer-human interaction in play.

Bartle, Richard (1996): Hearts, clubs, diamonds, spades. Players who suit MUDs. In: Journal of MUD research 1 (1), p. 19.

Bartle, Richard (2005): Virtual worlds. Why people play. In: Massively multiplayer game development 2 (1), p. 3–18.

Baumeister, Roy F.; Leary, Mark R. (1995): The need to belong. Desire for interpersonal attachments as a fundamental human motivation. In: Psychological bulletin 117 (3), p. 497.

Baxter, Ryan J.; Holderness, D. Kip; Wood, David A. (2015): Applying Basic Gamification Techniques to IT Compliance Training. Evidence from the Lab and Field. In: Journal of Information Systems 30 (3), p. 119–133. DOI: https://doi.org/10.2308/isys-51341.

Baxter, Ryan J.; Holderness, D. Kip; Wood, David A. (2017): The Effects of Gamification on Corporate Compliance Training. A Partial Replication and Field Study of True Office Anti-Corruption Training Programs. In: Journal of Forensic Accounting Research 2 (1), A20-A30. DOI: https://doi.org/10.2308/jfar-51725.

Bedny, Gregory Z.; Karwowski, Waldemar; Bedny, Inna S. (2012): Complexity evaluation of computer-based tasks. In: International Journal of Human–Computer Interaction 28 (4), p. 236–257.

Bell, David J.; Ruthven, Ian (2004): Searcher's Assessments of Task Complexity for Web Searching. In: Sharon McDonald und John Tait (Hg.): Advances in Information Retrieval. 26th European Conference on IR Research, ECIR 2004, Sunderland, UK, April 5–7, 2004. Proceedings. Berlin, Heidelberg: Springer (Lecture Notes in Computer Science, 2997).

Benabou, Roland; Tirole, Jean (2003): Intrinsic and extrinsic motivation. In: The review of economic studies 70 (3), p. 489–520.

Berger, Verena; Miesler, Linda; Hari, Jürg J. (Hg.) (2014): The potential of gamification in changing consumer behaviour towards a more sustainable nutrition behaviour. Academy of Marketing Conference 2014. Bournemouth, UK.

Berger, Verena; Schrader, Ulf (2016): Fostering sustainable nutrition behavior through gamification. In: Sustainability 8 (1), p. 67.

Bettman, James R.; Johnson, Eric J.; Payne, John W. (1990): A componential analysis of cognitive effort in choice. In: Organizational Behavior and Human Decision Processes 45 (1), p. 111–139.

Bitrián, Paula; Buil, Isabel; Catalán, Sara (2020): Flow and business simulation games. A typology of students. In: The International Journal of Management Education 18 (1), p. 100365.

Bittner, Jenny V.; Schipper, Jeffrey (2014): Motivational effects and age differences of gamification in product advertising. In: Journal of Consumer Marketing 31 (5), p. 391–400. DOI: https://doi.org/10.1108/JCM-04-2014-0945.

Blocher, Edward; Moffie, Robert P.; Zmud, Robert W. (1986): Report format and task complexity. Interaction in risk judgments. In: Accounting, Organizations and Society 11 (6), p. 457–470.

Blohm, Ivo; Leimeister, Jan Marco (2013): Gamification Design of IT-Based Enhancing Services for Motivational Support and Behavioral Change. In: Bus Inf Syst Eng 5 (4), p. 275–278. DOI: https://doi.org/10.1007/s12599-013-0273-5.

Blumberg, Boris; Cooper, Donald R.; Schindler, Pamela S. (Hg.) (2014): Business research methods. 4. ed. London: McGraw-Hill Education (McGraw-Hill Higher education).

Bogost, Ian (2011): Persuasive Games. Exploitaionware—Gamasutra. Retrived from: http://www.gamasutra.com/view/feature/134735/persuasive_games_exploitationware.php, accessed 18.08.2020.

Bonner, Sarah E. (1994): A model of the effects of audit task complexity. In: Accounting, Organizations and Society 19 (3), p. 213–234.

Bonner, Sarah E.; Hastie, Reid; Sprinkle, Geoffrey B.; Young, S. Mark (2000): A Review of the Effects of Financial Incentives on Performance in Laboratory Tasks. Implications for Management Accounting. In: Journal of Management Accounting Research 12 (1), p. 19–64. DOI: https://doi.org/10.2308/jmar.2000.12.1.19.

Bonner, Sarah E.; Lewis, Barry L. (1990): Determinants of auditor expertise. In: Journal of accounting research 28, p. 1–20.

Bonner, Sarah E.; Sprinkle, Geoffrey B. (2002): The effects of monetary incentives on effort and task performance. Theories, evidence, and a framework for research. In: Accounting, Organizations and Society 27 (4–5), p. 303–345. DOI: https://doi.org/10.1016/S0361-3682(01)00052-6.

Booth, Andrew; Sutton, Anthea; Papaioannou, Diana (2012): Systematic approaches to a successful literature review. First edition. Los Angeles, London, New Delhi: Sage.

Borlund, Pia; Dreier, Sabine (2014): An investigation of the search behaviour associated with Ingwersen's three types of information needs. In: Information processing & management 50 (4), p. 493–507.

Bortz, Jürgen; Döring, Nicola (2006): Forschungsmethoden und Evaluation. Für Human- und Sozialwissenschaftler; mit 87 Tabellen. 4., überarb. Aufl., [Nachdr.]. Heidelberg: Springer-Medizin-Verl. (Springer-Lehrbuch Bachelor, Master).

Braarud, P. Ø. (1998): Complexity factors and prediction of crew performance (HWR-521). In: Halden, Norway: OECD Halden Reactor Project.

Braarud, Per Øivind (2001): Subjective task complexity and subjective workload. Criterion validity for complex team tasks. In: International Journal of Cognitive Ergonomics 5 (3), p. 261–273.

Braarud, Per Øivind; Kirwan, Barry (2010): Task complexity. What challenges the crew and how do they cope. In: Simulator-based Human Factors Studies Across 25 Years: Springer, p. 233–251.

Brennan, Kathy; Kelly, Diane; Arguello, Jaime (2014): The effect of cognitive abilities on information search for tasks of varying levels of complexity. In: Proceedings of the 5th Information Interaction in Context Symposium, p. 165–174.

Brito, Jailson; Vieira, Vaninha; Duran, Adolfo (2015): Towards a Framework for Gamification Design on Crowdsourcing Systems. The G.A.M.E. Approach. In: Proceeding of the 12th international conference on information technology—new generations, p. 445–450. DOI: https://doi.org/10.1109/ITNG.2015.78.

Broadbent, Donald Eric (1971): Decision and stress.

Buckley, Patrick; Noonan, Seamus; Geary, Conor; Mackessy, Thomas; Nagle, Eoghan (2019): An Empirical Study of Gamification Frameworks. In: Journal of Organizational and End User Computing 31 (1), p. 22–38. DOI: https://doi.org/10.4018/JOEUC.2019010102.

Burke, Biran (2014): Gamify. How Gamification Motivates People to Do Extraordinary Things. Brookline: Taylor and Francis.

Bylund, Markus (Hg.) (2011): Proceedings of the 13th International Conference on Human Computer Interaction with Mobile Devices and Services. the 13th International Conference. Stockholm, Sweden. ACM Special Interest Group on Computer-Human Interaction; ACM Special Interest Group on Mobility of Systems, Users, Data and Computing. New York, NY: ACM.

Byström, Katriina (1999): Task complexity, information types and information sources. Examination of relationships: Tampere University Press.

Byström, Katriina; Järvelin, Kalervo (1995): Task complexity affects information seeking and use. In: Information processing & management 31 (2), p. 191–213.

Cafazzo, Joseph A.; Casselman, Mark; Hamming, Nathaniel; Katzman, Debra K.; Palmert, Mark R. (2012): Design of an mHealth app for the self-management of adolescent type 1 diabetes. A pilot study. In: Journal of medical Internet research 14 (3), e70.

Camerer, Colin F.; Hogarth, Robin M. (1999): The effects of financial incentives in experiments. A review and capital-labor-production framework. In: Journal of risk and uncertainty 19 (1–3), p. 7–42.

Campbell, Donald J. (1988): Task Complexity. A Review and Analysis. In: Academy of management review 13 (1), p. 40–52. DOI: https://doi.org/10.5465/amr.1988.4306775.

Campbell, Donald K. (1991): Goal levels, complex tasks, and strategy development. A review and analysis. In: Human Performance 4 (1), p. 1–31.

Campbell, Donald T. (1986): Relabeling internal and external validity for applied social scientists. In: New Directions for Program Evaluation 1986 (31), p. 67–77.

Campbell, Donald T.; Stanley, Julian C. (2015): Experimental and quasi-experimental designs for research: Ravenio Books.

Campbell, John P.; Pritchard, Robert D. (1976): Motivation theory in industrial and organizational psychology. In: Handbook of industrial and organizational psychology 63, p. 130.

Cardador, M. Teresa; Northcraft, Gregory B.; Whicker, Jordan (2017): A theory of work gamification. Something old, something new, something borrowed, something cool? In: Human Resource Management Review 27 (2), p. 353–365. DOI: https://doi.org/10.1016/j.hrmr.2016.09.014.

Cerasoli, Christopher P.; Nicklin, Jessica M.; Ford, Michael T. (2014): Intrinsic motivation and extrinsic incentives jointly predict performance. A 40-year meta-analysis. In: Psychological bulletin 140 (4), p. 980.

Chang, C. Janie; Yen, Sin-Hui; Duh, Rong-Ruey (2002): An Empirical Examination of Competing Theories to Explain the Framing Effect in Accounting-Related Decisions. In: Behavioral Research in Accounting 14 (1), p. 35–64. DOI: https://doi.org/10.2308/bria.2002.14.1.35.

Cheong, C.; Filippou, Justin; Cheong, France (2014): Towards the gamification of learning. Investigating student perceptions of game elements. In: Journal of information systems education. 25 (3).

Cherry, Todd L.; Ellis, Larry V. (2005): Does Rank-Order Grading Improve Student Performance? In: International Review of Economics Education 4 (1), p. 9–19. DOI: https://doi.org/10.1016/S1477-3880(15)30140-7.

Chidambaram, Laku; Tung, Lai Lai (2005): Is Out of Sight, Out of Mind? An Empirical Study of Social Loafing in Technology-Supported Groups. In: Information Systems Research 16 (2), p. 149–168. DOI: https://doi.org/10.1287/isre.1050.0051.

Chong, Dennis; Druckman, James N. (2007): A Theory of Framing and Opinion Formation in Competitive Elite Environments. In: Journal of Communication 57 (1), p. 99–118. DOI: https://doi.org/10.1111/j.1460-2466.2006.00331.x.

Chou, Yu-Kai (2016): Actionable gamification. Beyond points, badges, and leaderboards. Fremont, CA: Octalysis Media.

Cianciolo, Anna T.; Matthew, Cynthia; Sternberg, Robert J.; Wagner, Richard K. (2006): Tacit knowledge, practical intelligence, and expertise. In: The Cambridge handbook of expertise and expert performance, p. 613–632.

Cohen, Jacob (1988): Statistical Power Analysis for the Behavioral Sciences. 2nd ed. Hoboken: Taylor and Francis.

Collins, R. L. (2000): Among the Better Ones. In Handbook of Social Comparison, pages 159–171. Jerry Sulsand Ladd Wheeler.

Condly, Steven J.; Clark, Richard E.; Stolovitch, Harold D. (2003): The effects of incentives on workplace performance. A meta-analytic review of research studies 1. In: Performance Improvement Quarterly 16 (3), p. 46–63.

Cook, Thomas D.; Campbell, Donald Thomas; Day, Arles (1979): Quasi-experimentation. Design & analysis issues for field settings: Houghton Mifflin Boston (351).

Costa F.A., Viana J., Raleiras M. (2021): What Do Higher Education Students Have to Say About Gamification?. In: Kubincová Z., Lancia L., Popescu E., Nakayama M., Scarano V., Gil A. (eds) Methodologies and Intelligent Systems for Technology Enhanced Learning, 10th International Conference. Workshops. MIS4TEL 2020. Advances in Intelligent Systems and Computing, vol 1236. Springer, Cham. https://doi.org/10.1007/978-3-030-52287-2_6.

Cramer, Henriette; Rost, Mattias; Holmquist, Lars Erik (2011): Performing a check-in. In: Markus Bylund (Hg.): Proceedings of the 13th International Conference on Human Computer Interaction with Mobile Devices and Services. the 13th International Conference. Stockholm, Sweden. ACM Special Interest Group on Computer-Human Interaction; ACM Special Interest Group on Mobility of Systems, Users, Data and Computing. New York, NY: ACM, p. 57.

Crumlish, Christian; Malone, Erin (2009): Designing social interfaces. Principles, patterns, and practices for improving the user experience. 1st ed. Beijing, Cambridge: O'Reilly Media.

Csikszentmihalyi, Mihaly (2000): Beyond boredom and anxiety. The experience of play in work and games. San Francisco, Calif.: Jossey-Bass.

Cummings, M. L.; Sasangohar, F.; Thornburg, K. M.; Xing, Jing; D'Agostino, Amy (2010): Human-system interface complexity and opacity part i. Literature review. In: Massachusettes Institute of Technology, Cambridge, MA.

da Silva Brito, Richard D'arc; Contreras Pinochet, Luis Hernan; Luiz Lopes, Evandro; Oliveira, Mauri Aparecido de (2018): Development of a gamification characteristics measurement scale for mobile application users. In: Desenvolvimento de uma escala de mensuração de características de gamificação para usuários de aplicativos em dispositivos móveis 13 (1), p. 1–16. DOI: https://doi.org/10.18568/1980-4865.1311-16.

Davidson, Elizabeth J. (2002): Technology Frames and Framing. A Socio-Cognitive Investigation of Requirements Determination. In: MISQ 26 (4), p. 329. DOI: https://doi.org/10.2307/4132312.

Davies, Huw Talfryn Oakley; Crombie, I. K. (1998): Getting to grips with systematic reviews and meta-analyses. In: The British Journal of Hospital Medicine 59 (12), p. 955–958. Retrieved from: access under http://www.scopus.com/inward/record.url?scp=0032222908&partnerID=8YFLogxK , accessed 12.082020.

Deci, Edward L.; Eghrari, Haleh; Patrick, Brian C.; Leone, Dean R. (1994): Facilitating internalization. The self-determination theory perspective. In: Journal of personality 62 (1), p. 119–142. DOI: https://doi.org/10.1111/j.1467-6494.1994.tb00797.x.

Deci, Edward L.; Koestner, Richard; Ryan, Richard M. (1999): A meta-analytic review of experiments examining the effects of extrinsic rewards on intrinsic motivation. In: Psychological bulletin 125 (6), p. 627.

Deci, Edward L.; Ryan, Richard M. (1985): The general causality orientations scale. Self-determination in personality. In: Journal of research in personality 19 (2), p. 109–134.

Deci, Edward L.; Ryan, Richard M. (2000): The" what" and" why" of goal pursuits. Human needs and the self-determination of behavior. In: Psychological inquiry 11 (4), p. 227–268.

Deci, Edward L.; Ryan, Richard M. (2012): Self-Determination Theory. In: Paul A. van Lange (Hg.): Theories of social psychology. Los Angeles, Calif.: Sage, p. 416–437.

Deci, Edward L.; Schwartz, Allan J.; Sheinman, Louise; Ryan, Richard M. (1981): An instrument to assess adults' orientations toward control versus autonomy with children.

Reflections on intrinsic motivation and perceived competence. In: Journal of educational Psychology 73 (5), p. 642.

Denny, Paul (2013): The effect of virtual achievements on student engagement. In: Proceedings of Conference on Human Factors in Computing Systems (CHI 2013), p. 763–772. DOI: https://doi.org/10.1145/2470654.2470763.

Deterding, Sebastian; Dixon, Dan; Khaled, Rilla; Nacke, Lennart (2011): From game design elements to gamefulness. In: Artur Lugmayr, Heljä Franssila, Christian Safran und Imed Hammouda (Hg.): Proceedings of the 15th International Academic MindTrek Conference Envisioning Future Media Environments. the 15th International Academic MindTrek Conference. Tampere, Finland. Academic MindTrek 2011; ACM Special Interest Group on Computer-Human Interaction; ACM Special Interest Group on Multimedia. New York, NY: ACM, p. 9.

Dias, Joana (2017): Teaching operations research to undergraduate management students. The role of gamification. In: The International Journal of Management Education 15 (1), p. 98–111.

Domínguez, Adrián; Saenz-de-Navarrete, Joseba; de-Marcos, Luis; Fernández-Sanz, Luis; Pagés, Carmen; Martínez-Herráiz, José-Javier (2013): Gamifying learning experiences. Practical implications and outcomes. In: Computers & Education 63, p. 380–392. DOI: https://doi.org/10.1016/j.compedu.2012.12.020.

Easterbrook, J. A. (1959): The effect of emotion on cue utilization and the organization of behavior. In: Psychological review 66 (3), p. 183–201. DOI: https://doi.org/10.1037/h0047707.

Eickhoff, Carsten; Harris, Christopher G.; Vries, Arjen P. de; Srinivasan, Padmini (2012): Quality through flow and immersion. In: SIGIR '12: Proceedings of the 35th international ACM SIGIR conference on Research and development in information retrieval, p. 871–880. DOI: https://doi.org/10.1145/2348283.2348400.

Eisenhardt, Kathleen M. (1989): Agency theory. An assessment and review. In: Academy of management review 14 (1), p. 57–74.

Elsayed, Omar Khaled Shokry Mohamed; Sharifi, Hossein; Dyer, Ronald (2018): Towards a theoretical framework for gamification as complementary capabilities. In: Conference: British Academy of Management.

Ērgle, Daiga (2015): Fostering Employee Engagement Through Gamification. AirBaltic Forecaster Tool. In: Vzpodbujanje storilnosti zaposlenih s pomočjo gamifikacije: AirBalticovo orodje Forecaster 10 (3), p. 219–234. Online verfügbar unter http://search.ebscohost.com/login.aspx?direct=true&db=bth&AN=112760653&site=ehost-live.

Ērgle, Daiga (2016): AirBaltic Case Based Analysis of Potential for Improving Employee Engagement Levels in Latvia through Gamification. In: Economics and Business 28 (1), p. 45–51. DOI: https://doi.org/10.1515/eb-2016-0007.

Esteves, J.M., (2017): The perils of gamification triviliazation: How and why gamification is failing to deliver loyalty. Proceedings 2017 (1), 13560. https://doi.org/10.5465/AMBPP.2017.13560abstract.

Evangelisti, Donna; Whitman, Thomas; Johnston, Mary Beth (1986): Problem solving and task complexity. An examination of the relative effectiveness of self-instruction and didactic instruction. In: Cognitive therapy and research 10 (5), p. 499–508.

Evans, John H., III; Heiman-Hoffman, Vicky B.; Rau, Stephen E. (1994): The accountability demand for information. In: Journal of Management Accounting Research 6,

p. 24. retrieved from https://search.proquest.com/docview/210172809?accountid=14264, accessed 14.09.2020.

Eysenck, Michael (1982): Attention and arousal. Cognition and performance: Springer Science & Business Media.

Eysenck, Michael W. (1984): A handbook of cognitive psychology: L. Erlbaum Associates.

Fang, Meiyu; Gerhart, Barry (2012): Does pay for performance diminish intrinsic interest? In: The International Journal of Human Resource Management 23 (6), p. 1176–1196. DOI: https://doi.org/10.1080/09585192.2011.561227.

Fernandes, João; Duarte, Diogo; Ribeiro, Claudia; Farinha, Carla; Pereira, João Madeiras; Silva, Miguel Mira da (2012): iThink. A Game-Based Approach Towards Improving Collaboration and Participation in Requirement Elicitation. In: Procedia Computer Science 15, p. 66–77. DOI: https://doi.org/10.1016/j.procs.2012.10.059.

Ferro, Lauren S.; Walz, Steffen P.; Greuter, Stefan (2013): Towards personalised, gamified systems. An investigation into game design, personality and player typologies. In: Interactive Entertainment Conference 2013, p. 1–6. DOI: https://doi.org/10.1145/2513002.2513024.

Fessler, Nicholas J. (2003): Experimental Evidence on the Links among Monetary Incentives, Task Attractiveness, and Task Performance. In: Journal of Management Accounting Research 15 (1), p. 161–176. DOI: https://doi.org/10.2308/jmar.2003.15.1.161.

Festinger, L. (1954): A theory of social comparison processes. Human relations, 7 (2):117–140.

Field, Andy (2009): Discopering Statistics Using SPSS, Thrid Edition: SAGE publications.

Fisher, Diane J.; Beedle, Jon; Rouse, Sharon E. (2014): Gamification. A Study of Business Teacher Educators' Knowledge of, Attitudes toward, and Experiences with the Gamification of Activities in the Classroom. In: The Journal of Research in Business Education 56 (1), p. 1–16.

Fortune Business Insights (Hg.) (2020): Market Research Report. Gamification Market Size, Share & COVID-19 Analysis. Report ID: FBI100632. retrieved from https://www.fortunebusinessinsights.com/industry-reports/gamification-market-100632, accessed 24.08.2020.

Foster, Aroutis (2012): Assessing Learning Games for School Content. The TPACK-PCaRD Framework and Methodology. In: Dirk Ifenthaler, Deniz Eseryel und Xun Ge (Hg.): Assessment in Game-Based Learning. Foundations, Innovations, and Perspectives. New York, NY: Springer New York, S. 201–215.

Foster, Jason A.; Sheridan, Patricia K.; Irish, Robert; Frost, Geoffrey S. (2012): Gamification as a strategy for promoting deeper investigation in a reverse engineering activity. In: Proceedings of the 2012 American Society for Engineering Education Conference, pp. AC 2012–AC 5456.

Francisco-Aparicio, Andrés; Gutiérrez-Vela, Francisco Luis; Isla-Montes, José Luis; Sanchez, José Luis González (2013): Gamification. Analysis and application. In: New trends in interaction, virtual reality and modeling: Springer, p. 113–126.

Frey, Bruno S.; Jegen, Reto (2001): Motivation crowding theory. In: Journal of economic surveys 15 (5), p. 589–611.

Frey, Bruno S.; Oberholzer-Gee, Felix (1997): The cost of price incentives. An empirical analysis of motivation crowding-out. In: The American economic review 87 (4), p. 746–755.

Friedman, Sunder; Friedman, Daniel; Sunder, Shyam (1994): Experimental Methods. A Primer for Economists. Cambridge University Press.
Frost, Raymond D.; Matta, Vic; MacIvor, Erin (2015): Assessing the efficacy of incorporating game dynamics in a learning management system. In: Journal of information systems education. 26 (1), p. 6.
Fullerton, Tracy (2014): Game design workshop. A playcentric approach to creating innovative games. 2nd ed. Boca Raton: CRC press (Gama Network Series).
Funke, Joachim (2010): Complex problem solving. A case for complex cognition? In: Cognitive processing 11 (2), p. 133–142.
Furnham, Adrian (1986): Response bias, social desirability and dissimulation. In: Personality and Individual Differences 7 (3), p. 385–400. DOI: https://doi.org/10.1016/0191-8869(86)90014-0.
Furnham, Adrian; Argyle, Michael (1998): The psychology of money: Psychology Press.
Gagné, Marylène; Deci, Edward L. (2005): Self-determination theory and work motivation. In: Journal of Organizational behavior 26 (4), p. 331–362.
Gagné, Marylène; Forest, Jacques (2008): The study of compensation systems through the lens of self-determination theory. Reconciling 35 years of debate: Educational Publishing Foundation (49).
Gagné, Marylène; Forest, Jacques; Gilbert, Marie-Hélène; Aubé, Caroline; Morin, Estelle; Malorni, Angela (2010): The Motivation at Work Scale. Validation Evidence in Two Languages. In: Educational and Psychological Measurement 70 (4), p. 628–646. DOI: https://doi.org/10.1177/0013164409355698.
Gagné, Marylène; Forest, Jacques; Vansteenkiste, Maarten; Crevier-Braud, Laurence; van den Broeck, Anja; Aspeli, Ann Kristin et al. (2015): The Multidimensional Work Motivation Scale. Validation evidence in seven languages and nine countries. In: European Journal of Work and Organizational Psychology 24 (2), p. 178–196.
Garbers, Yvonne; Konradt, Udo (2014): The effect of financial incentives on performance. A quantitative review of individual and team-based financial incentives. In: Journal of occupational and organizational psychology 87 (1), p. 102–137.
García, Félix; Pedreira, Oscar; Piattini, Mario; Cerdeira-Pena, Ana; Penabad, Miguel (2017): A framework for gamification in software engineering. In: Journal of Systems and Software 132, p. 21–40. DOI: https://doi.org/10.1016/j.jss.2017.06.021.
Gartner Group (2011): Press release. "Gartner Says By 2015, More Than 50 Percent of Organizations That Manage Innovation Processes Will Gamify Those Processes".
Gåsland, Magne Matre (2011): Game Mechanics Based E-Learning. A case study. Master Thesis. Trondheim, Norway.
Gatautis, Rimantas; Vitkauskaite, Elena; Gadeikiene, Agne; Piligrimiene, Zaneta (2016): Gamification as a Mean of Driving Online Consumer Behaviour. SOR Model Perspective. In: EE 27 (1). DOI: https://doi.org/10.5755/j01.ee.27.1.13198.
Gears, Deborah; Braun, Karen (2013): Gamification in Business: Designing Motivating Solutions to Problem Situations. In: CHI (2013), 4503–1952.
Gibson, James J. (1977): The theory of affordances. In: Hilldale, USA 1 (2).
Gill, J., Johnson, P., Clark, M., 2010. Research methods for managers, 4th ed. SAGE, Los Angeles.
Gill, T. Grandon (1996): Expert systems usage. Task change and intrinsic motivation. In: MISQ, p. 301–329.

Gill, T. Grandon; Hicks, Richard C. (2006): Task complexity and informing science. A synthesis. In: Informing Science 9, p. 1.
Glucksberg, Sam (1962): The influence of strength of drive on functional fixedness and perceptual recognition. In: Journal of experimental psychology 63 (1), p. 36.
Goehle, Geoff (2013): Gamification and Web-based Homework. Primus: Probl. Resour. Issues Math. Undergrad. Stud. 23, 234–246. http://dx.doi.org/10.1080/10511970.2012.736451.
Gonzalez, Cleotilde; Vanyukov, Polina; Martin, Michael K. (2005): The use of microworlds to study dynamic decision making. In: Computers in Human Behavior 21 (2), p. 273–286.
Greiner, Ben (2015): Subject pool recruitment procedures. Organizing experiments with ORSEE. In: Journal of the Economic Science Association 1 (1), p. 114–125.
Greitzer, Frank L. (2005): Toward the development of cognitive task difficulty metrics to support intelligence analysis research. In: Fourth IEEE Conference on Cognitive Informatics (ICCI), p. 315–320.
Grolnick, Wendy S.; Ryan, Richard M. (1987): Autonomy in children's learning. An experimental and individual difference investigation. In: Journal of personality and social psychology 52 (5), p. 890.
Guin, Theo Downes-Le; Baker, Reg; Mechling, Joanne; Ruyle, Erica (2012): Myths and Realities of Respondent Engagement in Online Surveys. In: International Journal of Market Research 54 (5), p. 613–633. DOI: https://doi.org/10.2501/IJMR-54-5-613-633.
Gupta, Ashish; Li, Han; Sharda, Ramesh (2013): Should I send this message? Understanding the impact of interruptions, social hierarchy and perceived task complexity on user performance and perceived workload. In: Decision Support Systems 55 (1), p. 135–145. DOI: https://doi.org/10.1016/j.dss.2012.12.035.
Gwizdka, Jacek; Spence, Ian (2006): What can searching behavior tell us about the difficulty of information tasks? A study of Web navigation. In: Proceedings of the American Society for Information Science and Technology 43 (1), p. 1–22.
Hackman, Richard J.; Lawler, Edward E. (1971): Employee reactions to job characteristics. In: Journal of applied psychology 55 (3), p. 259–286. DOI: https://doi.org/10.1037/h0031152.
Hackman, Richard J.; Oldham, Greg (1976): Motivation through the design of work. Test of a theory. In: Organizational behavior and human performance 16 (2), p. 250–279.
Ham, Dong-Han; Park, Jinkyun; Jung, Wondea (2012): Model-based identification and use of task complexity factors of human integrated systems. In: Reliability Engineering & System Safety 100, p. 33–47.
Hamari, Juho (2013): Transforming homo economicus into homo ludens. A field experiment on gamification in a utilitarian peer-to-peer trading service. In: Electronic Commerce Research and Applications 12 (4), p. 236–245. DOI: https://doi.org/10.1016/j.elerap.2013.01.004.
Hamari, Juho (2017): Do badges increase user activity? A field experiment on the effects of gamification. In: Computers in Human Behavior 71, p. 469–478.
Hamari, Juho; Hassan, Lobna; Dias, Antonio (2018): Gamification, quantified-self or social networking? Matching users' goals with motivational technology. In: User Model User-Adap Inter 28 (1), p. 35–74. DOI: https://doi.org/10.1007/s11257-018-9200-2.
Hamari, Juho; Koivisto, Jonna (2015): Why do people use gamification services? In: International Journal of Information Management 35 (4), p. 419–431. DOI: https://doi.org/10.1016/j.ijinfomgt.2015.04.006.

Hamari, Juho; Koivisto, Jonna; Sarsa, Harri (2014): Does Gamification Work? -- A Literature Review of Empirical Studies on Gamification. In: Conference: the 47th Hawaii International Conference on System Sciences, p. 3025–3034. DOI: https://doi.org/10.1109/HICSS.2014.377.

Hammedi, Wafa; Leclerq, Thomas; van Riel, Allard C.R. (2017): The use of gamification mechanics to increase employee and user engagement in participative healthcare services. In: Journal of Service Management 28 (4), p. 640–661. DOI: https://doi.org/10.1108/JOSM-04-2016-0116.

Hammermann, Andrea; Mohnen, Alwine (2014): The pric(z)e of hard work. In: Journal of Economic Psychology 43, p. 1–15. DOI: https://doi.org/10.1016/j.joep.2014.04.003.

Handbook of social psychology, Vol. 1, 5th ed (2010). Hoboken, NJ, US: John Wiley & Sons, Inc.

Hannan, R. Lynn; McPhee, Gregory P.; Newman, Andrew H.; Tafkov, Ivo D. (2013): The effect of relative performance information on performance and effort allocation in a multi-task environment. In: The Accounting Review 88 (2), p. 553–575.

Hanus, Michael D.; Fox, Jesse (2015): Assessing the effects of gamification in the classroom. A longitudinal study on intrinsic motivation, social comparison, satisfaction, effort, and academic performance. In: Computers & Education 80, p. 152–161. DOI: https://doi.org/10.1016/j.compedu.2014.08.019.

Harms, Johannes; Wimmer, Christoph; Kappel, Karin; Grechenig, Thomas (2014): Gamification of online surveys. Conceptual foundations and a design process based on the MDA Framework. In: Proceedings of the 8th Nordic conference on human–computer interaction: Fun, fast, foundational, p. 565–568. DOI: https://doi.org/10.1145/2639189.2639230.

Harvey, Craig M.; Koubek, Richard J. (1998): Toward a model of distributed engineering collaboration. In: Computers & Industrial Engineering 35 (1-2), p. 173–176.

Harwood, Tracy (2012): Emergence of gamified commerce. Turning virtual to real. In: Journal of Electronic Commerce in Organizations (JECO) 10 (2), p. 16–39.

Heiss, Hans-Ulrich (Hg.) (2011): Informatik 2011. Informatik schafft Communities ; Beiträge der 41. Jahrestagung der Gesellschaft für Informatik e.V. (GI), 4.—7.10.2011 in Berlin. Bonn: Ges. für Informatik (GI-Edition : Proceedings, 192).

Hense, Jan; Klevers, Markus; Sailer, Michael; Horenburg, Tim; Mandl, Heinz; Günthner, Willibald (2014): Using gamification to enhance staff motivation in logistics. In: David Hutchison, Takeo Kanade und Josef Kittler (Hg.): Frontiers in Gaming Simulation. 44th International Simulation and Gaming Association Conference, ISAGA 2013 and 17th IFIP WG 5.7 Workshop on Experimental Interactive Learning in Industrial Management, Stockholm, Sweden, June 24–28, 2013. Revised Selected Papers. Cham: Springer International Publishing, p. 206–213.

Herbert, B.; Charles, D.; Moore, A.; Charles, T. (Hg.) (2014): An Investigation of Gamification Typologies for Enhancing Learner Motivation. 2014 International Conference on Interactive Technologies and Games. 2014 International Conference on Interactive Technologies and Games.

Herzig, Philipp (2014): Gamification as a service. Conceptualization of a Generic Enterprise Gamification Platform. Ph.D. Thesis. Dresden.

Heyvaert, M.; Maes, B.; Onghena, P. (2013): Mixed methods research synthesis. Definition, framework, and potential. In: Qual Quant 47 (2), p. 659–676. DOI: https://doi.org/10.1007/s11135-011-9538-6.

Hong, Goh Yung; Masood, Mona (2014): Effects of gamification on lower secondary school students' motivation and engagement. In: International Journal of Social, Education, Economics and Management Engineering 8 (12), p. 3483–3490.

Hunicke, Robin; LeBlanc, Marc; Zubek, Robert (2004): MDA: A formal approach to game design and game research. In: Proceedings of the challenges in Game AI Workshop, nineteenth national conference on artificial intelligence, p. 4–8.

Huotari, Kai; Hamari, Juho (2012): Defining gamification. In: Artur Lugmayr (Hg.): Proceeding of the 16th International Academic MindTrek Conference. Proceeding of the 16th International Academic MindTrek Conference. Tampere, Finland, 3/10/2012—5/10/2012. ACM Special Interest Group on Computer-Human Interaction; ACM Special Interest Group on Multimedia. New York, NY: ACM, p. 17.

Hutchison, David; Kanade, Takeo; Kittler, Josef (Hg.) (2013): Design, User Experience, and Usability. Health, Learning, Playing, Cultural, and Cross-Cultural User Experience. Second International Conference, DUXU 2013, Held as Part of HCI International 2013, Las Vegas, NV, USA, July 21–26, 2013, Proceedings, Part II. Berlin/Heidelberg: Springer Berlin Heidelberg (Lecture Notes in Computer Science).

Jacko, Julie A.; Salvendy, Gavriel; Koubek, Richard J. (1995): Modelling of menu design in computerized work. In: Interacting with Computers 7 (3), p. 304–330.

Jacko, Julie A.; Ward, Kenneth G. (1996): Toward establishing a link between psychomotor task complexity and human information processing. In: Computers & Industrial Engineering 31 (1-2), p. 533–536.

Jansen, Bernard J.; Spink, Amanda (2006): How are we searching the World Wide Web? A comparison of nine search engine transaction logs. In: Information processing & management 42 (1), p. 248–263.

Jenkins Jr, G. Douglas; Mitra, Atul; Gupta, Nina; Shaw, Jason D. (1998): Are financial incentives related to performance? A meta-analytic review of empirical research. In: Journal of applied psychology 83 (5), p. 777.

Jesson, Jill K.; Matheson, Lydia; Lacey, Fiona M. (2011): Doing your literature review. Traditional and systematic techniques. Los Angeles, Calif.: SAGE Publ.

Julius, K.; Salo, J. (2013): Designing gamification. Marketing. Master's Thesis. Oulu.

Jung, J. H.; Schneider, Christoph; Valacich, Joseph (2010): Enhancing the Motivational Affordance of Information Systems. The Effects of Real-Time Performance Feedback and Goal Setting in Group Collaboration Environments. In: Management Science 56 (4), p. 724–742. DOI: https://doi.org/10.1287/mnsc.1090.1129.

Kahneman, Daniel; Tversky, Amos (1979): Prospect Theory. An Analysis of Decision under Risk. In: Econometrica 47 (2), p. 263. DOI: https://doi.org/10.2307/1914185.

Kamel, Moataz M.; Watfa, Mohamed K.; Lobo, Brian; Sobh, Daniel (2017): Is Enterprise Gamification Being Cannibalized by Its Own Brand? In: IEEE Trans. Profess. Commun. 60 (2), p. 147–164. DOI: https://doi.org/10.1109/TPC.2017.2656598.

Kanfer, Ruth (1990): Motivation theory and industrial and organizational psychology. In: Handbook of industrial and organizational psychology 1 (2), p. 75–130.

Kanfer, Ruth; Ackerman, Phillip L. (1989): Motivation and cognitive abilities. An integrative/aptitude-treatment interaction approach to skill acquisition. In: Journal of applied psychology 74 (4), p. 657.

Kapp, Karl M. (Hg.) (2012): The gamification of learning and instruction. Game-based methods and strategies for training and education. San Francisco, Calif.: Pfeiffer (Essential resources for training and HR professionals).

Kappen, Dennis L.; Nacke, Lennart E. (2013): The kaleidoscope of effective gamification. In: Lennart E. Nacke, Kevin Harrigan und Neil Randall (Hg.): Gamification 2013. Proceedings of the First International Conference on Gameful Design, Research, and Applications : October 2–4, 2013, Stratford, Ontario, Canada. the First International Conference. Toronto, Ontario, Canada, 2/10/2013—4/10/2013. New York, New York: Association for Computing Machinery (ICPS), p. 119–122.

Kelly, Diane; Arguello, Jaime; Edwards, Ashlee; Wu, Wan-ching (2015): Development and evaluation of search tasks for IIR experiments using a cognitive complexity framework. In: Proceedings of the 2015 International Conference on The Theory of Information Retrieval, p. 101–110.

Khan, Khalid S.; Kunz, Regina; Kleijnen, Jos; Antes, Gerd (2003): Five Steps to Conducting a Systematic Review. In: J R Soc Med 96 (3), p. 118–121. DOI: https://doi.org/10.1177/014107680309600304.

Kim, Chankon; Khoury, Majeed (1987): Task complexity and contingent information processing in the case of couple's decision making. In: Journal of the Academy of Marketing Science 15 (3), p. 32–43.

Kim, Kyung-Sun; Allen, Bryce (2002): Cognitive and task influences on Web searching behavior. In: Journal of the American Society for Information Science and Technology 53 (2), p. 109–119.

Kim, SangBin; Lee, SinJae; Han, JungHyun (2017): StretchArms. Promoting Stretching Exercise with a Smartwatch. In: International Journal of Human–Computer Interaction 34 (3), p. 218–225. DOI: https://doi.org/10.1080/10447318.2017.1342408.

Kitchenham, Barbara; Charters, Stuart (2007): Guidelines for performing Systematic Literature Reviews in Software Engineering. Keele University and Durham University Joint Report. In: EBSE 2007–001.

Kleiman-Weiner, Max; Berger, Jonathan (Hg.) (2006): The sound of one arm swinging. A model for multidimensional auditory display of physical motion: Georgia Institute of Technology.

Knauer, Thorsten; Sommer, Friedrich; Wöhrmann, Arnt (2017): Tournament Winner Proportion and its Effect on Effort. An Investigation of the Underlying Psychological Mechanisms. In: European Accounting Review 26 (4), p. 681–702. DOI: https://doi.org/10.1080/09638180.2016.1175957.

Kocadere, Selay Arkün; Özhan, Şeyma Çağlar (2018): Gamification from Player Type Perspective. A Case Study. In: Educational Technology & Society 21 (3), p. 1436–4522.

Kumar, Janaki (2013): Gamification at Work. Designing Engaging Business Software. In: David Hutchison, Takeo Kanade und Josef Kittler (Hg.): Design, User Experience, and Usability. Health, Learning, Playing, Cultural, and Cross-Cultural User Experience. Second International Conference, DUXU 2013, Held as Part of HCI International 2013, Las Vegas, NV, USA, July 21–26, 2013, Proceedings, Part II, Bd. 8013. Berlin/Heidelberg: Springer Berlin Heidelberg (Lecture Notes in Computer Science), p. 528–537.

Kunz, Jennifer; Linder, Stefan (2012): Organizational Control and Work Effort—Another Look at the Interplay of Rewards and Motivation. In: European Accounting Review 76 (1), p. 1–31. DOI: https://doi.org/10.1080/09638180.2012.684498.

Kwon, K. Hazel; Halavais, Alexander; Havener, Shannon (2015): Tweeting badges. User motivations for displaying achievement in publicly networked environments. In: Cyberpsychology, behavior and social networking 18 (2), p. 93–100. DOI: https://doi.org/10.1089/cyber.2014.0438.

Lachmann, Maik; Stefani, Ulrike; Wöhrmann, Arnt (2015): Fair value accounting for liabilities. Presentation format of credit risk changes and individual information processing. In: Accounting, Organizations and Society 41, p. 21–38. DOI: https://doi.org/10.1016/j.aos.2014.08.001.

Lambert, Viktoria (2017): Gamification and the Quality of Informal Post-Experiential Learning. In: MNG 12 (3), p. 249–271. DOI: https://doi.org/10.26493/1854-4231.12.249-271.

Landers, Richard N. (2015): Developing a Theory of Gamified Learning. In: Simulation & Gaming 45 (6), p. 752–768. DOI: https://doi.org/10.1177/1046878114563660.

Landers, Richard N.; Armstrong, Michael B. (2017): Enhancing instructional outcomes with gamification. An empirical test of the Technology-Enhanced Training Effectiveness Model. In: Computers in Human Behavior 71, p. 499–507. DOI: https://doi.org/10.1016/j.chb.2015.07.031.

Landers, Richard N.; Callan, Rachel C. (2012): Training Evaluation in Virtual Worlds. Development of a Model. In: JVWR 5 (3). DOI: https://doi.org/10.4101/jvwr.v5i3.6335.

Landers, Richard N.; Landers, Amy K. (2014): An Empirical Test of the Theory of Gamified Learning. In: Simulation & Gaming 45 (6), p. 769–785. DOI: https://doi.org/10.1177/1046878114563662.

Lankton, Nancy K.; Speier, Cheri; Wilson, E. Vance (2012): Internet-based knowledge acquisition. Task complexity and performance. In: Decision Support Systems 53 (1), p. 55–65.

Leclercq, Thomas; Poncin, Ingrid; Hammedi, Wafa (2017): The Engagement Process During Value Co-Creation. Gamification in New Product-Development Platforms. In: International Journal of Electronic Commerce 21 (4), p. 454–488. DOI: https://doi.org/10.1080/10864415.2016.1355638.

Lee, T. W., Locke, E. A., & Phan, S. H. (1997). Explaining the assigned goal-incentive interaction: the role of self-efficacy and personal goals. Journal of Management, 23, 541–559.

Levin, Irwin P.; Gaeth, Gary J.; Schreiber, Judy; Lauriola, Marco (2002): A New Look at Framing Effects. Distribution of Effect Sizes, Individual Differences, and Independence of Types of Effects. In: Organizational Behavior and Human Decision Processes 88 (1), p. 411–429. DOI: https://doi.org/10.1006/obhd.2001.2983.

Li, Carol (2014): Evaluation of a Theoretical Model for Gamification in Workplace IS context. Doctoral dissertation. Vancouver: University of British Columbia.

Li, Kang; Wieringa, Peter A. (2000): Understanding perceived complexity in human supervisory control. In: Cognition, Technology & Work 2 (2), p. 75–88.

Li, Wei; Grossman, Tovi; Fitzmaurice, George (2012): GamiCAD. In: Proceedings of the 25th annual ACM symposium on User interface software and technology, p. 103. DOI: https://doi.org/10.1145/2380116.2380131.

Libby, Robert; Lipe, Marlys Gascho (1992): Incentives, effort, and the cognitive processes involved in accounting-related judgments. In: Journal of accounting research 30 (2), p. 249–273.

Lieberoth, Andreas (2015): Shallow Gamification. In: Games and Culture 10 (3), p. 229–248. DOI: https://doi.org/10.1177/1555412014559978.
Lin, Raymund J.; Ramakrishnan, Sreeram; Chang, Henry; Spraragen, Susan; Zhu, Xinxin (2013): Designing a web-based behavior motivation tool for healthcare compliance. In: Hum. Factors Man. 23 (1), p. 58–67. DOI: https://doi.org/10.1002/hfm.20519.
Lindenberg, Siegwart (2001): Intrinsic motivation in a new light. In: Kyklos 54 (2-3), p. 317–342.
Ling, Lynette Tan Yuen (2018): Meaningful Gamification and Students' Motivation. A Strategy for Scaffolding Reading Material. In: Online Learning 22 (2), p. 141–155.
Liu, De; Santhanam, Radhika; Webster, Jane (2017): Toward Meaningful Engagement. A Framework for Design and Research of Gamified Information Systems. In: MISQ 41 (4), p. 1011–1034. DOI: https://doi.org/10.25300/MISQ/2017/41.4.01.
Liu, Minyang; Huang, Yanqun; Zhang, Dawei (2018): Gamification's impact on manufacturing. Enhancing job motivation, satisfaction and operational performance with smartphone-based gamified job design. In: Hum. Factors Man. 28 (1), p. 38–51. DOI: https://doi.org/10.1002/hfm.20723.
Liu, Peng; Li, Zhizhong (2012): Task complexity. A review and conceptualization framework. In: International Journal of Industrial Ergonomics 42 (6), p. 553–568.
Liu, Yefeng; Alexandrova, Todorka; Nakajima, Tatsuo (2011): Gamifying intelligent environments, p. 7. DOI: https://doi.org/10.1145/2072652.2072655.
Locke, Edwin A. (1997): Self-efficacy. The exercise of control. In: Personnel Psychology 50 (3), p. 801.
Locke, Edwin A.; Latham, Gary P. (1990): A theory of goal setting & task performance: Prentice-Hall, Inc.
Locke, Edwin A.; Shaw, Karyll N.; Saari, Lise M.; Latham, Gary P. (1981): Goal setting and task performance. 1969–1980. In: Psychological bulletin 90 (1), p. 125.
Lourenço, Sofia M. (2016): Monetary incentives, feedback, and recognition—Complements or substitutes? Evidence from a field experiment in a retail services company. In: The Accounting Review 91 (1), p. 279–297.
Lussier, Denis A.; Olshavsky, Richard W. (1979): Task complexity and contingent processing in brand choice. In: Journal of Consumer Research 6 (2), p. 154–165.
MacKay, D.B., Villarreal, A., (1987): Performance differences in the use of graphic and tabular displays of multivariate data. Decision Sciences 18 (4), 535–546.
Mackay, Wendy E.; Brewster, Stephen; Bødker, Susanne (Hg.) (2013): CHI 2013. Changing perspectives ; the 31st Annual CHI Conference on Human Factors in Computing Systems, conference proceedings, 27 April—2 May 2013, Paris, France. the SIGCHI Conference. Paris, France. Association for Computing Machinery; CHI 2013; Annual CHI Conference on Human Factors in Computing Systems. New York, NY: ACM.
Malmi, Teemu; Brown, David A. (2008): Management control systems as a package—Opportunities, challenges and research directions. In: Management Accounting Research 19 (4), p. 287–300. DOI: https://doi.org/10.1016/j.mar.2008.09.003.
Mandl, H., Klevers, M.T.M., Sailer, M., (2015): Forschungsbericht zu dem IGF-Vorhaben GameLog—Gamification in der Intralogistik der Forschungsstellen Lehrstuhl für Fördertechnik Materialfluss Logistik, Technische Universität München und Lehrstuhl für Empirische Pädagogik und Pädagogische Psychologie, Ludwig-Maximilians-Universität

München. fml—Lehrstuhl für Fördertechnik Materialfluss Logistik Technische Universität München, Garching.

Manthei, Kathrin; Mohnen, Alwine (2013): The incentive impact of the fixed wage–A real effort experiment. In: German Journal of Human Resource Management 27 (4), p. 331–353.

Markets and Markets (Hg.) (2020): Gamification Market. Global Forecast to 2025. Online verfügbar unter https://www.marketsandmarkets.com/Market-Reports/gamification-market-991.html#:~:text=The%20gamification%20market%20size%20is,27.4%25%20during%20the%20forecast%20period., last checked on 13.08.2020.

Massung, Elaine; Coyle, David; Cater, Kirsten F.; Jay, Marc; Preist, Chris (2013): Using crowdsourcing to support pro-environmental community activism. In: Wendy E. Mackay, Stephen Brewster und Susanne Bødker (Hg.): CHI 2013. Changing perspectives; the 31st Annual CHI Conference on Human Factors in Computing Systems, conference proceedings, 27 April—2 May 2013, Paris, France.: ACM, p. 371–380.

Mavletova, Aigul (2015): Web Surveys Among Children and Adolescents. In: Social Science Computer Review 33 (3), p. 372–398. DOI: https://doi.org/10.1177/0894439314545316.

McCracken, J. H.; Aldrich, T. B. (1984): Analyses of selected LHX mission functions. Implications for operator workload and system automation goals. Anacapa Sciences Inc Fort Rucker Al.

McDaniel, Linda S. (1990): The effects of time pressure and audit program structure on audit performance. In: Journal of accounting research 28 (2), p. 267–285.

McDaniel, R.; Lindgren, R.; Friskics, J. (Hg.) (2012): Using badges for shaping interactions in online learning environments. 2012 IEEE International Professional Communication Conference. 2012 IEEE International Professional Communication Conference.

Mehrabian, Albert; Russell, James A. (1974): An approach to environmental psychology. Cambridge, MA, US: The MIT Press (An approach to environmental psychology).

Mekler, Elisa D.; Brühlmann, Florian; Tuch, Alexandre N.; Opwis, Klaus (2017): Towards understanding the effects of individual gamification elements on intrinsic motivation and performance. In: Computers in Human Behavior 71, p. 525–534. DOI: https://doi.org/10.1016/j.chb.2015.08.048.

Monterrat, Baptiste; Lavoué, Élise; George, Sébastien (2017): Adaptation of Gaming Features for Motivating Learners. In: Simulation & Gaming 48 (5), p. 625–656. DOI: https://doi.org/10.1177/1046878117712632.

Mora, Alberto; Riera, Daniel; González, Carina; Arnedo-Moreno, Joan (2017): Gamification. A systematic review of design frameworks. In: J Comput High Educ 29 (3), p. 516–548. DOI: https://doi.org/10.1007/s12528-017-9150-4.

Mosenthal, Peter B. (1998): Defining prose task characteristics for use in computer-adaptive testing and instruction. In: American Educational Research Journal 35 (2), p. 269–307.

Mussweiler, T. (2003): Comparison processes in social judgment: Mechanisms and consequences. Psychological Review, 110(3):472–489.

Musthag, Mohamed; Raij, Andrew; Ganesan, Deepak; Kumar, Santosh; Shiffman, Saul (2011): Exploring micro-incentive strategies for participant compensation in high-burden studies. In: UbiComp 2011: Ubiquitous Computing, 13th International Conference, UbiComp 2011, p. 435. DOI: https://doi.org/10.1145/2030112.2030170.

Nacke, Lennart E.; Deterding, Sebastian (2017): The maturing of gamification research. In: Computers in Human Behavior 71, p. 450–454. DOI: https://doi.org/10.1016/j.chb.2016.11.062.

Naylor, James C.; Clark, Roger D. (1968): Intuitive inference strategies in interval learning tasks as a function of validity magnitude and sign. In: Organizational behavior and human performance 3 (4), p. 378–399. DOI: https://doi.org/10.1016/0030-5073(68)90016-0.

Nelson, Mark J. (2012): Soviet and American precursors to the gamification of work. In: Artur Lugmayr (Hg.): Proceeding of the 16th International Academic MindTrek Conference. Proceeding of the 16th International Academic MindTrek Conference. Tampere, Finland, 3/10/2012—5/10/2012. ACM Special Interest Group on Computer-Human Interaction; ACM Special Interest Group on Multimedia. New York, NY: ACM, p. 23.

Nembhard, David A.; Osothsilp, Napassavong (2002): Task complexity effects on between-individual learning/forgetting variability. In: International Journal of Industrial Ergonomics 29 (5), p. 297–306.

Nicholson, Scott (2012): A User-Centered Theoretical Framework for Meaningful Gamification. In: Conference: Games+Learning+Society 8.0.

Nicholson, Scott (2014): Exploring the endgame of gamification. In: Mathias Fuchs, Sonia Fizek, Paolo Ruffino u.a. (Hg.): Rethinking Gamification. Lüneburg: meson press 2014, p. 289–303. DOI: https://doi.org/10.25969/mediarep/725.

Nix, Glen A.; Ryan, Richard M.; Manly, John B.; Deci, Edward L. (1999): Revitalization through self-regulation. The effects of autonomous and controlled motivation on happiness and vitality. In: Journal of experimental social psychology 35 (3), p. 266–284.

Nobre, Helena; Ferreira, André (2017): Gamification as a platform for brand co-creation experiences. In: J Brand Manag 24 (4), p. 349–361. DOI: https://doi.org/10.1057/s41262-017-0055-3.

Onwuegbuzie, Anthony J. (2000): Expanding the Framework of Internal and External Validity in Quantitative Research. In: Research in the Schools (10), p. 71–90.

Otley, David (2003): Management control and performance management. Whence and whither? In: The British Accounting Review 35 (4), p. 309–326. DOI: https://doi.org/10.1016/j.bar.2003.08.002.

Park, Jinkyun (2009): Complexity of Proceduralized Tasks: Springer.

Passos, Erick B.; Medeiros, Danilo B.; Neto, Pedro A. S.; Clua, Esteban W. G. (2011): Turning Real-World Software Development into a Game. In: Conference: Games and Digital Entertainment (SBGAMES), p. 260–269. DOI: https://doi.org/10.1109/SBGAMES.2011.32.

Patricio, Rui (2017): A gamified approach for engaging teams in corporate innovation and entrepreneurship. In: W J of Sci, Tech and Sus Dev 14 (2/3), p. 254–262. DOI: https://doi.org/10.1108/WJSTSD-10-2016-0057.

Payne, John W. (1976): Task complexity and contingent processing in decision making. An information search and protocol analysis. In: Organizational behavior and human performance 16 (2), p. 366–387.

Pedro, Lais Z.; Lopes, Aparecida M. Z.; Prates, Bruno G.; Vassileva, Julita; Isotani, Seiji (2015): Does gamification work for boys and girls? An exploratory study with a virtual learning environment. An exploratory study with a wirtual learning environment. In: Proceedings of the 30th annual ACM symposium on applied computing.

Pelham, Brett W.; Neter, Efrat (1995): The effect of motivation of judgment depends on the difficulty of the judgment. In: Journal of personality and social psychology 68 (4), p. 581.

Peng, Wei; Lin, Jih-Hsuan; Pfeiffer, Karin A.; Winn, Brian (2012): Need satisfaction supportive game features as motivational determinants. An experimental study of a self-determination theory guided exergame. In: Media Psychology 15 (2), p. 175–196.

Perryer, Chris; Celestine, Nicole Amanda; Scott-Ladd, Brenda; Leighton, Catherine (2016): Enhancing workplace motivation through gamification. Transferrable lessons from pedagogy. In: The International Journal of Management Education 14 (3), p. 327–335.

Pinder, Craig C. (2014): Work motivation in organizational behavior: Psychology Press.

Plant, Robert W.; Ryan, Richard M. (1985): Intrinsic motivation and the effects of self-consciousness, self-awareness, and ego-involvement. An investigation of internally controlling styles. In: Journal of personality 53 (3), p. 435–449.

Popa, D. M. (2013): Gamification of productivity software: A user-centered design approach. Master's Thesis. Copenhagen.

Przybylski, Andrew K.; Rigby, C. Scott; Ryan, Richard M. (2010): A Motivational Model of Video Game Engagement. In: Review of General Psychology 14 (2), p. 154–166. DOI: https://doi.org/10.1037/a0019440.

Puerta Melguizo, Mari Carmen; Vidya, Uti; van Oostendorp, Herre (2012): Seeking information online. The influence of menu type, navigation path complexity and spatial ability on information gathering tasks. In: Behaviour & Information Technology 31 (1), p. 59–70.

Putz, Lisa-Maria; Hofbauer, Florian; Treiblmaier, Horst (2020): Can gamification help to improve education? Findings from a longitudinal study. In: Computers in Human Behavior (110). DOI: https://doi.org/10.1016/j.chb.2020.106392.

Raftopoulos, Marigo (2014): Towards gamification transparency. A conceptual framework for the development of responsible gamified enterprise systems. In: journal of gaming & virtual worlds 6 (2), p. 159–178. DOI: https://doi.org/10.1386/jgvw.6.2.159_1.

Rapp, Amon; Cena, Federica; Gena, Cristina; Marcengo, Alessandro; Console, Luca (2015): Using game mechanics for field evaluation of prototype social applications. A novel methodology. In: Behaviour & Information Technology 35 (3), p. 184–195. DOI: https://doi.org/10.1080/0144929X.2015.1046931.

Rapp, Amon; Marcengo, Alessandro; Console, A.; Simeoni, L. (2012): Playing in the wild: enhancing user engagement in field evaluation methods. In: Conference: mindtrek. DOI: https://doi.org/10.1145/2393132.2393180.

Rechenberg, Tobias von; Gutt, Dominik; Kundisch, Dennis (2016): Goals as Reference Points. Empirical Evidence from a Virtual Reward System. In: Decision Analysis 13 (2), p. 153–171. DOI: https://doi.org/10.1287/deca.2016.0331.

Reeves, Byron; Read, J. Leighton (2009): Total Engagement. How Games and Virtual Worlds Are Changing the Way People Work and Businesses Compete. Boston: Harvard Business Review Press.

Reiners, Torsten; Wood, Lincoln C. (Hg.) (2015): Gamification in education and business. Switzerland: Springer.

Robertson, Margaret (2010): Can't Play, Won't Play. Hide & Seek. Online verfügbar unter http://hideandseek.net/2010/10/06/cant-play-wont-play/.

Robinson, David; Bellotti, Victoria (2013): Taxonomy of Gamification Elements for Varying Anticipated Commitment. In: Paper presented at the CHI 2013, Paris.

Robinson, Peter (2001): Task complexity, task difficulty, and task production. Exploring interactions in a componential framework. In: Applied linguistics 22 (1), p. 27–57.

Robson, Karen; Plangger, Kirk; Kietzmann, Jan; McCarthy, Ian P.; Pitt, Leyland (2014): Understanding Gamification of Consumer Experiences. In: ACR North American Advances.

Robson, Karen; Plangger, Kirk; Kietzmann, Jan H.; McCarthy, Ian; Pitt, Leyland (2015): Is it all a game? Understanding the principles of gamification. In: Business Horizons 58 (4), p. 411–420. DOI: https://doi.org/10.1016/j.bushor.2015.03.006.

Robson, K., Plangger, K., Kietzmann, J.H., McCarthy, I., Pitt, L., (2016): Game on: Engaging customers and employees through gamification. Business Horizons 59 (1), 29–36. https://doi.org/10.1016/j.bushor.2015.08.002.

Rouse, William B. (1979): Measures of complexity of fault diagnosis tasks. In: IEEE Tranactions on Systems, Man, and Cybernetics 11 (9), p. 720–727.

Ruhi, Umar (2015): Level Up Your Strategy. Towards a Descriptive Framework for Meaningful Enterprise Gamification. In: Technology Innovation Management Review 5 (8), p. 5–16. DOI: https://doi.org/10.22215/timreview918.

Ryan, R. M.; Kuhl, J.; Deci, E. L. (1997): Nature and autonomy. An organizational view of social and neurobiological aspects of self-regulation in behavior and development. In: Development and psychopathology 9 (4), p. 701–728. DOI: https://doi.org/10.1017/S0954579497001405.

Ryan, Richard M. (1982): Control and information in the intrapersonal sphere. An extension of cognitive evaluation theory. In: Journal of personality and social psychology 43 (3), p. 450–461. DOI: https://doi.org/10.1037/0022-3514.43.3.450.

Ryan, Richard M.; Connell, James P.; Plant, Robert W. (1990): Emotions in nondirected text learning. In: Learning and Individual Differences 2 (1), p. 1–17. DOI: https://doi.org/10.1016/1041-6080(90)90014-8.

Ryan, Richard M.; Deci, Edward L. (2000a): Intrinsic and Extrinsic Motivations. Classic Definitions and New Directions. In: Contemporary educational psychology 25 (1), p. 54–67. DOI: https://doi.org/10.1006/ceps.1999.1020.

Ryan, Richard M.; Deci, Edward L. (2000b): Self-determination theory and the facilitation of intrinsic motivation, social development, and well-being. In: American psychologist 55 (1), p. 68–78.

Ryan, Richard M.; Deci, Edward L. (2017): Self-determination theory. Basic psychological needs in motivation, development, and wellness: Guilford Publications.

Ryan, Richard M.; Koestner, Richard; Deci, Edward L. (1991): Ego-involved persistence. When free-choice behavior is not intrinsically motivated. In: Motivation and Emotion 15 (3), p. 185–205. DOI: https://doi.org/10.1007/BF00995170.

Ryan, Richard M.; Mims, Valerie; Koestner, Richard (1983): Relation of reward contingency and interpersonal context to intrinsic motivation. A review and test using cognitive evaluation theory. In: Journal of personality and social psychology 45 (4), p. 736–750. DOI: https://doi.org/10.1037/0022-3514.45.4.736.

Rybak, Jan; Balog, Krisztian; Nørvåg; Kjetil (2015): IR Game: How well do you know information retrieval papers? In: Proceedings of the GamifIR'15 Workshop, p. 7–12.

Rynes, Sara L.; Gerhart, Barry; Parks, Laura (2005): Personnel psychology. Performance evaluation and pay for performance. In: Annu. Rev. Psychol. 56, p. 571–600.

Sailer, Michael (2016): Die Wirkung von Gamification auf Motivation und Leistung: Springer.

Sailer, Michael; Hense, Jan; Mandl, Heinz; Klevers, Markus (2013): Psychological Perspectives on Motivation through Gamification. In: IxD&A 19, p. 28–37.

Sailer, Michael; Hense, Jan Ulrich; Mayr, Sarah Katharina; Mandl, Heinz (2017): How gamification motivates. An experimental study of the effects of specific game design elements on psychological need satisfaction. In: Computers in Human Behavior 69, p. 371–380. DOI: https://doi.org/10.1016/j.chb.2016.12.033.

Sailer, M., Sailer, M., (2020): Gamification of in-class activities in flipped classroom lectures. Br J Educ Technol 52 (1), 129. DOI: https://doi.org/10.1111/bjet.12948.

Sakamoto, Mizuki; Nakajima, Tatsuo; Alexandrova, Todorka (2012): Value-Based Design for Gamifying Daily Activities. In: 11th international conference on entertainment computing 7522, p. 421–424. DOI: https://doi.org/10.1007/978-3-642-33542-6_43.

Sanchez, Diana R.; Langer, Markus; Kaur, Rupinder (2020): Gamification in the classroom: Examining the impact of gamified quizzes on student learning. In: Computers & Education (144). DOI: https://doi.org/10.1016/j.compedu.2019.103666.

Sandelowski, Margarete; Docherty, Sharron; Emden, Carolyn (1997): Qualitative metasynthesis. Issues and techniques. In: Res. Nurs. Health 20 (4), p. 365–371. DOI: https://doi.org/10.1002/(SICI)1098-240X(199708)20:4<365::AID-NUR9>3.0.CO;2-E.

SAP (2011): Gamification examples @ SAP. Retrieved from: https://www.forbes.com/sites/sap/2011/03/04/the-gamification-of-sap/#7e0430c035ed, accessed: 06.10.2020.

Scheiner, Christian W. (2015): The Motivational Fabric of Gamified Idea Competitions. The Evaluation of Game Mechanics from a Longitudinal Perspective. In: Creativity and Innovation Management 24 (2), p. 341–352. DOI: https://doi.org/10.1111/caim.12115.

Scheufele, Dietram A. (1999): Framing as a Theory of Media Effects. In: Journal of Communication 49 (1), p. 103–122. DOI: https://doi.org/10.1111/j.1460-2466.1999.tb02784.x.

Schmider, Emanuel; Ziegler, Matthias; Danay, Erik; Beyer, Luzi; Bühner, Markus (2010): Is It Really Robust? Reinvestigating the Robustness of ANOVA Against Violations of the Normal Distribution Assumption. In: Methodology 6 (4), p. 147–151. DOI: https://doi.org/10.1027/1614-2241/a000016.

Schwab, Donald P.; Cummings, Larry L. (1976): A theoretical analysis of the impact of task scope on employee performance. In: Academy of management review 1 (2), p. 23–35.

Schwering, Anja (2016): Budgetierung im Kontext des Management Accounting. In: Ehrlichkeit in der Budgetierung: Springer, p. 11–25.

Seaborn, Katie; Fels, Deborah I. (2015): Gamification in theory and action. A survey. In: International Journal of Human-Computer Studies 74, p. 14–31. DOI: https://doi.org/10.1016/j.ijhcs.2014.09.006.

Seiffert-Brockmann, Jens; Weitzl, Wolfgang; Henriks, Magdalena (2018): Stakeholder engagement through gamification. In: JCOM 22 (1), p. 67–78. DOI: https://doi.org/10.1108/JCOM-12-2016-0096.

Sheldon, Kennon M.; Elliot, Andrew J. (1998): Not all personal goals are personal. Comparing autonomous and controlled reasons for goals as predictors of effort and attainment. In: Personality and social psychology bulletin 24 (5), p. 546–557.

Sheldon, Kennon M.; Kasser, Tim (1998): Pursuing personal goals. Skills enable progress, but not all progress is beneficial. In: Personality and social psychology bulletin 24 (12), p. 1319–1331.

Siemens, Jennifer Christie; Smith, Scott; Fisher, Dan; Thyroff, Anastasia; Killian, Ginger (2015): Level Up! The Role of Progress Feedback Type for Encouraging Intrinsic Motivation and Positive Brand Attitudes in Public Versus Private Gaming Contexts. In: Journal of Interactive Marketing 32, p. 1–12. DOI: https://doi.org/10.1016/j.intmar.2015.07.001.

Singer, Georg; Norbisrath, Ulrich; Lewandowski, Dirk (2013): Ordinary search engine users carrying out complex search tasks. In: Journal of Information Science 39 (3), p. 346–358.

Singer, Georg; Pruulmann-Vengerfeldt, Pille; Norbisrath, Ulrich; Lewandowski, Dirk (2015): The relationship between Internet user type and user performance when carrying out simple vs. complex search tasks. In: arXiv preprint arXiv:1511.05819.

Slack, Marion K.; Draugalis Jr, Jolaine R. (2001): Establishing the internal and external validity of experimental studies. In: American Journal of Health-System Pharmacy 58 (22), p. 2173–2181.

Smeddinck, Jan David; Herrlich, Marc; Roll, Max; Malaka, Rainer (2014): Motivational effects of a gamified training analysis interface. In: Mensch & Computer 2014-Workshopband.

Smith, M., 2015. Research methods in accounting, 3rd ed. SAGE, Los Angeles.

Smith, Tamarah (2017): Gamified Modules for an Introductory Statistics Course and Their Impact on Attitudes and Learning. In: Simulation & Gaming 48 (6), p. 832–854. DOI: https://doi.org/10.1177/1046878117731888.

Snyder, Erin; Hartig, Jason (2013): Gamification of board review: a residency curricular innovation. Med. Educ. 47, 524–525. http://dx.doi.org/https://doi.org/10.1111/medu.12190.

Soto-Acosta, Pedro (2020):COVID-19 Pandemic: Shifting Digital Transformation to a High-Speed Gear. In: Information Systems Management. p. 1–7. DOI: https://doi.org/10.1080/10580530.2020.1814461.

Speier, Cheri (2006): The influence of information presentation formats on complex task decision-making performance. In: International Journal of Human-Computer Studies 64 (11), p. 1115–1131.

Sprinkle, Geoffrey B. (2000): The Effect of Incentive Contracts on Learning and Performance. In: The Accounting Review 75 (3), p. 299–326. DOI: https://doi.org/10.2308/accr.2000.75.3.299.

Sprinkle, Geoffrey B.; Williamson, Michael G.; Upton, David R. (2008): The effort and risk-taking effects of budget-based contracts. In: Accounting, Organizations and Society 33 (4-5), p. 436–452. DOI: https://doi.org/10.1016/j.aos.2007.11.001.

Stajkovic, Alexander D.; Luthans, Fred (1997): A meta-analysis of the effects of organizational behavior modification on task performance, 1975–95. In: Academy of Management journal 40 (5), p. 1122–1149.

Stock, D., Watson, C.J., (1984): Human judgment accuracy, multidimensional graphics, and humans versus models. Journal of Accounting Research, 192–206.

Su, C-H; Cheng, C-H (2015): A mobile gamification learning system for improving the learning motivation and achievements. In: Journal of Computer Assisted Learning 31 (3), p. 268–286.

Su, Chungho (2017): The Effects of Students' Learning Anxiety and Motivation on the Learning Achievement in the Activity Theory Based Gamified Learning Environment. In: Eurasia J Math Sci T 13 (5). DOI: https://doi.org/10.12973/eurasia.2017.00669a.

Suh, Ayoung; Cheung, Christy M.K.; Ahuja, Manju; Wagner, Christian (2017): Gamification in the Workplace. The Central Role of the Aesthetic Experience. In: Journal of Management Information Systems 34 (1), p. 268–305. DOI: https://doi.org/10.1080/07421222.2017.1297642.

Suh, Ayoung; Wagner, Christian (2017): How gamification of an enterprise collaboration system increases knowledge contribution. An affordance approach. In: J of Knowledge Management 21 (2), p. 416–431. DOI: https://doi.org/10.1108/JKM-10-2016-0429.

Suh, Ayoung; Wagner, Christian; Liu, Lili (2018): Enhancing User Engagement through Gamification. In: Journal of Computer Information Systems 58 (3), p. 204–213. DOI: https://doi.org/10.1080/08874417.2016.1229143.

Sutcliffe, Alistair; Hart, Jennefer (2016): Analyzing the Role of Interactivity in User Experience. In: International Journal of Human–Computer Interaction 33 (3), p. 229–240. DOI: https://doi.org/10.1080/10447318.2016.1239797.

Tan, Hun-Tong; Ng, Terence Bu-Peow; Mak, Bobby Wai-Yeong (2002): The effects of task complexity on auditors' performance. The impact of accountability and knowledge. In: Auditing: A Journal of Practice & Theory 21 (2), p. 81–95.

Technavio (July 2020): Gamification Market by End-user, Need, Application, and Geography—Forecast and Analysis 2020–2024. retrieved from https://www.technavio.com/report/gamification-market-size-industry-analysis, accessed 13.08.2020.

Terlutter, Ralf; Capella, Michael L. (2013): The Gamification of Advertising. Analysis and Research Directions of In-Game Advertising, Advergames, and Advertising in Social Network Games. In: Journal of Advertising 42 (2–3), p. 95–112. DOI: https://doi.org/10.1080/00913367.2013.774610.

Tranfield, David; Denyer, David; Smart, Palminder (2003): Towards a Methodology for Developing Evidence-Informed Management Knowledge by Means of Systematic Review. In: Br J Management 14 (3), p. 207–222. DOI: https://doi.org/10.1111/1467-8551.00375.

Tsigilis, Nikolaos; Theodosiou, Argiris (2003): Temporal stability of the intrinsic motivation inventory. In: Perceptual and motor skills 97 (1), p. 271–280.

Tversky, Amos; Kahneman, Daniel (1981): The framing of decisions and the psychology of choice. In: science 211 (4481), p. 453–458.

Vakkari, Pertti (1999): Task complexity, problem structure and information actions. Integrating studies on information seeking and retrieval. In: Information processing & management 35 (6), p. 819–837.

van Roy, R., & Zaman, B. (2017). Why Gamification Fails in Education and How to Make it Successful: Introducing Nine Gamification Heuristics Based on Self-Determination Theory. In Ma, M., & Oikonomou, A. (eds.), Serious Games and Edutainment Applications, Volume II (pp. 485—509). Chan, Switzerland: Springer International Publishing AG.

Vansteenkiste, Maarten; Niemiec, Christopher P.; Soenens, Bart (2010): The development of the five mini-theories of self-determination theory. An historical overview, emerging trends, and future directions. In: The decade ahead: Theoretical perspectives on motivation and achievement: Emerald Group Publishing Limited.

Venkatesh, Viswanath; Johnson, Philip (2002): Telecommuting technology implementations. A within-and between-subjects longitudinal field study. In: Personnel Psychology 55 (3), p. 661–687.

Vroom, Victor Harold (1964): Work and motivation.

Walhout, Jaap; Brand-Gruwel, Saskia; Jarodzka, Halszka; van Dijk, Martin; Groot, Renate de; Kirschner, Paul A. (2015): Learning and navigating in hypertext. Navigational support by hierarchical menu or tag cloud? In: Computers in Human Behavior 46, p. 218–227.

Walhout, Jaap; Oomen, Paola; Jarodzka, Halszka; Brand-Gruwel, Saskia (2017): Effects of task complexity on online search behavior of adolescents. In: Journal of the Association for Information Science and Technology 68 (6), p. 1449–1461.

Walker, Geraldene; Janes, Joseph (1999): Online retrieval. A dialogue of theory and practice: Libraries Unlimited.

Wang, Ming-Te; Eccles, Jacquelynne S. (2013): School context, achievement motivation, and academic engagement. A longitudinal study of school engagement using a multidimensional perspective. In: Learning and Instruction 28, p. 12–23. DOI: https://doi.org/10.1016/j.learninstruc.2013.04.002.

Wang, Xiaohui; Goh, Dion Hoe-Lian; Lim, Ee-Peng; Vu, Adrian Wei Liang; Chua, Alton Yeow Kuan (2017): Examining the Effectiveness of Gamification in Human Computation. In: International Journal of Human–Computer Interaction 33 (10), p. 813–821. DOI: https://doi.org/10.1080/10447318.2017.1287458.

Wang, Xuequn; Schneider, Christoph; Valacich, Joseph S. (2012): Fine-Tuning Group Collaboration Environments. How Differences in General Causality Orientation and Performance Targets Shape Interaction and Performance. In: 45th Hawaii International Conference on System Sciences, Maui, p. 553–561. DOI: https://doi.org/10.1109/HICSS.2012.281.

Webster, Jane; Martocchio, Joseph J. (1992): Microcomputer playfulness. Development of a measure with workplace implications. In: MISQ, p. 201–226.

Werbach, Kevin (2014): (Re) defining gamification. A process approach. In: International conference on persuasive technology, p. 266–272.

Werbach, Kevin; Hunter, Dan (2012): For the Win. How Game Thinking Can Revolutionize Your Business. Chicago: Wharton Digital Press. Online access https://ebookcentral.proquest.com/lib/gbv/detail.action?docID=5482556.

Werbach, Kevin; Hunter, Dan (2015): The Gamification Toolkit. Dynamics, Mechanics, and Components for the Win. Chicago: Wharton Digital Press.

Wickens, Christopher D.; McCarley, Jason S. (2007): Applied attention theory: CRC press.

Wildemuth, Babara M.; Freund, Luanne (2012): Assigning search tasks designed to elicit exploratory search behaviors. In: Proceedings of the Symposium on Human-Computer Interaction and Information Retrieval, p. 1–10.

Willett, Peter; Wildemuth, Barbara; Freund, Luanne; Toms, Elaine G. (2014): Untangling search task complexity and difficulty in the context of interactive information retrieval studies. In: Journal of Documentation.

Wilson, Timothy D.; Aronson, Elliot; Carlsmith, Kevin (2010): The art of laboratory experimentation. In: Handbook of social psychology, Vol. 1, 5th ed. Hoboken, NJ, US: John Wiley & Sons, Inc, p. 51–81.

Witt, Maximilian; Scheiner, Christian W.; Robra-Bissantz, Susanne (2011): Gamification of online idea competitions: insights from an explorative case. In: Hans-Ulrich Heiss (Hg.): Informatik 2011. Informatik schafft Communities ; Beiträge der 41. Jahrestagung der Gesellschaft für Informatik e.V. (GI), 4.—7.10.2011 in Berlin. Bonn: Ges. für Informatik (GI-Edition : Proceedings, 192), p. 392.

Wood, Robert E. (1986): Task complexity. Definition of the construct. In: Organizational Behavior and Human Decision Processes 37 (1), p. 60–82.

Wood, Robert E.; Mento, Anthony J.; Locke, Edwin A. (1987): Task complexity as a moderator of goal effects. A meta-analysis. In: Journal of applied psychology 72 (3), p. 416.

Wright, William F.; Aboul-Ezz, Mohamed E. (1988): Effects of extrinsic incentives on the quality of frequency assessments. In: Organizational Behavior and Human Decision Processes 41 (2), p. 143–152.

Xiao, Yan; Hunter, William A.; Mackenzie, Colin F.; Jefferies, Nicolas J.; Horst, Richard L.; Group, Lotas (1996): Task complexity in emergency medical care and its implications for team coordination. In: Human Factors 38 (4), p. 636–645.

Xu, Yongwen; Johnson, Philip M.; Moore, Carleton A.; Brewer, Robert p.; Takayama, Jordan (2013): SGSEAM: Assessing serious game frameworks from a Stakeholder Experience perspective. In: Gamification '13: Proceedings of the First International Conference on Gameful Design, Research, and Applications 2013, p. 75–78. DOI: https://doi.org/10.1145/2583008.2583018.

Yerkes, Robert M.; Dodson, John D. (1908): The relation of strength of stimulus to rapidity of habit-formation. In: Punishment: Issues and experiments, p. 27–41.

Young, S. M. (2001): The effects of earnings predictability on optimism and accuracy in forecasts of financial analysts. Working paper, Emory University.

Zhang, Ping (2008): Technical opinion Motivational affordances. Reasons for ICT design and use. In: Commun. ACM 51 (11), p. 145–147.

Zhao, Baijun (1994): A structured analysis and quantitative measurement of task complexity in human-computer interaction.

Zichermann, Gabe; Cunningham, Christopher (2011): Gamification by design. Implementing game mechanics in web and mobile apps. First edition.

Zichermann, Gabe; Linder, Joselin (2013): The gamification revolution. How leaders leverage game mechanics to crush the competition. New York, NY: McGraw Hill Education.

Zimmerman, Barry J. (2011): Motivational sources and outcomes of self-regulated learning and performance. In: Barry J. Zimmerman und Dale H. Schunk (Hg.): Handbook of self-regulation of learning and performance. 1. publ. New York: Routledge (Educational psychology handbook series), p. 49–64.

Zimmerman, Barry J.; Schunk, Dale H. (Hg.) (2011): Handbook of self-regulation of learning and performance. 1. publ. New York: Routledge (Educational psychology handbook series).

The manufacturer's authorised representative in the EU is Springer Nature Customer Service Centre GmbH, Europaplatz 3, 69115 Heidelberg, Germany. If you have any concerns regarding our products, please contact ProductSafety@springernature.com

Printed and bound by CPI Group (UK) Ltd, Croydon, CR0 4YY
30/09/2026
02225659-0001